W9-DEN-895

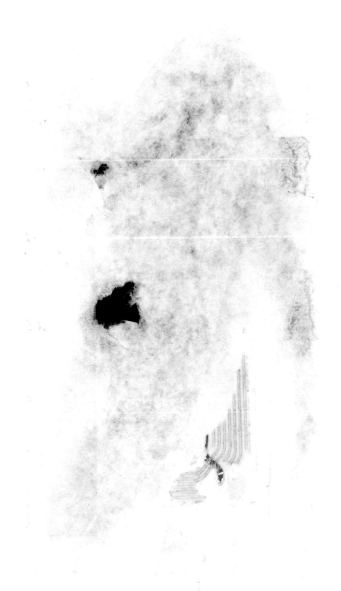

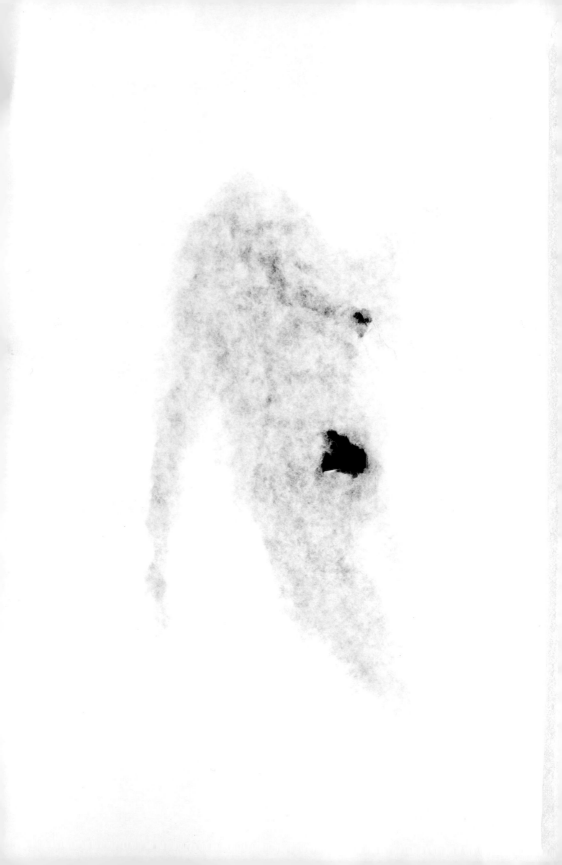

Protectors of Privacy

Protectors of Privacy

Regulating Personal Data in the Global Economy

Abraham L. Newman

Cornell University Press
Ithaca and London

First published 2008 by Cornell University Press

Printed in the United States of America

Library of Congress Cataloging-in-Publication Data

Newman, Abraham, 1973–
    Protectors of privacy : regulating personal data in the global economy / Abraham L. Newman.
        p. cm.
    Includes bibliographical references and index.
    ISBN 978–0–8014–4549–1 (cloth : alk. paper)
    1. Data protection—Law and legislation—European Union countries. 2. Privacy, Right of—European Union countries. 3. Globalization—Economic aspects—Europe. 4. Europe—Economic integration. I. Title.

    KJE6071.N495   2008
    342.2408'58—dc22

                                                        2008011614

Cornell University Press strives to use environmentally responsible suppliers and materials to the fullest extent possible in the publishing of its books. Such materials include vegetable-based, low-VOC inks and acid-free papers that are recycled, totally chlorine-free, or partly composed of nonwood fibers. For further information, visit our website at www.cornellpress.cornell.edu.

Cloth printing   10 9 8 7 6 5 4 3 2 1

To Barbara and Phil Newman

Contents

Acknowledgments

This project began as I arrived in the San Francisco Bay Area in 1999, at the height of the dotcom boom, and evolved over the following years marked by the dotcom collapse, terrorist attacks, and research in Europe. As I grappled with the fierce debates over personal identity, civil liberties, the new economy, and the emerging information society, I am indebted to the numerous people who helped me along the way. Countless individuals answered questions, read and reread draft chapters, lifted my spirits, and provided the space necessary to complete my work.

Let me begin by thanking my mentors: John Zysman, Stephen Cohen, Jonah Levy, and Steven Weber. Each had his own unique style and focus, and I could not imagine a better set of scholars to guide such a project. They demonstrated academic excellence at its best. Alongside my formal advisers, a large group of peers and academics both at Berkeley and at other universities played a critical role in the development of the project. I am particularly grateful to David Bach, Pat Egan, Alisa Gaunder, Elliot Posner, Sara Watson, and Sarah Williarty, who encouraged me as I swung from excitement to despair. I also thank Jeff Anderson, Chris Ansell, Tanja Börzel, Tim Büthe, Roger Chickering, John Cioffi, Burkhard Eberlein, Henry Farrell, Orfeo Fioretos, Ed Fogerty, Jane Gingrich, Virginia Haufler, Dorothee Heisenberg, Nicolas Jabko, Kate McNamara, Sophie Meunier, Dan Nexon, Kathy Olesko, Mark Pollack, Armin Shaffer,

Katrin Sieg, Holger Wolf, Cornelia Woll, and Nick Ziegler, all of whom challenged and encouraged me in the process. Roger Haydon at Cornell University Press and three anonymous reviewers offered invaluable comments that greatly improved the manuscript.

Several organizations made important contributions to the completion of the project. I spent five years at the Berkeley Roundtable on the International Economy (BRIE), and I am indebted to its graduate students and the staff. Similarly, the project would not have been possible without the financial and intellectual support of the Max Planck Institute for the Study of Societies in Cologne. I am particularly grateful for the opportunity to work with Wolfgang Streeck and the team of scholars who populate the institute. I thank the Center for Information Technology Research in the Interest of Society (CITRIS) at the University of California and the American Council on Germany, which provided critical financial assistance. Most recently, the faculty, students, and staff at the BMW Center for German and European Studies at Georgetown University provided the support and intellectual inspiration to finish the project. Finally, I acknowledge the cafés in San Francisco and Berkeley—Strada, Milano, Maxfields, Morning Dew, and Jumpin Java—that permitted me to sit for hours on a $1.50 tea. They are a public resource unparalleled in the country.

Of course, the project would not have been possible without the scholars, politicians, civil servants, and business officials who took the time to talk to me about data privacy debates in the United States and Europe. I extend a special thanks to Marie Georges, Spiros Simitis, and the staff at the Gesellschaft für Datenschutz und Datensicherheit, who met with me for countless hours and graciously helped me access the world of European data privacy.

In addition to the academic community, my family and friends stood by as I obsessed over the nitty-gritty of the project. My parents patiently listened as I battled with ideas. My brother and sister inspired me to keep plugging away. And a host of friends, including Thomas Butler, Ellie Heckscher, and Becca Hong, talked me down and pepped me up.

Finally, I thank Craig Pollack. Although we often joked about the words I would write here, I cannot express my gratitude. His tireless engagement with my project was breathtaking. It is not something that I expected, but it is something that I treasure.

Protectors of Privacy

You have zero privacy anyway. Get over it.

Scott McNealy, Chief Executive Officer of Sun Microsystems

Everyone has the right to the protection of personal data concerning him or her.

Article 8-1, Charter of Fundamental Rights of the European Union

CHAPTER 1

Data Privacy and the Global Economy

The digital revolution has radically increased the amount of personal information produced and collected. In 2004, Wal-Mart alone stored more than 460 terabytes of customer information, twice as much data as housed in all the webpages of the Internet. Commercial credit reporting agencies in the United States have amassed roughly 500 million individual credit reports. That number translates into two credit reports for every man, woman, and child in the country. Bureaucracies and businesses process intimate personal information, including social security numbers, credit card purchases, website clicks, mobile phone logs, thumb prints, and now even retina scans. The theft of millions of customer records from Bank of America, MasterCard, Visa, and the Veterans Administration highlights the serious security issues surrounding these tremendous data warehouses.[1] Already the U.S. economy suffers more than $50 billion in losses annually due to identity theft and fraud.[2]

Although all advanced industrial societies face essentially the same dilemma—how to manage a vast pool of personal information flows—their governments have chosen substantially different solutions. Some countries—including the United States and many nations in Asia—have developed limited systems of regulations that focus attention on the public sector and a select number of sensitive industries. Implementation and enforcement stress self-regulation among both industry and government administrations. Personal information is readily available in the economy and for many firms has become central to their business models. In contrast to these limited systems, other countries—most notably those in Europe—have adopted an alternative vision privileging consumer protection and individual privacy against the efficiency and economic interests of firms and public officials. Beginning in the 1970s, nations such as France and Germany adopted comprehensive rules about data privacy for both governments and business. With the passage of the EU data privacy directive in 1995, all twenty-seven members of the European Union now have comprehensive regulations in place.[3] These regulations include clear rules regarding the collection, transfer, and use of personal information that are monitored and enforced by independent regulatory agencies—data privacy authorities. These agencies are dedicated to the protection of personal privacy, much like a Federal Trade Commission with sole responsibility for data privacy.

In contrast to the extensive data commodification in countries with limited rules, countries with comprehensive systems produce less personally identifiable information, and clear procedures exist to deter misuse. In France, for example, there are no private-sector credit reports, and the data privacy agency has worked closely with credit card companies to make credit card transaction records anonymous. These rules do not create an absolute right to privacy or solve all the problems associated with privacy in a modern society. Under the banner of new security threats, national governments have in recent years sought to expand data collection and surveillance.[4] Nevertheless, in terms of balancing individual and societal interests, Europe and non-European countries with comprehensive rules have set the default strongly in favor of the individual.

Because digital data networks facilitate the rapid transfer of personal information across jurisdictional boundaries, these divergent approaches to data privacy have brought nations into conflict with one another. Disputes over data privacy regulations have roiled trade relations and raised new security concerns, providing a critical window into the evolving role that Europe plays in shaping the rules of the global economy. In the face of fierce international industry resistance, EU-style regulations have nonetheless spread rapidly across the industrial world, with most members of the Organisation for Economic Cooperation and Development (OECD)—the United States is the major exception—adopting similar rules for privacy protection or having legislation pending in their legislatures. Although the exact administrative structures differ, over forty nations have adopted some form of comprehensive regulations, including countries that long maintained more limited regulations such as Australia, Canada, and Japan. And even the United States signed an international agreement that requires U.S. firms active in European markets to comply with European rules.

Despite intense opposition from the United States and other major governments, Europe not only has developed an alternative to the laissez-faire mentality concerning personal information but is leading the race to set global privacy rules. This outcome is quite striking given fears that national regulatory protections would fall victim to the pressures of the international economy. It is even more surprising given the general dominance of U.S. regulatory preferences in most other governance concerns of the digital economy, ranging from intellectual property to Internet domain names. Europe, long viewed as the little brother of international economic governance, has transformed the global privacy debate by pressing for high levels of protection, especially in the private sector. My goal in this book is to explain why. Why did the European Union ratchet up privacy regulations in the 1990s, and how has Europe shaped policy decisions in other countries? I investigate how societies have resolved the question: Who should be allowed to know what about whom? And I then ask: How do these systems interact in a global digital economy in which markets are rarely contained within a single national jurisdiction? More generally, I examine when and why the European Union built and promoted its own agenda for globalization.

I invoke two sets of arguments, linked but distinct, to answer these questions. The first is a sequenced, stepwise process whereby domestic and intra-European politics shape outcomes occurring at the international level. National legislation passed in the 1970s in several European countries was exported upward regionally, forging the regulatory tools necessary to influence international market regulations. The other argument focuses on the agents of change. European data privacy leadership depends on the protectors of privacy, who both advocate for strong individual safeguards within Europe and have the resources to enforce European rules internationally.

Why Privacy Regulations Matter

Privacy policies have implications for individual liberty, the powers of the state, and the global economy. Complemented by technology and self-regulation, government rules establish an important framework for how societies produce and share personal information. These rules balance the needs of organizations that use such data against the potential harm such use could cause to individuals.

Because industries, including banking, insurance, telecommunications, and marketing, employ personal data to customize products and minimize fraud, there is a very real danger of discrimination.[5] Personalized risk assessments and more differentiated pricing, for instance, facilitate cherry-picking and the exclusion of less attractive groups.[6] People whose mobile phones indicate that they drive frequently through low-income neighborhoods become high risks for car insurance. Employees who purchase cigarettes on the Web at work find their health insurance premiums rise. Already data mining is used to identify bad apples in insurance pools; it is not far-fetched to imagine that insurers will soon use genetic testing to exclude large populations of costly clients. The danger exists that, as more and more information about an individual's behavior is known, societies will reduce their support for risk pooling. The healthy and wealthy may join together against those at risk. Ultimately, extreme differentiation threatens to weaken the political bargains that underpin the modern welfare state.

Private-sector monitoring of customer behavior multiplies the eyes conducting surveillance, potentially altering the character of the relations among state, industry, and society. As companies collect and network more information, the threat exists that everyday behavior will be aggregated by industry and deployed by governments to augment social control. While civil libertarians have showered criticism on the expansion of state police powers in legislation such as the Patriot Act or domestic surveillance efforts in the United States, mounting public- and private-sector partnerships have emerged under the radar of public scrutiny. U.S. private-sector information aggregators have billions of pieces of information about the citizenry. A Government Accountability Office study estimates that four federal agencies alone purchased $30 million in personal information from these firms in 2005.[7] The blurring of public- and private-sector surveillance neutralizes traditional safeguards against government abuse and reframes the role of industry as the projection of police power.[8] A scandal involving JetBlue, whereby the company released some 5 million passenger records to Defense Department contractors, the government subpoena of Google search records, and the creation of a massive databank by the National Security Agency of consumer telephone logs provide revealing examples of the outsourcing of Orwellian tasks.[9]

Internationally, the regulation of personal information has become an increasing source of economic and security disputes. The 1995 EU data privacy directive raised European protection levels and limited member-state transfers of information to countries without adequate safeguards. This extraterritorial provision prompted other countries, including the United States, to reconsider their data privacy policies and endangered the integration of markets such as financial services and telecommunications. By the end of the 1990s, the transatlantic partners had entered into a full-blown trade conflict, threatening to disrupt information flows between the largest economic areas in the world.[10] The tensions raised by the directive continue to plague transatlantic information policy.[11]

In addition to transatlantic disputes, data privacy concerns broadly affect the further development of international economic integration. The blockage of data flows hinders the expansion of international trade, especially in the service sectors. Multinational corporations rely on the free flow of personal information about clients and personnel to manage their complex networks of affiliates. The failure to respect data privacy within these channels threatens the cross-border transmission of personal information. Attempts to outsource services and move them offshore have already raised data privacy issues. Leaks of personal medical records by stenographers in India, for example, have forced U.S. firms to reconsider the importance of privacy laws in their international strategy.[12] European workers, by contrast, find that privacy laws create an additional shield against the outsourcing of service jobs to such distant lands.

Data privacy issues have also become a point of conflict between the United States and Europe in the new security environment, complicating transatlantic cooperation on counterterrorism.[13] As a result of heightened security concerns, the U.S. government has called for access to increasing amounts of data about foreign citizens. In 2004, for example, U.S. requests for detailed airline records of passengers arriving from Europe conflicted with EU privacy regulations. Tense rounds of negotiations between the two trading partners and North Atlantic Treaty Organization (NATO) allies ensued.[14] These disputes have intensified with the revelation in 2006 that a European-based financial services consortium provided the U.S. Treasury Department with detailed personal information concerning international money transfers.[15]

Far from being simply an abstract legal concern, the regulation of personal information affects patterns of information exchange: how individuals express their identity, how companies differentiate markets, and how governments manage risk. International interdependence marked by expanded communication, cross-border trade, and global financial markets has transformed previously domestic privacy bargains into an international debate.

Existing Accounts of European Privacy Leadership

Given the domestic and international significance of data privacy rules, it is critical to explain Europe's role in this policy field. In examining the rise of European leadership, I find three distinct yet interlinked phases: (1) the initial passage of privacy legislation in the 1970s; (2) the adoption of the EU privacy directive in the 1990s; and (3) the promotion of strong privacy protections around the globe. Existing research has looked at these phases in isolation; in this book, I take a comprehensive approach, examining developments at each historical moment to understand future policy decisions. This sequenced, stepwise argument emphasizes the importance of regulatory capacity and the role of independent regulators as transgovernmental policy entrepreneurs. Before presenting the core of the argument, however, I review some alternative explanations.

First a functional approach: in a purely rational world, developments at each phase would be the result of policymakers responding to new problems and frictions that arose from technological and market changes. This functional explanation, however, is immediately confronted by politics—efficient adjustments often raise real distributional consequences and in turn fierce resistance. The proliferation of computer technology posed the same challenges to civil liberties for all policymakers across the advanced industrial democracies, but the types of privacy regimes adopted in response differed dramatically. Similarly, regional and international efforts to promote the comprehensive regime resulted in long-fought political battles. The story is not one of inevitable and efficient policy change; on the contrary, a number of firms and bureaucracies lobbied to stop reform and at times, at least partially, succeeded.

Turning from this functional explanation, the standard political argument employed to understand national variations in privacy policies that began in the 1970s stresses authoritarian, or fascist, legacies. That is, as

European nations dealt with privacy concerns raised by computer technology, their direct historical experiences with fascist abuses led to the adoption of strict privacy rules.[16] In the aftermath of horrendous government atrocities, somewhat paradoxically, Europeans looked to their governments to guard them against future individual-rights violations. And the absence of such experience in the United States, the argument continues, undercut efforts to pass sweeping privacy regulation.

The fascist legacies argument, however, has difficulty accounting for the initial cross-national variation in privacy policy in the 1970s. As chapter 3 demonstrates in more detail, a cursory examination of early national privacy legislation casts significant doubt on the fascist legacy claim. The United Kingdom, which never experienced authoritarian leadership, passed comprehensive rules; Germany and Japan, which once had direct fascist rule, chose different policies, with Germany adopting strong legislation and Japan adopting weaker rules. And countries such as Spain and Italy that had extensive fascist pasts were among the last countries in Europe to adopt privacy legislation. In addition, the argument does not fit well with the U.S. case. The modern notion of "the right to privacy" is credited to late-nineteenth-century U.S. scholars.[17] Although it seems attractive to associate a fascist legacy with national privacy policies, such arguments obscure rather than illuminate specific differences in the scope of privacy regulations across the advanced industrial democracies.

Scholars invoke a second set of arguments to explain the EU initiative in the 1990s to establish comprehensive rules across Europe. These accounts contend that data privacy became an issue at the European level because of a regulatory asymmetry that penalized the largest and most powerful member states. Five member states—Belgium, Greece, Italy, Portugal, and Spain—had no privacy regulations, thus creating an economic burden for firms in France, Germany, and the United Kingdom, which had long before adopted comprehensive rules. Hoping to level the playing field for their national firms within the single market, the French and German governments pushed for supranational regulation.[18] This part of the argument follows closely a strand of liberal intergovernmental thinking in the European integration literature that stresses the importance of national government preferences from the largest member states in regional policymaking.[19]

But a liberal intergovernmental story that the largest member-state governments forced pan-European action faces several problems. The German government opposed a European directive to harmonize regulation

prior to the European Commission release of such a draft directive in
1990. Similarly, the French government was reluctant to push for European regulations that might alter national rules. The most vocal opponent
of the directive was another country with comprehensive legislation—the
United Kingdom. Firms in these three countries also strongly opposed
the directive. A representative from the largest German industry trade association noted that, despite the cost of divergent rules to German firms,
the trade association did not support supranational legislation. The en-
gine for regulatory harmonization was neither the national executives nor
the major industries in the three most powerful European economies.
Given the conventional explanations for how regulations are produced in
Europe, the passage of the directive is quite startling.

The third and final part of the story focuses on the adoption of comprehensive regulations by non-European countries. Once Europe had
established strict rules, according to existing accounts, its large market provided a natural adjustment incentive for other countries.[20] Non-European
multinational firms, fearing the loss of lucrative European markets, mobilized on behalf of comprehensive privacy rules in their home markets.[21]
The cost of complying with multiple, distinct national privacy rules raised
the incentive for firms to advocate the passage of similar regulations
domestically.[22]

But this account simplifies the causal relationship, focusing on the
material scale of markets and providing an incomplete understanding
of regulatory power. Domestic politics, as noted above, often gets in the
way of efficiency-based adjustment processes. Europe has a large market,
but it does not always prevail in international regulatory debates. There
are many cases in the global economy, ranging from banking regulation
to social welfare policy, in which the European Union has failed to win
international converts to the European system.[23] Indeed, European reforms are often isolated as examples of convergence around U.S. regulatory preferences. The case of financial securities regulation in the
1980s provides an important case in which the United States projected
its rules and Europe has Americanized its industry.[24] In other words, size
does not necessarily guarantee influence, especially when markets of
similar size compete.

An industry report estimated that global electronic commerce would
grow to $12 trillion in 2006. Of this, the U.S. market would be roughly
$7 trillion, compared with $3 trillion in Europe. And this disparity in market size has been true since the diffusion of the comprehensive model

began in the 1990s.[25] Europe has a robust information economy but it does not clearly dominate the international economy in electronic commerce, a critical market for personal information. The European market is not trivial, but clearly economic strength cannot be the sole factor at work.

Given the inconsistencies between the historical record and the existing explanations, I construct an argument highlighting the importance of time and the development of regulatory institutions to explain outcomes at the three phases.[26]

The Argument in Brief

My central thesis in this book is that government officials with regulatory capacity played a critical role in creating and expanding privacy protection within Europe and around the world. Regulatory capacity encompasses the ability of a jurisdiction to define, monitor, and enforce a set of market rules.[27] Agencies forged to supervise markets in personal information emerged as political actors in their own right, with preferences for strong privacy protections. These subnational actors relied on their power resources—technical expertise, domestically delegated authority, and network ties—to lobby successfully for EU action. After the implementation of the directive, the regulations and agencies built over a thirty-year period provided Europe with the resources to motivate other countries to adjust. Political institutions created new actors, shaped their preferences, and influenced the resources available to them to achieve their goals. A critical finding of this book is that the regulatory institutions that govern internal markets affect the ability of a jurisdiction to formulate and implement rules at home and abroad.

In order to explain why the European Union promoted the comprehensive model within Europe and why it was able to alter policy debates in other countries, I examine the historical timing of data privacy rules. Displaying an increasingly clear pattern in Europe, the national, regional, and global contexts exist in dialogue with one another, shaping (often unintentionally) outcomes at all levels. The spread of comprehensive privacy rules globally is tied to the passage of the EU data privacy directive, which is conditioned on the historical development of national data privacy regimes in Europe and the lack of parallel developments in the United States. Building on comparative historical institutional work, which isolates the importance of timing and temporality within national

institutional trajectories, I examine the relative sequencing of events globally.[28] The empirical narrative takes each phase of this process, highlighting the effect that political institutions created at one historical moment
have on international outcomes in later periods.

The initial adoption of data privacy regulation in the 1970s was primarily addressed in national debates concerned with the spread of computer
technology. This phase laid the foundations for cross-national variation in regulatory capacity.[29] Countries faced new and powerful machines
(i.e., mainframe computers) that permitted enhanced levels of data collection, processing, and networking. Governments developed initiatives
to employ computers to enhance economic planning and rationalize operations. Business also saw the potential inherent in this technology.
At the same time, politicians and citizen groups became concerned that
computers would threaten individual liberties and, therefore, called for
legislative action.

The historical configuration of business and politics played a critical
role in shaping the scope of national legislation. Faced with the demands
of privacy advocates, business had to navigate a course that would mitigate the effect of legislation. Industry lobbies in many countries hoped
to block private-sector data privacy regulation. They viewed the protection of individual rights and enforcement powers as regulatory burdens
and feared that privacy rules would hinder the exploitation of new markets. The organization of business within the economy shaped the intensity of firm preferences. Companies from fragmented sectors that relied
on information exchange for their primary business had a greater incentive to attack proposals for comprehensive data privacy rules. Companies in more oligopolistic markets, however, had a much larger internal
consumer base. They were less affected by the legislation (and may have
even benefited from restrictions on data flows) and thus less vocal in
their opposition.

During these national debates, privacy advocates demanding sweeping legislation faced off against business interests lobbying to constrain
government intervention in the private sector. National political institutions, which determine the ability of interest groups to hinder new
regulations, shaped the relative power of privacy advocates and business
lobbies to influence the final legislation. Privacy advocates could better
fend off attacks against comprehensive privacy rules in countries with less
fragmented political systems. In contrast, business curtailed the scope of
privacy rules by activating legislative blocks such as the presidential veto,

bicameralism, and federalism.[30] By the end of the 1970s, several large countries in Europe had passed strict rules enforced by independent regulatory agencies, and many countries in North America and Asia had adopted limited rules without parallel institutions.

In the second phase, these national systems confronted the changing market structures brought on by European integration and new digital technologies. Data privacy authorities, which were established in some countries and were delegated considerable authority to regulate the use of personal information, played a critical role in promoting data privacy concerns at the European level. The initial rounds of privacy regulation quite unintentionally created policy feedbacks that facilitated the adoption of regional privacy rules.[31]

Data privacy authorities developed their own preferences for greater European regulation. These agencies had a dual motivation: the belief that all Europeans deserved basic privacy protection and a desire to protect their regulatory authority from assault during the creation of the internal market. An internal market in which a third of the members had no data privacy rules posed a threat to their authority. Fearing that firms would relocate their data processing operations to countries without data privacy rules, regulators in countries such as France and Germany formed transgovernmental networks to lobby for European action. Transgovernmental actors include substate officials such as regulators, judges, and parliamentarians who interact internationally and relatively independently of their national executives.[32]

Acting as transgovernmental policy entrepreneurs, government agencies from multiple countries working alone and in cooperation with one another used their regulatory capacity to forge a coalition in support of European rules.[33] Transgovernmental actors are not merely expert groups or epistemic communities endowed with information; they have power both in terms of their relationships with national constituencies and their domestically delegated authority.[34] Each has a stable of domestic constituencies that it has developed by carrying out its job nationally. The reputation that the transgovernmental actors have built can be mobilized to lobby national and international actors in support of their agenda. Moreover, many regulators enjoyed considerable delegated authority to regulate the flow of personal information into and out of their national market and to sanction bureaucratic behavior. In short, they have the authority to disrupt cross-border data exchanges. Working collectively in a network served as a multiplier, coupling agencies with varying levels of domestic authority and amplifying the scope of their relative bully pulpit.

Distinct from arguments emphasizing the neofunctional spillover effects of market integration, the transgovernmental claim presented here stresses coercive power and shrewd politics.[35] Although in some instances substate actors serve to resolve technical fixes that result from market integration, I contend that transgovernmental actors create the very need for policy action. In counterfactual terms, if the creation of the European internal market had proceeded *prior* to the establishment of independent regulatory authorities empowered to disrupt cross-border data flows, the European policy community would *not* have adopted transnational rules.[36]

Thus, the movement toward strict European data privacy rules did not arise from demands by the typical drivers of European integration, such as powerful member states, the Commission, European industry, or the European Court of Justice. National regulators acting as transgovernmental entrepreneurs foisted their preferences onto the European agenda. The resulting privacy directive forced reforms that strengthened privacy protection and civil liberties within the member states and created a structured system of oversight for the entire region. This is particularly remarkable given the widespread belief that the single-market initiative had so focused the European Community on market making and economic concerns that policies pertaining to sociopolitical concerns were deemed impossible.[37]

The third phase of the story is marked by the increased international economic interdependence and communication that brought diverse national regulatory systems into contact with one another. The demands for data exchange inherent in the digital era accentuated the differences between the privacy regimes, engendering international economic and security disputes. Nowhere were these differences more pronounced than between the countries on the two sides of the Atlantic, first as an economic debate about the future of electronic commerce and then as a security debate about the information requirements of a war on terrorism. In both instances, the United States (and many of its economic and strategic partners) lined up behind efficiency arguments, claiming that business and government had to have relatively unfettered access to personal data to guarantee economic growth and national security. European officials, on the other hand, influenced by previous rounds of privacy legislation, argued that privacy was critical to the founding of a robust information society. That is to say, citizens would continue to participate in an online environment only if they felt that their privacy was guaranteed against ubiquitous business and government surveillance.

The European Union turned to regulatory capacity developed at the national and regional levels over a thirty-year period to activate its market power globally. Far from this being a natural diffusion of EU rules based on market efficiency, the European Union had to deploy its regulatory capacity to define, monitor, and enforce a clear set of market rules so as to persuade other countries to adjust.[38] Although European rules offer citizens considerable leverage over the collection and use of personal information in the economy, they have serious financial implications for firms. As such, important interest groups across the industrial world resisted the adoption of comprehensive rules. Non-export-oriented firms that relied on information exchange (e.g., direct marketers and insurance providers) vocally opposed the new laws. They stood to lose from a reduction in data sharing and benefited little from a guarantee of data trade with Europe. Multinational corporations, on the other hand, feared exclusion from the European market. The European Union used its regulatory resources as both carrots and sticks to shape the policy choices of the political actors in foreign countries.

The European Union relied on regulatory capacity to send a coherent signal concerning the set of rules that it wished to export and to assist other countries in their transition to the new regulatory regime. After formulating an EU initiative, national experts were sent to other countries to teach how best to build compliant institutions. By laying the groundwork, these capacity-building efforts lowered the adjustment costs to other nations. EU delegates provided statutory roadmaps that could be modeled, supervised implementation, and benchmarked progress to pressure for adjustment. Representatives of the EU system employed their expertise to persuade other nations that regulatory change was in their best interest. By contrast, the United States, with no dedicated data privacy agency, often found itself lacking the necessary expertise to defend its position in international debates.

Regulatory capacity also provided the European Union with coercive tools. Nations adjust their regulatory policies when they perceive the costs of inaction to be greater than the costs of policy change.[39] The European market size determines the magnitude of *potential* costs to other countries of inaction but not the *real* cost. The probability of suffering nonadjustment costs has less to do with market size. Rather, it is a function of the credible threat of enforcement by European regulators. Critical in the adjustment equation is the perception of Europe's ability to monitor and punish regulatory infractions. The European Union is well positioned to promote its economic agenda internationally in those sectors in which it has extensive internal regulatory resources. And the existence of such resources is highly dependent on the sequencing of political institutional development. The argument, then, offers clear expectations about variation in influence across sectors given different institutional trajectories.

My focus in this book is on the tools available to the European Union to shape policy choices in other countries, but the extent of regulatory adjustment by other countries depends on the constellation of national interests and institutions within them. Where there was little domestic opposition to European demands, countries followed closely the basic principles of the European privacy regime; in countries where there was sizable domestic opposition and adjustment costs, reforms often deviated from the original model.[40] Europe relies on its regulatory capacity to respond to such challenges, emphasizing the benefits and disadvantages of resisting regulatory change. The European Union can use its regulatory tools to mobilize political activity in support of its desired outcome in foreign jurisdictions. National outcomes result from the interaction of external European pressure with such national factors as interest-group configuration, existing regulatory structures, scandal, levels of technological development, and subnational governmental policy.

The European Union used multiple mechanisms to encourage other countries to adopt its regulatory system, ranging from strategies stressing learning to those relying on coercion. It taught other countries about the comprehensive model, placed conditions on eventual membership, threatened to block market entry to firms from nations with inadequate protections, and promoted EU rules through expert policy networks. The existence of these tools is predicated on the historical development of regulatory capacity that began in the 1970s with the passage of national laws and evolved over time with subsequent regional initiatives.

The European Union as a Leader in a Global Economy

In addition to contributing to discussions of global privacy debates, the argument that I develop in this book has several important theoretical implications. First, the analysis demonstrates the global dimensions of the regulatory state and, in turn, Europe's changing role in international relations. Since the 1990s, comparative political economy has identified the shift in governance from positivist to regulatory strategies, that is, for example, the move by governments away from running companies and toward setting the rules by which companies compete. Privatization, liberalization, and market integration have elevated regulation over direct fiscal intervention as the primary tool of governance. Nowhere is this more pronounced than in Europe.[41]

At the national level, member states have built regulatory capacity through a dual reregulation process. Faced with international pressure and the European internal market project, national governments liberalized large segments of their economies. Sectors such as telecommunications, energy, and transportation were deregulated and then reregulated. Governments created new agencies to enforce market rules and, at times, to achieve societal objectives.[42] Far from shrinking the state, the liberalization effort transformed state activities from the direct provision of services to the provision of market rules.[43] At the same time, Europe experienced a social-rights revolution. Responding to protests arising from the student movements in the late 1960s, legislatures expanded social protection standards. From the environment to consumer protection, Europe has established regulatory institutions to safeguard individual interests.[44]

Simultaneously, a set of Europeanwide developments—the single-market project, followed by the Maastricht Treaty and the creation of the single currency—consolidated regulatory authority at the European level. The European Union has jurisdiction over an expanding set of issue areas, the institutions of the European Union have been strengthened by these reforms, and national regulators have been integrated into European policymaking. This has occurred through a daisy chain of delegation whereby national governments have empowered the political actors of the European Union to oversee new areas of governance and these EU actors have, in turn, relied on newly created national regulatory bodies to implement and enforce EU policy. The proliferation of regulatory bodies organized in transgovernmental networks has the potential to inject a number of new political actors into regional politics altering the trajectory of European integration.

The shift in governance at the national and regional levels has clear implications for global governance, as well. International market regulation—the international exposure of nationally regulated markets—has become the next wave of globalization.[45] Conflicts over national rules, ranging from food safety to chemicals, have reached the highest levels of international political dialogue. And the European Union, increasingly, has a powerful voice in such debates. Regulatory institutions constructed to manage competition policy within Europe, for example, have had significant international effects as the EU competition directorate intervened in cases concerning major U.S. firms.[46] Despite the French and Dutch rejection of the EU Constitution and, with it, the post of EU foreign minister, this research demonstrates the much subtler but potentially equally powerful effect of regulatory policy on international affairs. Due to the complex systems of governance within the European Union, this regulatory capacity differs considerably across issue areas. In sectors in which regulatory capacity has been built, Europe has a host of resources to challenge U.S. dominance in the production and maintenance of international economic governance.[47] At the same time, the United States has allowed its regulatory infrastructure to erode in many domains. The European Union, then, may be best positioned to forge an alternative vision of globalization in those market sectors in which it has the densest market rules internally.

Second, in this book I highlight the need for scholars to take seriously the study of the European Union in international politics. Because they have long been considered a sui generis case in the international relations field, the external relations of the European Union have been given relatively little scrutiny. But this assumption obscures the unique roles that all great powers play in the international system. Despite the limited generalizability of such research, the few large markets, such as the United States and the European Union, define international regulatory debates. It is therefore necessary to reconsider the EU role in global governance. In issue areas ranging from trade to the environment, international negotiations increasingly occur between EU representatives and representatives from non-EU nations rather than between German, Spanish, or Polish negotiators and negotiators from other nations. And these EU negotiators have influenced the terms of international outcomes even in the face of global pressures to ratchet down such rules.[48] In this book, I examine how and why this has occurred, adding to a burgeoning literature that takes seriously the role of the European Union as an international actor.[49]

Researchers need to examine how the political institutions of the EU shape the way it interacts in the international environment.[50] It is not enough to accept that the European Union plays a role in international affairs; it is necessary, in addition, to investigate the way in which the institutional design of the European Union affects its behavior. To take one example of multilevel governance, the distribution of political authority within the European Union varies across issue areas.[51] In some policy spheres, such as defense, national authority dominates, whereas in others, such as commercial policy, supranational authority is supreme. Examining the variation in institutional authority and its interaction should not be limited to domestic decision making. If transgovernmental actors and regulatory institutions play an increasing role in EU external affairs, EU behavior may be explained by differences in these internal institutions. On a normative level, the prospect of unelected national bureaucrats driving EU foreign policy raises important questions of accountability and democratic legitimacy.[52] Just as the presidential system has been found to influence U.S. foreign policy, an institutional analysis of regulatory institutions within the European Union will provide a fruitful research agenda for those interested in international economic governance in the twenty-first century.

Third, the stepwise argument adapts sequencing arguments developed in comparative historical institutional research to international questions. Whereas a growing body of international relations literature has identified the importance of domestic institutions in international affairs, this work has relied primarily on rationalist insights from comparativist and Americanist scholarship.[53] The argument in the book complements these efforts by drawing on an equally rich tradition of historical institutional research.[54] A critical finding of historical institutional research is that the sequencing of political events matters; the timing of state building, for example, affects the politicization of national civil services.[55]

The sequencing argument developed in the book translates this argument to the international realm, underscoring the importance of domestic political events in one country relative to similar developments in other countries. Governments construct political institutions with particular historical parameters in mind. As international challenges emerge, countries rarely have the ability to forge new institutions; they are left with the institutions that were created in earlier times. Few policymakers, for example, could have predicted that the U.S. Securities and Exchange Commission (SEC), which was created in the wake of the Great Depression to guarantee the national market, would play a central role in international financial market governance.[56] The strength of the SEC and

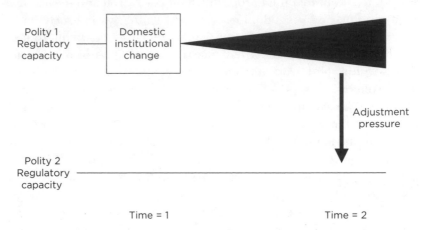

Figure 1. Relative institutional sequencing.

the absence of a credible regulator in European markets for much of the post–World War II period solidified U.S. financial hegemony.[57] The timing of institutional developments in one country when compared with those in others, then, can have a significant effect on international regulatory influence.[58] This, then, creates a systemic dimension whereby the global distribution of domestic regulatory institutions shapes international interactions. Figure 1 offers a simple visual demonstration of the argument, following the development of regulatory capacity in two polities over time. As the two polities come to interact, their relative institutional developments shape the relationship.

Fourth, and finally, in this book I examine a new area of international concern—transnational civil liberties. Privacy, free speech, and the freedom of the press protect citizens from the concentration of power by governments and business. Advanced industrial democracies continually struggle to strike the proper balance between individual freedom and societal order. Long viewed primarily as a domestic debate, these delicate compromises increasingly take on an international dimension. As economic transactions span political boundaries on data networks and terrorism and criminality cross borders, citizens are simultaneously subject to multiple civil liberties regimes. Questions arise as to whose rules should apply. In the late 1990s, for example, a French court fined Yahoo for the distribution of Nazi paraphernalia through its website. Yahoo was found guilty even though the illegal content was not on its French site but was accessed by a French citizen on the U.S. Yahoo service. The French ruling typifies this new area of international conflict and cooperation. Traditional notions of sovereignty become blurred, and new regulatory battles emerge concerning transnational civil liberties.[59] The ways that nations resolve these conflicts have important societal and economic implications. Privacy provides a cutting-edge case of the shifting responsibilities of governance in transnational markets and the possibility for political entrepreneurial intervention to shift the definition of basic fundamental rights on a global scale.

Research Methodology

The book is organized around a historical narrative that examines the global governance of privacy by systematically analyzing a sequencing of national and regional efforts.[60] Bringing together research from comparative political economy and international political economy, I take seriously the findings from comparative work that micro-institutional configurations are important for economic outcomes and highlight the international implications of such domestic institutional changes.[61] This research strategy is a response to the call in the discipline for scholars to examine the origins and evolution of institutional change as they relate to one another.[62] In other words, I examine how regional institutions affect international politics at the same time that I address the prior question of where institutions come from. This strategy is particularly useful in identifying sequencing effects and focusing on how time shapes political outcomes.

My findings emerge from a detailed analysis of historical events. By examining the development and adoption of privacy rules over time, I specify and evaluate competing causal pathways. Critical in this effort is the identification of actor preferences and capabilities. In addition to examining the significant secondary literature on the topic, I conducted numerous expert interviews with the relevant actors involved in the decision-making process.[63] The information from these interviews is corroborated by primary sources—national and EU documents, interest-group position papers, and newspaper accounts of the political debates. When appropriate, I employ counterfactuals and statistical analyses to test the claims that emerge from the historical narrative.

To explicitly address the question of generalizability, the final two chapters provide comparative research that examines the critical arguments of the book using examples across sectors and jurisdictions.

Transatlantic examples from the field of national security, financial services, and aviation safety bolster the central argument of the book and
allay concerns that the findings represent merely quirks of the 1995 data
privacy directive. At the same time, the additional historical examples
flag important boundary conditions for my argument.

The effort to understand the origins and evolution of institutional
change in the global economy requires a tiered approach that examines
national, regional, and international events. Although such a strategy
risks the infinite regression of analysis through prior temporal moments,
I make a good faith effort to ground the research project in its proper
historical context. Nowhere is this more appropriate than in the study of
modern European politics, in which policy at any level is deeply rooted
in historical events at other levels.

The Plan of the Book

In chapter 2, I elaborate the types of privacy regimes that are examined
in the book. The chapter begins with a detailed description of comprehensive and limited data privacy regimes, both their institutional features
and their implications for society and the economy. Although differences
in the scope of regulation (i.e., comprehensive vs. limited) set the stage
for many privacy debates, particularly the extraterritorial effects of European regulations, there is also considerable variation within the regimes.
The chapter, therefore, examines how the implementation and administrative structures differ within the regime types. The second part of the
chapter deals with international trends in regime adoption.

The rest of the book is organized around the three periods that frame
international privacy debates. In chapter 3, I examine the political story
surrounding the emergence of national privacy laws. These initial legislative efforts place the United States and Europe on distinct trajectories for privacy protection. I argue that the historical organization of
business and politics affects the character of privacy regimes. This hypothesis is first tested across a broad range of early-adopter nations, complemented by detailed case studies of legislative action in the United
States, France, and Germany. The case studies underscore the importance of political veto points (political institutions where legislation can
be derailed) and industry structure for the resultant regimes. These countries offer useful case studies because they represent a mix of different
privacy regimes in nations with varying levels of political fragmentation.

Whereas some European countries, most notably Sweden, enacted policies earlier, France and Germany are considered here because of their central role in the European Union. These initial forays into data privacy regulation at the national level laid the foundations for events that later transpired regionally and globally.

In chapter 4, I examine the creation of European rules in the 1990s. Initial data privacy regulation established strong independent regulators in several European countries. Working individually and in networks, data privacy authorities overcame opposition by the European Commission, national governments, and firms. Arguing that the internal market could proceed only with EU-wide rules, the data privacy authorities lobbied the various groups and threatened to block cross-national data transfers, thus reframing the interests of critical actors. The European Union adopted the 1995 data privacy directive, becoming the world leader in data privacy protection. In the chapter, I demonstrate how the institutionalization of data privacy authorities with expertise, statutory authority, and network ties transformed the group into a powerful transgovernmental force capable of foisting their preferences onto the European agenda.

The rapid global diffusion of European privacy regulations is explained in chapter 5. Over forty countries, ranging from Albania to Argentina, have adopted comprehensive legislation. Far from this being a natural, costless adjustment process, the European Union leveraged its regulatory capacity to shape the policy choices in the non-European countries. Relying on control over market access, enlargement, centralized negotiating authority, and oversight networks, the European Union successfully promoted its regulatory regime. Data privacy officials traveled to other nations to teach about the comprehensive regime, accession discussions imposed the adoption of comprehensive rules, market access by firms from other nations was made conditional on adequate protection, and European regulators developed and promoted international best practices. The construction of a regulatory state in Europe to manage the single market simultaneously expanded Europe's ability to influence international market regulation.

The central argument of the book that regulatory capacity plays an important role in both regional and international politics is analyzed in chapter 6. With the terrorist attacks in the United States, Spain, and the United Kingdom since 2001, governments in the advanced industrial world have introduced numerous proposals to expand surveillance efforts. This new national security environment presents significant challenges to personal privacy. In chapter 6, I examine two examples from the new national security environment: the retention of communication data in Europe and negotiations between the United States and Europe over the transfer of airline passenger records. I conclude the chapter by underscoring the importance of transgovernmental actors regionally and regulatory capacity in the international politics of privacy. At the same time, I demonstrate that data privacy (even in countries with strong privacy rules) is not an absolute right; rather, it is a freedom balanced against other societal concerns.

In the final chapter, I return to the theoretical argument posed in the book. The institutional transformation underway in Europe over the last several decades has created a host of new regulatory institutions in sectors ranging from air transport to financial securities. Examining additional cases of European Union policymaking provides further evidence for my claim that internal regulatory capacity affects international regulation. I conclude the chapter by offering several implications of the argument for international politics, stressing the role of regulatory power for international affairs.

Data privacy has emerged as one of the top public policy problems of the information age. European action has transformed the debate, raising the level of protection across the globe. The resulting spread of comprehensive legislation fundamentally shapes individual liberty, state-society relationships, and the international economy. Simultaneously, the case of data privacy demonstrates how and why Europe is an increasingly important player in global governance.

CHAPTER 2

Privacy Regimes

Comprehensive and Limited Approaches

Starting in the 1970s, countries devised legislation to regulate the collection and exchange of personal information. The advanced industrial democracies generally based these rules on a common set of principles, but the fundamental institutional features of national privacy regimes varied. In light of international debates, I distinguish these regimes by differences in the scope of regulation and the character of oversight institutions. The chapter sets out the landscape of these privacy regimes, their basic features, their effects on markets and politics, and their evolution over time. This establishes the foundation for my explanation of the causes of cross-national legislative differences, the EU effort to expand comprehensive regulations regionally, and the proliferation of comprehensive rules across the globe, addressed in the following chapters.

Although national implementation structures vary, two general images of privacy regimes exist: comprehensive and limited. *Comprehensive regimes* cover both the public and private sectors with a similar set of data privacy principles. These principles are enforced by specialized independent regulatory agencies devoted to privacy protection. *Limited regimes* cover the public sector with clearly enforceable data privacy principles but do not impose these general principles on the entire private sector of the economy. Instead, market solutions dominate, with some legislation for a select number of sensitive sectors. Limited approaches rarely have a dedicated enforcement agency or redress mechanisms for both the public and private sectors.[1]

In the most fundamental sense, the comprehensive system anticipates that individuals, because of power and information asymmetries, have difficulty asserting their preferences for privacy protection. It, therefore, creates a set of legal norms that balance individual privacy interests against those of industry and bureaucracy. Individual consent is often required before organizations collect or transmit information to others. Government institutions proactively monitor public- and private-sector behavior and are empowered to identify and sanction the misuse of personal data.

The limited system puts faith in the market to check inappropriate activity. The potential for abuse must be balanced against possible economic and efficiency gains. Consumer demand and industry self-regulation, rather than government regulations, drive the protection of privacy.

The distinction between comprehensive and limited regimes is critically important for understanding the global politics of privacy. Although the two systems long competed as viable alternative solutions to data privacy problems, the limited approach has come under intense pressure to adjust since the passage of EU rules in the 1990s. The European privacy directive includes an important extraterritorial provision that makes access to the European market conditional on the adoption of comprehensive rules. The European Union repeatedly enforced these demands, scrutinizing privacy legislation in countries such as Australia, the Czech Republic, and the United States, which either lacked an independent enforcement agency or did not cover the entire economy. This raised tremendous trade friction among the advanced industrial economies and forced many nations to reconsider their national privacy policies.

The depiction of the two stark regime types—comprehensive and limited—captures essential differences between the majority of national regulations for the purpose of international negotiations. At the same time, domestic institutional structures and implementation mechanisms vary considerably within each category. These differences do not play a significant role at the international level; they affect the domestic organization of privacy regulation. In Europe, for example, member states must adopt the comprehensive regime, but the privacy directive (as is typical with many EU directives) permits national governments considerable maneuverability in implementing general privacy principles. Some nations, such as France, have a relatively centralized administrative system that focuses monitoring and enforcement in a single national oversight body. Others, such as Germany, have a decentralized structure that relies on federal, state, and internal-firm privacy officers to monitor regulations. Both meet the EU requirements, and they have very different effects on the domestic political economy. Similarly, countries, such as Japan and Australia, that have only recently adopted comprehensive rules rely on distinct enforcement and implementation structures.[2]

In this chapter, I offer a detailed description of the global variety of privacy regimes. I begin with a brief overview of the basic principles that underpin all data privacy legislation. Next, I examine the differences between the two regime types—comprehensive and limited—with a discussion of their effects on society and the economy more generally. This section concludes by examining the different implementation and enforcement mechanisms that exist within the regime types. In the final two sections, I identify broad changes in privacy regimes over time, noting the rise of comprehensive rules and the isolation of countries relying on limited systems.

The Underlying Principles

During the 1970s, a group of legal scholars in western Europe and the United States began debating the implications of the mainframe computer for the law. Broadening their focus, these experts transitioned from studying the effect of computers on the law to larger questions surrounding the relationship between computers and society.[3] These discussions produced a set of general norms based on the principle that individuals about whom data are collected have certain rights that must be balanced against the interests of those who collect and process the personal information. The principles include, among others, the right to be notified before the collection of the information, the right to consent to the further distribution of the information, the right to access the data held by a data controller, the right to object to incorrect data, and the right to demand the erasure of incorrect or disputed information. Labeled the Fair Information Practice Principles (FIPPs; see table 1), they were first elaborated in national privacy legislation in Sweden and the United States and were latter codified internationally in the OECD *Guidelines on the Protection of Privacy and Transborder Flows of Personal Data* of 1980 and the Council of Europe *Convention for the Protection*

TABLE 1
The Fair Information Practice Principles

	Description
Collection limitation	Personal information collection should be limited and lawful
Purpose	The purpose of data collection should be disclosed and data should not be used for other purposes without consent
Openness	Individuals should be informed about privacy policies
Accuracy	Data should be accurate, complete, and current
Participation	Individuals may request information about data held by organizations and challenge incorrect data
Security	Stored data must be secure from theft or corruption
Accountability	Organization must be held accountable to measures that implement these principles

of Individuals with Regard to Automatic Processing of Personal Data, which came into force in 1985.[4]

Despite expert consensus concerning data privacy principles, the scope of enforcement and implementation mechanisms has varied across countries, especially with regard to the private sector.[5] I present the two most general categories—comprehensive and limited regimes—before addressing the diversity of implementation structures within the regimes.[6]

The Comprehensive System

In comprehensive privacy regimes, regulatory agencies monitor and enforce privacy regulations to protect individuals against privacy intrusions across the entire economy, including the public and private sectors. Some countries, such as France, have a single law that covers all data processing. Others, such as Denmark, have distinct laws that tailor legislation to the public and private sectors. Rules for additional sectors may extend protection levels, but regardless of such additional legislation, a regulatory floor exists for firms and administrative bodies.[7] The comprehensive regime adopts the FIPP norms to balance the interests of individuals in protecting their privacy against the interests of companies and bureaucracies in collecting and processing personal information.

Data privacy authorities enforce data privacy rules and work with legislatures to identify new regulatory needs. Although the exact institutional designs may vary, many of these authorities are set up as independent agencies with long-term leadership appointments and secure budgets. In guaranteeing leadership tenure for multiple election cycles, most data privacy authorities enjoy considerable protection from direct political influence by their governments.[8]

Data privacy authorities employ a broad range of tools to encourage regulatory compliance. Some focus on national registration or licensing systems, whereby organizations that process information must notify the regulatory agency of data collection efforts. Other agencies rely on codes of conduct developed between data processors in the public and private sectors and the data privacy agency. Still others work with data privacy officers embedded within firms and government agencies to monitor and enforce national rules. All these tools promote a dialogue between organizations exploring new uses of technology and the regulatory authority. At the same time, a powerful bureaucracy constrains the ability of industry and government to exploit unchecked the processing of personal information. Opponents of comprehensive systems argue that these regulations unduly burden industry and government, preventing the productive use of personal information to create new markets and enhance domestic security.

The exact enforcement powers delegated to such agencies vary, with some enjoying broad investigatory and sanctioning powers and others serving a more constrained ombudsperson function. Typical agency duties include drafting or commenting on emerging regulations, managing complaints and enforcement issues, and maintaining a registry of or licensing data banks.[9] In the United Kingdom, for example, between April 2005 and March 2006, the data privacy agency opened over 20,000 cases. In half of these cases, the data protection agency provided advice and guidance. In roughly 1,500 cases, the agency determined a breach of the law had occurred. It required remedial action in two-thirds of these cases, such as the correction of individual data records or staff training. The agency successfully prosecuted fifteen of the sixteen cases it brought against firms that persisted in noncompliance.[10] Increasingly, agencies have used surprise audits to encourage firm compliance. The French privacy agency Commission Nationale de l'Informatique et des Libertés (CNIL), for example, conducted over fifty random audits in 2002 and over thirty in 2003.[11] In addition to overt enforcement, data privacy agencies work with firms and bureaucracies to manage their privacy policies.

The composition, structure, and resources of these agencies differ across countries. In a number of countries, regulatory authority is concentrated in a single commissioner, who is in charge of the data privacy office. In other countries, the data privacy authority is composed of a commission that shares responsibility among its members. At times, these agencies and commissions are supported by tribunals, which manage dispute settlement. In terms of both budget and staff, they have grown into substantial organizations. In 2007, for example, the German federal data protection commissioner had a budget of nearly 4 million euros and a staff of sixty-seven, doubling the number of people working for the organization since 1987.[12] Similarly, the data privacy commission in France has more than doubled its staff since the 1980s, with a budget of 7 million euros and eighty employees in 2004.

Comprehensive regimes enforced by these agencies limit and even prevent the commodification of certain forms of personal information.[13] For example, banks may be barred from trading or selling data to other parties. To illustrate the point, take the case of financial services mergers between insurance companies and banks that occurred in Germany in the 1990s. Companies hoped to use the wealth of customer information warehoused by firms from the two sectors to energize cross-marketing strategies, for example, to encourage customers of a bank affiliate to open accounts with an insurance affiliate. Data privacy rules, however, limited the ability of companies to share personal information and stymied these efforts.[14] A round of regulatory negotiations occurred between insurance companies such as Alliance and Provinzal, which hoped to cash in on bank data bases, with state privacy regulators. The compromise solution required each customer to sign a consent form permitting transfers between the affiliates, slowing the transformation of financial services marketing.

Similarly, data privacy rules have hindered the application of prospective marketing and profiling in the economy. Prospective marketing is a commonplace strategy used in the United States, which identifies potential new clients using personal information purchased from other sources. Many companies in the United States deploy information technology to organize publicly available data, such as driver's licenses and voter registries, along with privately held customer lists to solicit new customers. Data privacy regulations in many European countries, however, limit the transfer of publicly available data. Aside from basic information such as names and addresses, legislation protects the information contained in public registries. Similarly, data privacy regulations limit the ability of credit-reporting agencies to collect and aggregate diverse pools of information and use that information to identify new customers. In France, for example, credit-reporting agencies are public-sector institutions that provide only negative credit information such as loan defaults or bankruptcies. These agencies do not collect positive financial information concerning spending habits, investment information, or successful credit repayment. Given these barriers to data collection, customer lists used to profile individuals are much more expensive than in the United States and more difficult to trade. Limits on access to customer information affect business models in a wide range of sectors. The lack of a robust subprime mortgage market, in which lenders identify high-risk clients and provide customized real estate products, is due in large part to data privacy rules. More generally, organizations have less incentive to produce and share personal information.

At the same time, comprehensive rules affect the ability of the public and private sectors to share information with one another. Because the regime covers the entire scope of the economy and society, all companies that aggregate personal information must comply with national privacy regulations. This limits the ability of companies to acquire personal information from public records, such as voting patterns, judicial decisions, and real estate sales. Privacy rules also constrain the ability of the public sector to rely on the private sector for personal data. In some cases, privacy regulations require private-sector companies to erase customer data. Similarly, information that the private sector transfers to government agencies falls under the comprehensive regime. Legislative proposals that require data retention by telecommunications companies, for example, face very different regulatory requirements in the comprehensive system than in the limited regime.[15] Data retention legislation mandates that telecommunications and Internet firms retain customer information for a specified period in order to assist law enforcement. Although there are a number of exemptions for national security, data transfers from a firm to the government generally must comply with data privacy rules and fall under the regulatory purview of data privacy authorities.

The logic of the comprehensive system assumes that the use of information by organizations is not transparent. Regulations, therefore, assure that individuals are provided with notice of data collection and rights of consent concerning the collection and transfer of such data. The imposition of these regulations, although certainly not eliminating information production or establishing an absolute right to privacy, discourages excessive individual profiling and empowers the regulatory agency to defend individuals against abuse. As external shocks increase pressure for data exchange, such as the rise of international terrorism and criminality, less information exists to be exploited, and a regulatory authority stands ready to protect the citizenry against abuse.

The Limited System

The limited system focuses regulation on the public sector, granting private-sector actors wide latitude in their use of personal information. Regulatory provisions implement the FIPPs in the public sector, shaping the collection and transfer of personal information among government agencies. Although sensitive sectors including health care and telecommunications may face government rules, the regime disperses oversight across a host of public and private bodies. Some countries, such as the United States and Thailand, relegate enforcement to executive ministries ranging from justice ministries to budget offices. Other countries, such as Canada and Australia (prior to their recent legislative reforms), established privacy ombudsmen, who oversaw public sector data processing. The limited regime generally permits the collection and transfer of personal information, relying on self-regulation and market mechanisms to prevent the abuse of personal data exchange.

Working within the limited regime, firms often use personal data to maximize company revenues. Companies buy, sell, and trade data in ways similar to more traditional commodities.[16] A survey conducted by the Financial Services Roundtable, a trade organization for the ninety largest financial services companies in the United States, estimated that the free flow of information earns the financial services industry $17 billion annually.[17] Similar studies report the value of personal information exchange for direct marketing, charities, and credit reporting in the United States. A study financed by the direct marketing industry reports that charities earn $80 billion through direct marketing activities. The sector could face costs of over $16 billion if European-style privacy rules were adopted.[18]

A group of companies known as data compilers have emerged that gather information from diverse sources and sell data to other firms.[19] For example, Experian Corporation, which specializes in consumer profiling, has annual sales of over $1 billion. Experian maintains profiling data on roughly 215 million consumers in over 100 million unique homes in the United States. These data are used to send more than 20 billion pieces of direct mail to more than 100 million households annually.[20]

The U.S. government has increasingly turned to these organizations as a rich surveillance resource. Companies such as ChoicePoint scour personal records to sell to government agencies. The Government Accountability Office estimated that in 2005 four government agencies alone purchased $30 million worth of information from data compilers.[21] In the limited regime, organizations constantly scrutinize citizens and construct detailed individual profiles.

The transfer of data between firms facing different sectoral regulations presents a growing challenge to the limited privacy regime. In the United States, for example, there are a multitude of unregulated sectors in the economy that offer a source of personal information for regulated sectors. Although financial services have faced government regulation since 1999, no rules prevent banks or insurance companies from purchasing personal information from other sources such as direct marketers. Financial services firms have developed affinity-marketing programs whereby they purchase membership lists from organizations such as alumni or professional associations to target low-risk customers. MBNA, the leading affinity marketer in the credit card sector, maintains relationships with nearly five thousand organizations that receive millions of dollars from marketing contracts in return.[22] Similarly, financial services firms collect information from a range of sources to identify high-risk customers, who become targets for high-interest loans.[23]

Companies must balance the benefits of data trade, however, against the fear of a public backlash against privacy intrusions. Inherent in the data trade associated with the limited system lies the risk that personal information will be misused. Privacy violations and industry scandals have the potential to promote consumer resistance to data processing. To protect the reputation and acceptability of data processing, a limited number of sensitive sectors, such as telecommunications, banking, and health care, face government regulations. In other sectors, market mechanisms determine the extent of data trade. Privacy protection itself becomes a marketing tool for firms that wish to distinguish themselves in the market. At the same time, nongovernmental organizations publicize industry scandals and raise consumer awareness. Lacking a government privacy agency with authority to regulate the private sector, civil society plays a more central role in monitoring industry actions. Much of the enforcement and implementation of privacy norms—legislation, self-regulation, and technological solutions—result from a dance between the threat of legal or government action and the hope of industry to

TABLE 2
Characteristics of data protection regimes

Comprehensive	Limited
Public and private sectors regulated	Public sector focus of regulation with a few limited sensitive sectors
Regulation overseen by a regulatory agency	No single regulatory oversight agency exists
Norms balance individual rights against data production and exchange	High levels of data use and exchange
Limits on the transfer of information between the private and public sectors	Data exchange between regulated and unregulated sectors possible
Bureaucratic restrictions on information commodification	Scandal and market forces limit information exchange

minimize the cost of bad privacy press.[24] Table 2 summarizes the differences between the two main regimes.

Institutional and Enforcement Differences within Regimes

Although ideal types are useful for social scientific categorization, they oversimplify the empirical realities. The two regimes are extreme cases of a spectrum of regulatory systems and do not fully capture the richness of the empirical cases. Focusing on formal rules and regulatory institutions, they do not describe the nuance of on-the-ground implementation, technological efforts, or the activities of civil society. They can, however, serve as important benchmarks for comparison within and between regulatory systems. Particularly at the international level, the scope of legal regulation and the independence of enforcement institutions play a critical role.

Within the two systems, however, national enforcement institutions differ considerably and affect the political economy of privacy regulations nationally. Most important, the structure of regulatory oversight varies.[25] Structures differ in their level of centralization, ranging from highly centralized to highly decentralized. These structural differences appear in both comprehensive and limited regimes. The data privacy authorities of South Korea and France, for example, have centralized regulatory institutions, but the South Korean mandate focuses on the public sector, whereas the French authority extends throughout the public and private sectors.

In countries with a centralized authority, the agency often has the right to draft or comment on emerging regulations, decide on enforcement issues, and maintain a registry of data banks within its respective jurisdiction. The regulator works with organizations to establish an appropriate balance between individual privacy concerns and organizational needs. The national regulator is the primary spokesperson for privacy concerns, but at the same time has limited resources and personnel to spend on compliance. The centralized agency within the comprehensive regime is particularly well suited to manage industries in which there are a concentrated number of large firms, as was long the case in the telecommunications sector. A potential disadvantage of the centralized system, however, is that it can have a top-down flare, with data privacy agencies developing policies that are then imposed on regulated organizations.

A decentralized structure, also found in both the limited and comprehensive regimes, does not limit rule development and enforcement to one single institution. Federal countries, such as Canada, Switzerland, and the United States, have both national and state-level agencies with the task of overseeing privacy concerns in their respective jurisdictions. Decentralized structures often promote the incorporation of private actors into the regulatory process. In some countries, such as Germany, companies are required to appoint chief privacy officers who monitor the use of personal information within the firm. In other countries, notably the Netherlands, firms participate in industry organizations to develop codes of conduct and offer advice on pending data privacy regulations. Such strategies promote close working relationships between regulators and their regulatory constituents whereby a large number of organizations become actively involved in the regulatory process. In the decentralized structure, regulators at the national, state, and firm levels share oversight responsibility. As the number of regulatory actors involved multiply, establishing common positions becomes more difficult. When a policy consensus exists, however, the decentralized system has a large number of advocates that can be mobilized for a political cause.

Although nations have constructed a variety of institutional enforcement systems, the differences in the scope of regulation (i.e., whether a country has a comprehensive or limited regime) provide an overarching framework that modifies the effect of the differences in regulatory structure. Comprehensive regimes that stress decentralized enforcement mechanisms, for example, employ the shadow of government sanction to shape private-sector governance. Under a system of co-regulation, adopted by countries such as the Netherlands and Australia, comprehensive privacy rules exist but industry associations have the right to work with data privacy authorities to develop tailored codes of conduct for their sector. These codes supersede national rules, creating best practices that minimize the regulatory burden and maximize appropriate privacy protection for the sector. Industry codes legally bind firms and data privacy agencies have the authority to rescind them and sanction nonenforcement. The motivation to initiate private-sector solutions in this form of co-regulation, in which industry codes offer an alternative to direct government regulation, differs considerably from industry efforts in limited regimes, such as the United States, where the threat of scandal often drives firm participation. Self-regulation in limited systems must rely on the commitment of other industry participants to enforce codes because they lack a clear government backstop to assure industry compliance.[26]

Data privacy legislation is not the sole mechanism by which a society manages the use and exchange of personal information. In addition to the self-regulatory efforts already described, technology plays a critical role in meeting emerging privacy challenges. Companies have developed a number of innovative systems, known collectively as privacy-enhancing technologies (PETs). These include software filters that assist individuals as they disclose personal information online and security measures that prevent criminal behavior.[27] There are also a number of nongovernmental organizations that actively promote privacy protection. Privacy International, the Electronic Privacy Information Center, and Statewatch are among some of the most active. They monitor government and business activities, exposing abuses and pressing for greater attention to the issue. As is the case with industry efforts, however, both technologies and nongovernmental efforts should be evaluated within the broader regulatory context. Data privacy authorities in comprehensive systems have played an important role in promoting PETs; they actively support their development and encourage their adoption by firms and government agencies.[28] Although industry in limited regimes has shown interest in PETs, coordination has proven more difficult, with many competing standards emerging. Similarly, privacy advocates in Europe often find support in the statements and actions of data privacy authorities; something unavailable to similar groups working in limited regimes.

Neither regime—comprehensive or limited—creates an absolute right to privacy.[29] The push for national identification cards since the turn of the twenty-first century in a number of European countries, including the Netherlands and the United Kingdom, powerfully demonstrates that comprehensive rules do not eliminate data collection.[30] Rather, privacy regimes construct a framework that attempts to balance the privacy interests of individuals against the need of an organization for information, and the two regimes establish different defaults. In so doing, they shape flows of personal information in society and the economy and the organization of political interests concerning privacy issues.

The Comprehensive System Gets a Boost

During the 1970s and 1980s, the comprehensive and limited systems coexisted in relative parity. A broad swath of nations, such as Australia, Canada, Japan, Switzerland, and the United States, had adopted limited protection, whereas a group of European nations, such as France, Germany, and the United Kingdom, had comprehensive rules. Although Europe was the locus of comprehensive protection, in 1985 fewer than half of the twelve members of the European Community had any privacy legislation.

After fifteen years of debate, however, the European Union in 1995 adopted a directive designed to regulate data privacy for the entire community. The directive required member states to implement comprehensive privacy legislation by 1998 and to create independent regulatory agencies devoted to the monitoring and enforcement of the law. The legislation attempted to harmonize rules so as to permit the free flow of information within Europe. At the same time, the directive called for a high level of protection, signaling EU commitment to individual data privacy rights. The directive maintains that the harmonization effort should not weaken privacy protection within Europe.[31] In addition to Belgium, Greece, Italy, Portugal, and Spain, which did not previously have national privacy rules, the eastern enlargement of the European Union in 2004 guaranteed that ten more countries adopted the comprehensive model.

The European data privacy directive has mitigated some important differences in regulatory structure across the member states. Enforcement powers were harmonized to afford regulators a high degree of authority. All data privacy agencies won the power to investigate and sanction; this authority had been previously limited to only a few agencies. The directive authorizes all national regulatory authorities to employ a diversity of regulatory structures, including registries, codes of conduct, and internal private-sector privacy officers. Since the passage of the directive, countries that had originally adhered rather strictly to one institutional structure have experimented with those of other systems. France, for example, has encouraged firms to appoint internal privacy officers, integrating decentralized mechanisms into a previously highly centralized regulatory structure.[32]

The directive also influences the way that Europe interacts with the rest of the world. Article 25 of the directive requires that international data transfers be limited to countries with adequate data privacy rules. The article is modeled on earlier national legislation, such as that in France and Sweden, which authorized the regulation of transborder data flows. These original provisions were motivated primarily by fears associated with the rise of multinational corporations in the 1970s. Given the inherent mobility of information, policymakers argued that successful supranational regulation had to protect EU data transferred outside of the European Union. In addition, the existence of national laws granting national regulators these powers pushed the commission to include a provision to coordinate the application of this authority at the EU level. A failure to do so in the directive risked a fragmentation, whereby member states might highjack the legislation to magnify their individual extraterritorial reach.

The Comprehensive Regime Goes Global

In contrast to the early years of data privacy legislation when comprehensive regulations were mainly a European phenomenon, since the 1990s it has become the de facto international model. Nations across the globe have crafted comprehensive legislation that covers the public- and private-sector use of personal information and establishes a clear enforcement mechanism.[33] Over thirty countries from five continents passed comprehensive legislation between 1990 and 2006. Emerging-market financial centers, including Dubai, Hong Kong, and Taiwan, have as well. This trend contrasts sharply with the fifteen years prior to 1990, when only thirteen countries (all European, with the exception of Israel) had adopted legislation.

In addition to a rise in the number of countries adopting comprehensive regimes, a transformation has occurred whereby nations that previously regulated primarily the public sector have adopted private sector legislation as well. Since the first data privacy policies emerged in the 1970s, an alternative policy strategy existed that focused on public-sector records. More recently, eight countries have reformed their limited privacy policies to move toward comprehensive rules: Australia, Canada, the Czech Republic, Japan, Lithuania, New Zealand, Slovakia, and Switzerland.[34] Due to Canadian federalism, for example, employee data were originally covered by provincial rules, and some provinces did not have data privacy regulations. In 2004, however, federal Canadian legislation was reformed to preempt provincial law, largely eliminating this loophole. Organizations conducting commercial activity in Canada are now required to protect employee data.[35] The trend indicates that late adopters have moved ever closer to the ideal-typical comprehensive regime.

Despite the widespread diffusion of the comprehensive regime, late adopters have not merely copied European institutions. In those countries new to comprehensive legislation, a variety of regulatory structures exist. Some countries, including many in eastern Europe, have closely replicated the centralized regulatory structure familiar to some EU member states. Others, especially in the Asia-Pacific region, have combined a variety of regulatory instruments. The European Union has not universally accepted the reforms in other countries as meeting its definition of adequate protection, highlighting the diversity of approaches.[36] These patterns of mimicry and experimentation are common in diffusion processes.[37] Nevertheless, late adopters share a fundamental similarity; enforceable regulations cover information collection and transfer in the public and private sectors.

The proliferation of the comprehensive model does not mean that the limited system has been eliminated as an option for regulating privacy. Several countries, for example, the United States, South Korea, and Thailand, maintain limited regulatory regimes. A group of countries, under the auspices of Asia-Pacific Economic Cooperation (APEC), formulated a privacy framework that attempted to broaden the forms of acceptable implementation strategies and potentially provide an alternative to the EU comprehensive regime.[38] The initial proposal included a provision that would allow countries to self-certify their privacy regime as providing internationally adequate privacy protections. Countries with limited regimes might have argued that their specific sectoral regulations qualified the country for international data exchanges.[39] Despite the adoption of the privacy framework, which reaffirmed many of the FIPPs, the group did not reach an agreement on how to evaluate the levels of protection in other countries. The APEC initiative may eventually shift international privacy politics, but over the last thirty years the limited regime has become increasingly marginalized. This shift toward comprehensive protection, which started in the 1990s, is depicted in figure 2.

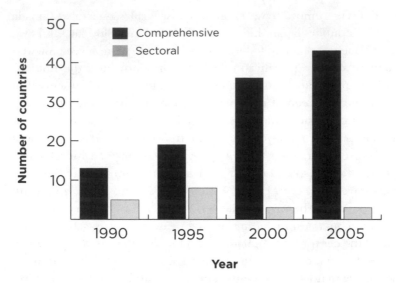

Figure 2. International diffusion of the comprehensive regime, 1990–2005.

Data on national regulatory policy is available through Privacy International and the Council of Europe. Data available at: http://www.privacyinternational.org and http://www.coe.int/T/E/Legal_affairs/Legal_co-operation/Data_protection/ Documents/National_laws.

Despite mounting security concerns related to international terrorism, countries have not abandoned the comprehensive regime or increasingly turned to the limited regime. Within the comprehensive regime, the balance between individual privacy concerns about and organizational interests in data has been recalibrated. Data retention policies and new national identification cards in Europe indicate that governments are looking for means to acquire more and different types of data. At the same time, these data still generally receive some scrutiny under data privacy laws. Governments have not eliminated data privacy authorities or sanctioned them as they criticize many of these surveillance efforts. As I examine at length in chapter 6, data privacy laws have deeply affected the construction of new surveillance systems and data privacy authorities have remained extremely active in the new security environment. More generally, countries have continued to adopt comprehensive regulations since 2001.

Not only have governments adapted to the comprehensive regime, but so too have multinational businesses. The most telling example is the

Safe Harbor Agreement reached between the United States and Europe in 2000. The agreement permits U.S. firms to transfer data between their European and U.S. affiliates as long as the firms comply with European regulatory standards. In practical terms, the U.S. Department of Commerce maintains a list of firms that have agreed to follow the agreement.[40] The principles of the agreement are binding on companies, and businesses must choose whether they will be monitored and enforced by self-regulation or by self-certification. Under self-regulation, the company agrees to comply with the principles and joins an independent dispute-settlement body. These dispute-settlement bodies include a range of private organizations, such as the Better Business Bureau or TRUSTe, that process and mediate complaints. The Federal Trade Commission agrees to act as a regulatory backstop, monitoring firm compliance with their self-regulatory agreements. Because the Federal Trade Commission jurisdiction does not extend to financial services or telecommunications, these sectors are excluded from the agreement. Under self-certification, firms register with a national European data privacy authority and agree to be regulated by that agency. If companies transfer human resources data, they are required to self-certify. A 2004 review of the implementation of the agreement found that 75 percent of firms self-certified, de facto placing themselves under the supervision of data privacy authorities in Europe.[41]

Although the uptake of the Safe Harbor Agreement began slowly, roughly one thousand U.S. companies have signed on and some eighty Fortune 500 companies have adopted the agreement. Excluding financial services and telecommunications firms, which are not eligible for the compromise, this represents nearly 20 percent of the largest firms in the United States. These numbers, however, underrepresent the impact of the agreement. Since the conclusion of negotiations, U.S. firms have moved on many fronts to satisfy European regulatory demands. Survey data suggest that many multinational companies integrate national data privacy regulations into their international operations.[42] In addition, such companies now routinely appoint chief privacy officers who oversee data use. This new management position signals that industry takes such privacy concerns seriously. Firms in emerging markets, hoping to attract the outsourcing of service contracts from European companies, have adjusted their business practices to comply with European privacy demands.[43]

That being said, many critics of the agreement argue that it has not garnered the adoption rate originally predicted and that actual enforcement has been rare. The very novelty of the compromise might have weakened its appeal. U.S. companies have expressed concern that the obligations of the agreement are not clear and that it creates a rather complicated framework for complying with European demands.[44] On the other hand, the agreement has existed for less than a decade; membership has more than doubled in the last few years from roughly four hundred in 2003 to nearly one thousand in 2006, and the coverage of the largest corporations in the United States has reached a substantial level.

European rules have also motivated international business associations to develop international standards and technology to minimize burdensome government intervention. The Global Business Dialogue (GBD), a network of leading multinational businesses, has worked to promote privacy-enhancing technology and corporate contracts to comply with European rules and to lessen the direct intervention of government regulators in internal firm operations.[45] These contracts require that companies uphold basic privacy principles, but, instead of government regulation, courts and mediation are used to enforce these standards. The usefulness of these solutions remains unclear because they too raise many issues of regulatory uncertainty and put much more responsibility on individual firms to devise and defend their privacy practices.

The international harmonization around comprehensive rules has real consequences for the polity and the economy. Politically, comprehensive rules limit the ability of firms to profile individuals. Because businesses are only able to transfer personal information to other companies with the consent of the consumer, it is much more complicated for companies to aggregate data across sectors. Discriminating against those that are most at risk is much more difficult under comprehensive regimes. Governments in Europe have argued that comprehensive protection increases consumer confidence in the new information technologies and is therefore critical for the successful economic diffusion and use of such innovations. Comprehensive systems hinder the flow of information between the public and private sectors, limiting the outsourcing of social control by governments to firms.

Whereas national rules continue to vary in terms of some implementation and enforcement practices, alternatives to the comprehensive regulatory regime developed in Europe seem to be disappearing at the international level. With the notable exception of those in the United States and several Asian countries, consumers living in industrial democracies increasingly enjoy enforceable rights of consent, notice, and access to personal information collected in the public and private sectors. This heightened level of protection holds even in cases in which the corporate headquarters of an international firm is located in a country with rules that fail to meet EU standards. Although security concerns have raised many new privacy challenges, countries have not turned away from the comprehensive regime. From national debates of the 1970s to international practice in the twenty-first century, few politicians and businesses question the importance of data privacy protection.

This shift toward the comprehensive system is quite striking. Since the 1970s, the two regulatory systems have coexisted, with the majority of the population living in the industrialized world favoring the limited regime. A functional argument—that the comprehensive system is simply more effective at easing market frictions—cannot easily explain the timing of the global shift to the comprehensive regime in the 1990s. The comprehensive model existed long before EU entry into the policy space. Through 1985, Israel was the only non–western European nation to adopt comprehensive rules, and considerable political opposition existed to the comprehensive system. Non-export-oriented domestic industries in countries such as the United States, Japan, and Australia vehemently protested that comprehensive rules would stifle innovation and crush the information technology revolution and predicted that the imposition of EU rules would cost billions of dollars. This opposition spilled over into international affairs, with the United States and Europe threatening a trade war over the diverging privacy policies.[46] OECD ministers met in 1999 to discuss data privacy and concluded that, although it was a major concern of the digital era, national strategies should be allowed.

Given the vocal international opposition to the comprehensive regime and the consequences of adopting such legislation for the economy and society, it is important to consider the political development of privacy regimes during the second half of the twentieth century. Following the three-step narrative introduced in chapter 1, the next chapters take each phase in turn—explaining the roots of cross-national variation in initial privacy legislation, the implications of these rules for regional politics within Europe, and the effects of constructing a European data privacy regime for data privacy rules around the globe. The historical narrative points to the importance of intra-European institutional developments in the area of regulatory capacity for the subsequent global adoption of the comprehensive regulatory model.

CHAPTER 3

The Computer Age

Similar Problems, Different Solutions

To understand regional European efforts concerning data privacy and the subsequent international diffusion of comprehensive legislation, I examine in this chapter the historical roots of varying data privacy regimes. National decisions made in the middle of the twentieth century created distinct regulatory institutions; these decisions, then, marked the first step in the sequencing argument outlined in chapter 1. The goal of the chapter is to explore the birth of domestic data privacy regimes in the advanced industrial democracies in order to better understand the constraints and resources that governments face as they manage global data privacy issues in the twenty-first century.

The rise of the mainframe computer spawned the initial data privacy debates; for the first time, unprecedented amounts of personal information could be collected, warehoused, and processed. Governments and business hoped to employ this new technology to promote efficiency, reduce fraud, and strengthen security. Over the course of the 1970s, however, technological advances and executive branch abuses propelled nightmarish images of social control to the top of the public policy agenda. National scandals involving personal data such as Watergate in the United States and the Système Automatisé pour les Fichiers Administratifs et le Répertoire des Individus (SAFARI) affair in France taught policymakers and the public a new appreciation for the powerful role that personal information plays in the emerging information era.

Societies around the globe faced a similar challenge—how to manage the rapid expansion of personal information flows. Despite this common policy problem, national governments differed in their responses. The U.S. government, for example, passed the Privacy Act in 1974, establishing a limited regulatory framework that focused attention on the public sector. Continental Europe, notably France and Germany, adopted legislation in the late 1970s that created comprehensive rules for the public and private sectors, enforced by independent regulatory agencies.[1] The contrast in initial regulatory strategies set the two regions on very different trajectories for privacy protection. Here I use a historical institutional framework to explain why this divergence came to pass—that is, why some countries adopted limited rules in the 1970s but key continental nations constructed comprehensive regimes for privacy protection.[2]

The story is puzzling given the fact that legislators considered comprehensive rules in all three nations. A motley alliance of legal scholars, technologists, and politicians emerged in each country in response to the fear that computer technology would centralize power within their respective societies. They forged a social libertarian coalition that drafted comprehensive proposals and lobbied governments to construct legislative checks against the rampant exchange of personal data. An international expert consensus concerning the basic principles that underpin appropriate privacy protection supported these efforts. Despite the common call across countries for comprehensive regulations, they did not universally succeed.

As argued in chapter 1, popular accounts often emphasize the authoritarian legacies of countries to explain differences in national privacy regimes—that is, countries that had first-hand experiences with fascism were more sensitive to such issues. This claim, however, does not address the variation in regulatory *scope* between the United States and Europe or even within Europe: the choice by some governments to concentrate regulation primarily on the public sector versus the public and private sectors. In keeping with the historical sequencing argument presented in chapter 1, I invoke an institutional explanation that emphasizes the organization of business and politics to explain this variation in industry preferences and policy outcomes across countries. The extent to which industry viewed these rules as burdensome and their ability to influence political outcomes depended, in large part, on the structure of the national political economy. The requirements of the comprehensive system raise the costs of transferring personal information across firms. These costs are higher for firms in sectors characterized by a fragmented industry structure, in which there is greater dependence on information exchange. Firms in concentrated markets, those that have enough internal data from their sizable customer bases, view such rules as a helpful barrier against new entrants. Following a strategy well known to scholars of political economy, business lobbies that opposed data privacy rules used political veto points, positions within the political system where legislation can be blocked, to prevent the adoption of comprehensive rules. In terms of preferences, firms in fragmented industries tended to be more vocal in their opposition to privacy rules than did firms in oligopolistic market structures. In terms of outcomes, business was more successful in limiting privacy rules in nations with a greater number of veto points. The environments that structured both preferences and veto points were often the result of long-term institutional developments.

The organization of the domestic political economy further influenced the structure of national implementation and enforcement institutions. States within federal countries, for example, demanded the decentralized administration of privacy laws, whereas legislation in unitary governments centralized administration in a single body. Similarly, regulatory structures mirrored existing public-private sector coordination arrangements, with statist economies emphasizing centralized, top-down enforcement; corporatist economies emphasizing collaborative regulatory networks; and liberal economies emphasizing arms-length, market-based solutions.[3]

In this chapter, I first establish the common policy challenge posed by the computer revolution, including its threat to individual liberties. I follow this with a discussion of the similar proposals that emerged across countries before detailing the sources of cross-national policy differences.

The Computer Revolution

In the years following World War II, the tasks of the modern central government—from economic management to internal security—expanded rapidly. Between 1950 and 1970, total government expenditures in the United States rose 7 percent, from 21 to 28 percent of GDP. During the same period, federal employment swelled from roughly 1.5 million to 2.2 million. Similarly, welfare expenditures for new social insurance programs such as Social Security and Medicare exploded from less than $1 billion in 1950 to over $36 billion by 1970.[4] Similar trends across the advanced industrial democracies mirrored the U.S. experience.[5] As governing became more complicated, public officials searched for mechanisms by which to improve economic planning and rationalize operations.

Computer technology emerged as one potential mechanism to resolve the growing complexity of governing and competing in the industrial era. The civilian government entered the computer age in 1951, when the U.S. Bureau of the Census purchased its first mainframe computer. Public- and private-sector adoption of computer technology spread rapidly as data storage became more economical and efficient. The cost of storing 1 million characters of information for one month dropped from $130 in 1956 to $4.55 in 1973, and the time required to access that information fell from eight-tenths of a second to thirty-thousandths of a second.[6] By 1971, just twenty years after the purchase of the first civilian computer, the U.S. government had deployed nearly six thousand computers, and some fifty-four federal agencies had developed over 850 data banks.[7] Between 1965 and 1975, computers-in-use per one thousand people had grown from 0.01 to 0.9, demonstrating the rapid diffusion of the technology (see table 3). Data processing units in Germany jumped from 1,650 to 25,000 during a similar period.[8] Company managers as well as public administrators looked to the computer as a vital tool to increase operational efficiency.

Centralizing Information

With the proliferation of computer technology in large organizations, governments proposed linking previously discrete information from diverse

TABLE 3
Computers in use per 1,000 people in the United States, 1965–1995

	Year-end					
	1965	1975	1980	1985	1991	1995
Computers per 1,000 people	0.01	0.9	14	90	245	365

Source: Egil Juliussen and Karen Petska-Juliussen, *The 8th Annual Computer Industry Almanac* (Incline Village, Nev.: Computer Industry Almanac, 1996).

collection points. The goal of such efforts was to enhance efficiency and oversight of growing public and business services. Across the OECD countries, governments created over two hundred data bank projects.[9] The U.S. Social Science Research Council developed one of the first proposals in 1965, calling for the creation of a national data center that would link various agency statistics into a clearinghouse for government information. The Bureau of the Budget expanded on the idea and in 1966 drew up plans to establish the National Data Center, which was to centralize twenty agency data banks.[10]

A similar regional effort was underway in the German state of Hesse. Begun in 1965, the Hesse First plan attempted to centralize economic and regional planning for the state in an attempt to promote growth.[11] As part of the ongoing efforts in Hesse to coordinate economic development, the government created a central data processing system for state and communal data in 1969. This effort provided the motivation for the Data Protection Act of the State of Hesse in 1970. This subnational legislation covered public-sector data use and was one of the first efforts in the world to regulate privacy concerns.[12]

Similarly, the German federal government in 1966 began a discussion of how to incorporate information technology into the public administration. Establishing a data processing committee in 1968, the government studied over a five-year period how computer innovations could be integrated into burgeoning planning efforts.[13]

As part of this data coordination program, the government proposed that government information collection be centralized around a single unique identification number. The release in 1971 by the Willy Brandt administration of an initial draft of a registry law was the culmination of much of this effort. The German Länder and communal governments already had citizen registries that contained personal information, including address, phone, religion, age, sex, and occupation. The government proposed to coordinate the Länder registries into a single computer-powered national database, whereby individuals would receive unique identifiers.

In the early 1970s, the French government explored a number of similar efforts. The most famous was a pilot project to centralize personal information, given the unfortunate code name SAFARI. The project examined using personal identification numbers as a mechanism to link disparate national databases. Governments saw in these efforts the possibility of reducing welfare fraud, increasing law enforcement efforts, and more generally navigating the boom and bust cycle of the capitalist state.

The Threat of Surveillance

With the proliferation of computer technology in the late 1960s and government efforts to use this technology to centralize information resources, societal concern over privacy threats grew. These fears evolved over nearly a decade, culminating in the call for comprehensive privacy legislation. Governments on both sides of the Atlantic held hearings in the late 1960s in response to proposals to centralize government data banks. National data banks quickly became synonymous with the Orwellian nightmare—Big Brother government using such systems to isolate political dissidents and eliminate them.[14] Although opposition blocked efforts to create unified national computer databases in many countries, the computer revolution could not be stopped.

A set of scandals that erupted during the late 1960s and early 1970s underscored the potential for abuse and the need for legal protections. In the United States, the domestic surveillance efforts of the army along with Watergate raised the salience of privacy concerns. In 1969, an army official leaked information concerning army efforts to monitor political dissidents such as members of the National Association for the Advancement of Colored People (NAACP) and the American Civil Liberties Union (ACLU) and a set of Democratic congresspeople, including a representative and senator-elect from Illinois.[15] As the news hit that a group tied to the president had stolen personal records in an attempt to win political advantage, privacy became a galvanizing issue. The presidential scandal clearly demonstrated the growth of executive power and the political danger of the collection of personal information.[16]

In spring 1974, the newspaper *Le Monde* set off a national privacy debate in France with an article titled, "SAFARI, or the Hunt for the French."[17] The perceived secrecy surrounding the database project enraged the political elite, who saw it as a potential power grab. This came on the heels of another data bank scandal surrounding children's medical data. The government had proposed to set up a centralized registry of children's medical information known as Gestion Automatisée de la Médicine Infantile (GAMIN, slang for child). The program was supposed to follow each child from birth through school. Protests emerged as citizen groups protested that the data bank would be used to target "problematic" youth, radically increasing government social control.[18] Elite and public outcry surrounding these government initiatives forced the administration to convene a national Commission on Data Processing and Freedom (known as the Tricot Commission) to examine the implications of computer technology for personal liberty. The final report of the commission provided the basis for initial French data privacy legislation.[19]

Common Proposals—Varying Legislation

In response to the threat to privacy posed by computer technology, policymakers across the industrial world developed a set of basic policy principles.[20] The principles, labeled the Fair Information Practice Principles (FIPPs), included norms concerning consent, notification, accuracy, security, and accountability (a full list of the principles can be found in chapter 2, table 1). These principles, later codified by international organizations, offered a framework for emerging privacy regulations.[21] The proposals that sprang up in legislatures from the United States to Europe looked surprisingly similar. Policymakers called for the creation of regulatory agencies capable of monitoring and enforcing the FIPPs in the public and private sectors.[22] Championed by an alliance of social libertarian politicians concerned with the concentration of power in society, such proposals quickly encountered opposition from business interests and administrative agencies, which resisted additional regulation.

The discussion in the United States began in 1972 when the Department of Health, Education, and Welfare (HEW) organized a committee to study the use of personal information in society. The final report outlined a set of FIPPs that processors of personal information should follow when handling data.[23] Similarly in Germany, the federal government commissioned a set of recommendations from the University of Regensburg concerning the regulation of personal information, known as the *Recommendation on Data Protection*, which were released in 1972.[24] The Tricot Commission in France presented its findings in 1975, calling on the government to enact "measures to ensure the development of data processing in the semi-public and private sectors will take place in the context of respect for private life, individual liberties, and public liberties."[25]

Politically active lawyers and computer scientists provided the backbone of the intellectual effort needed to construct realistic policy proposals.

Meeting nationally to provide information to their governments and internationally to develop a coherent set of privacy standards, these privacy experts produced the original research that inspired privacy rules.[26] Unable to obtain support from the European Commission, these actors worked internationally through the OECD and the Council of Europe. Because legislative efforts were confined to the national level in this first phase of regulation, they actively lobbied their respective governments to take action to assure the responsible diffusion of computer technology.

This intellectual agenda resonated with policy actors interested in social libertarian issues. These politicians feared that the concentration of power in government and big business would endanger individual liberty. After roughly twenty years of closed, regimented postwar politics, political actors—inspired by the student movements of the 1960s—saw a window of opportunity to open up government. Social libertarians pushed to free individuals from control and check the further expansion of centralized authority. The threats to liberty posed by computer technology offered a natural policy agenda.

At the forefront of the privacy movement in the United States stood Sam Ervin (D-S.C.). Clearly established in the old guard of the Southern Democrats, Ervin headed the Subcommittee for Constitutional Rights of the Judiciary Committee. Ervin used his post to hold a series of hearings on privacy issues, including the privacy of federal employees, military surveillance, and comprehensive legislation. Far from a member of the progressive wing of the Democratic Party, Ervin considered himself a constitutionalist who believed that the government should play a limited role in constraining liberty.[27] With the rise of new technology and executive scandal, Ervin became a specialist on information technology and individual rights issues. In addition to leading the Senate investigation of the Watergate affair and being a staunch opponent of President Richard Nixon, Ervin fought for comprehensive privacy rules in the Senate.[28]

On the House side, an unusual alliance formed between Edward Koch (D-N.Y.) and Barry Goldwater Jr. (R-Calif.). Young members of their respective parties, the progressive Koch and the conservative Goldwater found common ground on issues concerning the potential abuse of personal information—in both the public and private sectors—in the modern political economy.[29] Citing the threat of centralized data banks to individual liberty, the congressmen went on to sit on the Privacy Protection

Study Commission that emerged from the Privacy Act of 1974 and championed privacy issues throughout their congressional careers.[30] Despite the oft-cited odd-couple character of their cooperation, their common belief that unchecked power threatened liberty forged a logical alliance for the support of comprehensive privacy rules.

In France, with the 1974 election of Valéry Giscard d'Estaing, a new push for democratic openness entered French politics. As the twenty-year iron grip of the center-right Gaullist party weakened, Giscard d'Estaing's Independent Republicans offered an alternative that championed a social libertarian agenda. Promising to inject civil liberties, social reform, and participation into an ossified French political culture, the Giscard administration worked on a range of issues, including easing abortion restrictions, lowering the voting age, expanding freedom of information, and minimizing divorce restrictions.[31] Culminating in the publication of his book *Démocratie française*, in which he advocates a real liberalism that "recognizes the individual as the sole source and exclusive end of all social and political organization,"[32] Giscard d'Estaing committed himself, at least rhetorically, to democratizing French politics. Politically, the reform platform moved Giscard's center-right coalition enough to the left to lure critical socially libertarian votes away from the Socialist party.[33]

In its effort to increase transparency and promote civil liberties, the new government championed data privacy. Interior Minister Michel Poniatowski, who was a close ally of Giscard and had played a substantial role in his electoral victory, had long supported data privacy legislation. In 1970, as an Independent Republican member of parliament, Poniatowski introduced legislation to create an independent authority to oversee personal information collection.[34] As interior minister, he argued for the creation of data privacy rules.[35]

Louis Joinet, an official in the Ministry of Justice at the time, was given the task of coordinating data privacy policy in France and was sent as the French liaison to international data privacy working groups at the OECD and the Council of Europe. Having served on the Tricot Commission, he understood data privacy issues. Joinet quickly rose in importance at the international meetings, taking on the responsibility of chair at the Council of Europe and vice chair at the OECD of their respective working groups on data privacy. Through this international experience, Joinet became fluent in international data privacy policy problems and responses and a respected expert in the French administration on these issues.[36]

Within the German government, the social liberal wing of the Free Democratic Party (FDP) examined the implications of computer technology for society.[37] This small party represented liberal interests of the German electorate and played a decisive king-maker role in German coalition governments through much of the postwar period. The social-liberal wing incorporated progressive reforms into the economic libertarian positions, which had dominated the party platform.[38] Concerned with issues that included abortion, divorce, and due process rights, the group attempted to minimize state involvement in private affairs, democratize society, and limit the concentration of power.[39]

Aside from a four-year period of Christian Democratic Union (CDU) absolute majority, the FDP had governed in coalition with the CDU since 1949. The decision of the CDU to form a grand coalition with the Sozialdemokratische Partei Deutschlands (SPD) in 1966, thereby excluding the FDP, shook the party. A group of FDP social-liberal party members seized the opportunity to elevate their status within the party ahead of the traditionally dominant economic libertarian wing. Blaming the economic libertarian wing for becoming too dependent on the CDU chancellor Konrad Adenauer and for losing the power position of the FDP, the progressive wing transformed the party during the late 1960s. The Grand Coalition between the CDU and the SPD thus shifted the balance of power within the FDP toward the social-liberal wing.[40]

This group of social-liberal FDP members, including two future federal interior ministers, Werner Maihofer and Gerhart Baum, and one Land (German state) interior minister, Burkhart Hirsch, actively followed the data privacy debate. Concerned with the effect of information technology on power relations within society, this core group of FDP members elevated data privacy to a party priority;[41] with rising public concern regarding computer use by large organizations, the social-liberal wing of the FDP hoped to leverage data privacy as a means both to guarantee technological diffusion and to protect individual rights.[42] Initially presented under Hans-Dietrich Genscher's watch as interior minister and pushed through by Baum, the FDP committed itself to data privacy legislation in the 1970s.[43] Beyond limiting the proliferation of information technology, the group hoped to guarantee the protection of democracy in a computerized world.

Drawing on recognized privacy principles developed by legal scholars, all of these social libertarian alliances successfully drafted privacy legislation across their regions. Ervin's initial bill in the Senate and those

emerging from his German and French counterparts proposed comprehensive rules. Considerable public debate quickly ensued, with opposition focusing on two issues. First, government bureaucracy and industry
opposed the construction of independent regulatory agencies capable
of monitoring information use. Second, the private sector, especially in
the United States and Germany, opposed private-sector rules. Industry
claimed that research had produced no empirical evidence of private-
sector abuse and therefore there was no need to regulate it. Moreover,
privacy rules threatened fundamental business practices and could dev-
astate many critical sectors. Finally, industry argued that privacy rules
created a new set of bureaucratic constraints that hindered innovation
and risked excessive government intervention in the economy. Business
communities argued that regulation should be limited to the public sector and that the private sector should be left to self-regulate. If industry proved incapable of maintaining privacy interests, future legislation
could right the situation.[44]

Despite very similar proposals across the advanced industrial democracies, the actual policy responses varied on the two critical issues. Some
policymakers, including those in France and Germany, largely fended
off the opposition and constructed independent regulatory agencies to
monitor and enforce privacy rules in the public and private sectors. In
the United States, by contrast, industry opposition successfully lobbied
to restrict the scope of legislation and prevent the establishment of an
independent regulator.

A Response to Fascist Legacies?

The common wisdom holds that variation in cross-national privacy rules
resulted from different experiences with government abuse early in the
twentieth century. Proponents of this argument explain the limited nature of U.S. privacy legislation and the comprehensive scope of European rules as a product of past authoritarian experiences. European
countries, the argument goes, due to the brutality of fascist regimes, constructed comprehensive privacy regulations.[45]

This, however does not fit well with the historical record in the U.S.
case. Although not a direct victim of fascism, the United States has a long
tradition in the field of privacy. The modern concept of the right to privacy
was invented in the United States at the hands of U.S. legal scholars concerned with the dehumanizing effects of end-of-the-nineteenth-century
innovations. The efforts of these scholars resulted in the development of

an elaborate tort of privacy, which protects individuals from the publication of embarrassing information by private companies.[46] Other countries have looked to this tort of privacy as they developed their own law in the post–World War II period. Although the privacy tort focuses on the publication, not the internal processing, of personal information and therefore fails to resolve many data privacy issues, it clearly demonstrates that private-sector privacy issues fall under government purview in the United States.[47]

In addition, the fascist legacies argument cannot explain the scope or structure of the regulations adopted as part of the Privacy Act. Numerous instances exist, from environmental regulation in the 1970s to tobacco restrictions in the 1990s, which demonstrate the ability of the U.S. government to regulate the private sector.[48] The United States popularized the concept of the independent regulatory agency during the 1930s under the New Deal and again in the 1960s under the Great Society. Far from being a cultural pariah, the independent regulatory agency is a foundational U.S. institution.[49] European policymakers actively modeled their data privacy authorities on U.S. independent regulators such as the Federal Trade Commission and the Federal Communications Commission.[50] And in the case of privacy, initial U.S. legislative drafts proposed a comprehensive system with an independent commission, as in the other countries examined.

The authoritarian legacies argument faces similar difficulties explaining differences between the United States and Europe. The rhetoric on both sides of the Atlantic cited concern over government abuse of computer technology.[51] I found no evidence that the atrocities of the early twentieth century provided political entrepreneurs different resources in their struggle to legislate data privacy rules in the 1970s. In fact, a French privacy expert involved in the French lobbying effort noted the similarity of the campaigns in the United States and Europe.[52] Legislators relied on the same fundamental privacy principles to formulate national legislation; historical experience did not produce different legislative norms.

One could credibly make the case (and many private-sector lobbies did) that in Europe a limited regime focused on public-sector efforts resolved the concerns raised by its authoritarian past. Even when the German Constitutional Court ruled on the issue of data privacy in the 1980s and recognized a constitutional right to informational self-determination, it limited the scope of this right to interactions between individuals and the public sector.[53] Without isolating a specific mechanism that helped

advocates of the comprehensive system defend their proposal to incorporate the private sector, the legacies argument seems to obscure more
than it clarifies.

The fascist legacies argument also fails to explain the tremendous
variation that emerged in the scope of privacy regimes. It is not obvious
why Germany and Japan, which both experienced authoritarian rule,
would have divergent privacy policies; Germany was among the first to
pass comprehensive rules, and Japan was a long-standing advocate of
the limited regime. And, similarly, it is not obvious why cultures such as
Germany and the United Kingdom, which most agree have very different fascist legacies, adopted similar comprehensive systems. In addition,
Italy and Spain, both countries with extensive authoritarian legacies,
were among the last countries in Europe to adopt comprehensive rules.
The statistical analysis conducted in the next section confirms that the
fascist legacy of a nation did not have a statistically significant effect on
the scope of data privacy legislation it adopted. Although the Nazi experience sensitized the advanced industrial democracies on both sides of
the Atlantic to the potential of government abuse, the fascist legacy argument cannot explain why countries adopted comprehensive rules over
limited ones.

The Organization of Business and Politics Matters

The political coalition that promoted comprehensive rules represented
a social libertarian agenda concerned with the dangers of enhanced data
collection by both the government and large private-sector conglomer-
ates. Groups of privacy advocates, primarily legal scholars, developed a
data privacy agenda that they attempted to translate into public policy.

Faced with the demands of privacy advocates, business had to navigate
a course that would mitigate the passage and effect of any legislation.
Industry interests, especially in the early phases of regulation, hoped to
minimize data privacy regulation. They viewed data subject rights and enforcement conditions as new regulatory burdens and feared that consent
rules would hinder the exploitation of new markets. Industry was better
positioned to block regulation in systems in which they were better able to
enter the political processes and shape political outcomes, often through
veto points—moments in the political system when actors can mobilize to
block legislation. These include presidentialism, single-member districts,
bicameralism, referendums, and judicial review. Countries with fewer

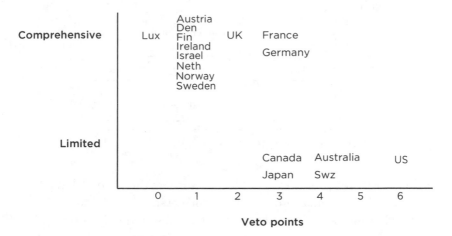

Figure 3. Types of data privacy legislation passed prior to 1990 and number of veto points. Den, Denmark; Fin, Finland; Lux, Luxembourg; Neth, Netherlands; Swz, Switzerland; UK, United Kingdom; US, United States.

veto points were able to impose stricter data privacy regulations, regardless of private-sector interests.[54]

Figure 3 lists the countries that passed some form of data privacy legislation prior to or during 1990.[55] From the figure, we can see that countries with multiple veto points tended to adopt limited regimes and that countries with few veto points tended to adopt comprehensive regimes.

The significance of political veto points is bolstered by a series of regression analyses that test the relative importance of the fascist legacy of a country (the standard hypothesis) and the configuration of political institutions. I used a binary measure of the dependent variable representing the scope of national regulations.[56] The fascist legacy of a country indicates whether the country had a fascist government or was occupied by a fascist power.[57] I used a modified composite measure for veto points based on data collected by Evelyne Huber, Charles Ragin, and John Stephens.[58]

The first regression (model 1 in table 4), which isolates the relationship between the fascist legacy of a nation and the scope of national regulation, does not produce a significant result at $p < 0.05$. In addition, the R^2 value indicates that the model offers a relatively poor fit. The second regression (model 2), which examines the effect of veto points on

TABLE 4
OLS regression results for the effect of fascist legacy and
institutional veto points on the scope of national
privacy regulations[a]

	Fascist legacy	Veto points	R-squared
Model 1	0.39		0.18
Model 2		−0.24*	0.63
Model 3	0.13	−0.22*	0.65

[a]*indicates result is significant for $p < 0.01$; OLS, ordinary least squares; n = 17.

regulatory scope, produces a significant result at the $p < 0.01$ level. The coefficient is substantial and carries the correct sign. The R^2 value also indicates that the model fits relatively well. Finally, in the third regression (model 3), the two causal explanations are pitted against one another. Here the veto-points measure continues to produce a statistically significant correlation but the addition of the fascist legacy indicator does not improve the model fit. This result supports the logical notion that firms were better able to achieve their desired policy outcome in systems with multiple legislative blocks.

The small sample size raises some concerns about these findings, and they should therefore be viewed critically.[59] It is, for example, not possible to conduct a definitive test of the veto-points variable against a large number of competing causal factors. This initial statistical exercise, however, acts as a critical jumping-off point for the more detailed historical narratives that follow and casts considerable doubt on the standard argument that focuses on the fascist legacy of a country.

Despite the revealing statistical results, veto points do not determine outcomes but, instead, merely isolate moments in the decision-making process when legislation can be stopped or threatened. It is necessary to consider business preferences and their relative influence to understand why the veto points were or were not employed. The organization of business sectors, often institutionally imposed over time, shaped both industry preferences and the ability of industry to leverage the political process.[60] In addition, the structure of information flows in a sector influenced firm preferences.[61] Firms in fragmented sectors, which required greater levels of information exchange, more fervently opposed comprehensive rules; firms in oligopolistic sectors, which had large warehouses of personal information, found their interests reinforced by privacy legislation because such legislation increased entry barriers to firms that lacked data. To demonstrate this, I next explore the position of political actors and their ability to take advantage of various political blockades in three case studies: the United States, France, and Germany. The German case demonstrates how veto points are neutralized by historical context, hindering industry efforts to prevent comprehensive rules. The examination of the legislative processes of the initial data privacy laws in the United States, France, and Germany underscores the importance of historical analysis for understanding how the structure of business and politics can affect political outcomes.

The Origins of the Limited Regime in the United States

In summer 1974, the U.S. Senate and the House of Representatives took their first pass at comprehensive legislation. Led by Ervin in the Senate and Koch and Goldwater in the House, the hearings considered proposals to establish rules for the public and private sectors, as well as to create a privacy board to monitor privacy issues. The debates quickly laid out the various actor positions. Industry attacked comprehensive rules as excessive and warned that such legislation would hinder essential information flows. An alliance formed among the administrative bureaucracy, efficiency-minded congresspeople, and the private sector against the establishment of a regulator. These groups argued that such an institution would hamper needed information exchanges, would add an additional layer of bureaucratic inefficiency, and could become a superregulator capable of dominating public- and private-sector behavior.[62]

Two bills emerged. The Senate bill called for comprehensive rules for the public and private sectors and for the creation of a regulatory authority. The House bill, by contrast, focused on the public sector and eliminated any form of privacy board.

Industry Opposition

Representatives of the private sector, especially from banks, credit agencies, and retail marketers, virulently opposed private-sector rules. Fifteen of the twenty industry lobbies that provided statements to the Senate hearing on the bill argued that legislation should not cover the private sector, and no industry lobby advocated the adoption of the legislation.[63] Patterns of information flows within the U.S. political economy fostered business opposition. For multiple historical reasons, information-intensive sectors such as financial services, retail, and direct marketing were highly fragmented in the postwar period. Take, for example, the banking sector. Owing to extensive regulation that prevented interstate banking and limited universal banking, the U.S. financial services sector was highly fragmented and populated by an enormous number of small, local banks.[64] These sectors developed a complex network of information sharing to overcome the inherent information asymmetries of working in a limited geographic area. Companies used information exchange to identify risk and segment customers.[65] The perceived threat to the credit industry, for example, is seen in the following statement by National Bank Americard:

> NBI [National Bank Americard] is concerned that various legislative proposals, as presently drafted, are overly broad and would impede the consumer credit process to the extent of reducing the availability of credit to individuals and generally crippling the authorization systems and credit reporting systems that are an integral and essential part of the bank credit card industry.[66]

Firms such as banks, credit-based retailers, and direct marketers, therefore, saw privacy legislation as a very real threat to their livelihood. Branches of these firms were strewn across virtually every congressional district, making them a potent lobby in a legislature composed of single-member districts.[67]

Few Allies

Despite increased lobbying against private-sector rules, few public-interest voices emerged to defend comprehensive rules. The ACLU was overjoyed that any legislation had progressed so far, and the consumer movement was absent from the debates.[68] The ACLU generally supported the legislative efforts, but it had a limited ability to criticize or shape legislative amendments. From the 1960s, the ACLU actively monitored privacy issues during the proliferation of computer technology through the ACLU Privacy Project.[69] Although not concerned exclusively with public-sector use of personal information, the ACLU focus on civil liberties certainly highlighted government abuses before private-sector issues.[70]

Despite a flurry of activity by the executive in summer 1974, the Nixon and Gerald Ford administrations did not support private-sector rules.

The administration believed that computer technology offered the private sector an important tool that could promote economic growth. Unwilling to dampen potential efficiency gains, the executive focused its attention on public-sector threats to privacy and warned against the over-regulation of business. In addition to executive-administration testimony that called for limiting privacy rules to the public sector, Nixon directed his Domestic Council Committee on Privacy, "Let's not all dump on industry, let's worry about the 'Big Brother' problem."[71]

Faced with considerable resistance from the business community and the administration, Ervin realized that he did not have the support he needed to push through private-sector rules, and he dropped that portion of regulation from the Senate bill.[72]

Veto Threat Blocks Regulatory Agency

As autumn approached, the major point of contention was the monitoring and enforcement mechanism that would oversee privacy legislation. Ervin was committed to the creation of a privacy board that would act as an ombudsman for privacy issues. The board would not have the power to hand down administrative decrees or regulations, but it would hear disputes, offer recommendations, and monitor the development of privacy issues in the private sector. The administration and business lobbies continued to oppose private-sector rules, culminating in the threat of a presidential veto on the creation of a privacy agency.[73] President Ford repeatedly signaled his resistance to the birth of an additional regulatory apparatus. He argued very bluntly that his administration hoped to constrain the expansion of the bureaucratic state, and he found support in the majority of Republican officials.[74] Similar concerns about potential rogue-agency behavior struck not only the administration but a series of congresspeople.[75] Fearing the creation of a superregulator able to act without government oversight, Ford withdrew his support from any legislation that included a privacy commission. Not only did the president use a veto threat to block the creation of a privacy body, but he leveraged the power of an executive order to speed legislation. Ford let it be known that if Congress could not agree on public-sector rules, he would push through similar regulations via an executive order; the executive order, however, would not include a privacy commission. This executive position held Congress double-hostage using presidential powers. If it passed legislation with a privacy agency, it faced a presidential veto;

if it waited to legislate in the future when presidential support might be more forthcoming, it risked being scooped by the president through an executive order.[76]

In the final hours of the legislature, staffers from the House and the Senate worked out a compromise that basically followed interest-group demands. Private-sector rules had already been eliminated from the proposed bills, leaving the privacy agency as the major hurdle. Despite Ervin's passionate belief in the need for such an agency, he was unable to overcome the broad opposition. He therefore agreed to the creation of a study commission that would conduct a survey of private-sector privacy policy and report to the Congress on the need for additional action. Far from an administrative agency with monitoring or enforcement power, the Privacy Protection Study Commission was not a permanent institution and had no regulatory authority. The passage of the Privacy Act, which focused on the federal bureaucracy, established the foundation of the limited regime in the United States. The conclusions of the Study Commission in 1977 further legitimized and entrenched the regime by arguing that, rather than adopting sweeping rules, private-sector regulation should be restricted to sensitive sectors such as health care and banking.[77]

This narrative underscores the critical importance of the organization of business and politics in the origins of the limited system in the United States. The highly fragmented nature of the financial services sector resulted in strong industry opposition. Industry was able to leverage several institutional veto points, including the bicameral nature of the U.S. Congress and the presidential system, to limit the scope of U.S. regulations.

Comprehensive Rules in France

The SAFARI affair, which publicized the creation by the French government of a large data bank system, placed the administration under intense political pressure. Given its electoral commitment to individual rights and Interior Minister Poniatowski's pledge to protect privacy in the information age, the scandal unleashed a wave of criticism.[78] In response, the administration commissioned the Tricot report to quell opposition. After the release of the Tricot Commission report in 1975, which spelled out the need for comprehensive privacy rules, the Giscard d'Estaing administration put together a team in the Ministry of Justice to draft the appropriate legislation. Led by Joinet, the ministry used the findings of the Tricot Commission as the basis for legislation that would be negotiated over the following three years. Industry opposition found limited traction in the unified political system, where strong commitment by the administration to comprehensive rules set the tone of the legislative process.

The Administration Commitment
to the Information Society

In addition to the natural affinity between the administration social agenda and data privacy policy, advocates of data privacy received a boost from governmental support of information technology. Since the 1950s, when the U.S. government restricted the export of high-end supercomputers to France, the French government had concerned itself with the French technological dependence on the United States.[79] In response, the Charles de Gaulle administration created the Plan Calcul, which attempted to establish an internationally competitive national computer and data processing industry so that, as described by Michel Debré, then finance minister, "our country remains master of its own destiny."[80]

The Giscard d'Estaing administration prioritized information technology and saw it as critical to the future of the French economy. Early in his administration, Giscard commissioned a report on the future of information technology by Simon Nora, a high-ranking official responsible for monitoring public finance.[81] The report became a best-seller in France, spelling out the threat of technological dependence on the United States. It highlighted the critical importance of information technology for the economic future of France and warned the government of the need to continue to develop a healthy data processing sector. In addition to calling on the government to create a ministry in charge of information technology policy and to subsidize technological development, the report highlighted the importance of protecting individual rights in the emerging information age; the SAFARI affair had highlighted for the administration the risk of pursuing technological advances without first establishing a system of legal protections.

A group of politically active computer scientists lobbied the government to take action on privacy. This group believed that the successful diffusion of computer technology required strong comprehensive privacy rules.[82] Members argued that for consumers and business to use information technology, the government had to construct a set of safeguards to protect against abuse. The administration believed that comprehensive data privacy rules were integral to its broader goals.[83] Data privacy legislation nicely dovetailed with both the government social agenda and technology policy, eliminating any threat of presidential resistance (a major veto point in the French system) to the proposal.

Muted Industry Opposition

In contrast to the United States and Germany, industry played a much more muted role in privacy debates in France. This relative silence and at times passive support are linked to the organization of the French political economy. Unlike the other countries examined here, the French government had nationalized many of the most affected service industries, such as banking.[84] And even private companies were highly dependent on government-controlled subsides, low-interest loans, and financial favors from the public sector.[85] This limited the options of industry leaders. Although they could offer input on government policy, direct criticism would be an attack on the very administration to which they belonged and constrained the ability of industry to wage a public campaign against the legislation. The management of Renault, for example, could offer suggestions to the Ministry of Justice, but had to be careful about any public statements. In the end, the centralized character of French government meant that the ministry-drafted legislation could override the concerns of industries.

The structure of the financial services sector around a limited number of large institutions further minimized the legislative impact.[86] In contrast to the United States and Germany, no independent, private, credit-reporting agencies existed.[87] Banks did not need to exchange intense amounts of information because they had relatively large, national customer pools and access to a wide range of information about those customers. Privacy regulations protected the storehouse of customer data of a firm from its competitors and hindered the entry of new challengers. As a result of the limited number of veto points available and the structure of the French political economy, industry played only a modest role in legislative negotiations and was less threatened by such rules compared with similar firms in the United States.[88]

Fights over Enforcement

The main conflict in the French debate centered on regulatory enforcement. The draft legislation proposed the creation of a national independent regulatory institution, named the Commission Nationale de l'Informatique et des Libertés (CNIL), to oversee data protection issues. The agency was charged with maintaining a registry for public- and private-sector databases, as well as investigatory and sanctioning authority over data privacy issues. French officials modeled the CNIL on U.S. New Deal institutions, becoming among the first independent regulatory agency to be created in France.[89]

A number of public-sector officials, including representatives of the police and the army, protested the creation of an independent regulatory body that had oversight authority over their operations. A broad coalition in parliament, however, including the socialist and communist opposition, supported the government proposal for strong independence and representation for the agency's administrative board. The parliamentary opposition argued that to offer a reasonable check on executive power, any such agency had to be independent.[90] With the final passage of legislation in 1978, France created an independent regulatory agency with broad powers across the public and private sectors. Given the strong commitment of the government to the proposal and the lack of industry involvement, the final legislation reflects the organization of the French political economy at the time.

A Last-Minute Deal for Comprehensive Rules in Germany

The effort to forge national data privacy legislation in Germany occurred during a hotly contested five-year political battle between 1973 and 1978. Three major legislative hearings were published, along with scores of interest-group position papers and trade press articles. When we analyze the possible public policy alternatives, the preferences of various actors, and the final outcome, it is clear that political actors—most notably industry lobbies and privacy advocates—leveraged political institutions, such as veto points, to shape the legislation. Despite fierce opposition by industry, the privacy alliance benefited from the historical configuration of domestic political institutions to achieve comprehensive regulations. Although Germany is often viewed as a country with multiple veto points (including a bicameral legislature and judicial review), the particular alignment of political actors at that time neutralized key barriers to the passage of the policy.

Government Support for Comprehensive Rules

The government presented its first-draft legislation in May 1973. This draft included rules governing the use and transfer of personal informa-tion in both the public and private sectors and relied on a tiered enforce-ment system.[91] Mirroring the federal structure of German government, legislators proposed a federal data privacy commissioner with oversight powers for federal institutions and nationalized industries. Länder gov-ernments monitored public data at the Land level and were responsi-ble for businesses located within their jurisdictions.[92] In keeping with the coordinated nature of the German political economy, the legislation required that firms appoint internal privacy officers. These privacy offi-cers worked with government regulators to manage private-sector pri-vacy issues.

The government draft legislation and position during the ensuing hearings committed the government to action in both the public and private sectors. Herbert Auernhammer, the civil servant from the Min-istry of the Interior responsible for the law, argued that effective data privacy had to cover both sectors. Given the increased communication between the public and private sectors, it would be foolish to attempt to regulate only one, recognizing that data transfers between the pub-lic and private sectors blurred any distinction between public and pri-vate surveillance. In addition, private-sector adoption of information technology posed considerable risk to individual liberty.[93] He specifically noted the potential threat to individuals of networked data banks being developed by the insurance and banking industry.[94] Minister of the Inte-rior Hans-Dietrich Genscher's statement at the 1972 hearing concern-ing the law clearly articulated the government commitment to individual liberties by regulating the private sector:

> Many sides are urgently advising more or less that the private sector be taken out of the law and following the example of the Data Protection Law of Hesse only regulate the public sector. This would be just as false as the opposite tendency, which may be observed in many other European coun-tries. The relationships in our modern world are so interdependent and intertwined that isolated solutions have only limited applicability. That

proves particularly true for information technologies and its companion data protection in national as in international areas. Additionally, no one could claim that the collection of personal information in the private sector does not pose a threat to the private sphere of individual citizens. We would be closing our eyes to reality if we were to exclude this important area and we would be leaving citizens defenseless.[95]

The adoption of a limited regime in the state of Hesse in 1970 offered the federal government a clear model for national legislation. The government, however, explicitly rejected the limited path, opting for comprehensive rules.

The legal community reinforced the government position, agreeing that private-sector action was necessary.[96] The legal community argued that pure self-regulation did not make sense in the area of data protection because of the great economic drive to exchange information. With the increasing sharing of governance responsibilities between public and private bodies, the traditional state-society boundaries had broken down. An unregulated private sector could provide a dangerous data warehouse for bureaucracies; the concentration of information in the hands of a few large corporations threatened to ossify power within society. The specter of large multinational corporations transferring personal information across borders further raised the stakes of uncontrolled private-sector data processing.

Industry Opposition

Between 1972 and 1976, the draft came under intense scrutiny by the private sector. At a set of hearings held during this period, a wide range of industry representatives, including those from financial services and marketing, argued that the new regulations would create economic ruin. Industry feared that rules governing the exchange of personal information promoted economic fraud, limited the deployment of new technology, increased administrative costs, and raised the level of government control over private-sector economic activity.[97]

The most powerful industry trade associations argued against the adoption of private-sector data privacy legislation.[98] Following the logic of their U.S. counterparts, they claimed that no abuse had occurred in the private sector and, therefore, no need for legislation existed. Furthermore, the private sector did not represent the same kind of threat as the public sector. Individuals were not forced to give data to businesses, as they were to bureaucracies, and therefore individuals could choose not to provide personal information. And the structure of the German economy necessitated the sharing of information between firms. The Zentraler Kreditausschuss, which is the peak trade association for the banking sector, summed up the industry position:

> You must demonstrate to us—and here would have been the appropriate place—that according to the analysis of relationships in the private sector, as you see it, that a legal regulation is necessary. We find that missing. We have thoroughly read through all of the justifications and I would like to say something rather provocative: I appeal for a limitation of the regulation to the public sector.[99]

Many lobby groups conceded the need for public-sector legislation and asked the government to proceed in two phases—first with public sector regulation and then with a study examining the possibility of private-sector rules.[100]

At the same time that industry attempted to prevent new legislative rules, it lobbied to weaken restrictions on transfers within corporate groups. Trade associations claimed that the modern corporation relied on communication among its affiliated partners, arguing that the bureaucratic drag of rules hindering the exchange of information among affiliates would negate any savings brought about by integrating data processing technology into company operations. Rules, which would break up the corporate family, would increase costs and contradict government regulations that promoted or required affiliation. Firms, which relied on affiliation or network structures such as insurance and cooperative banks, attacked the proposed affiliate rules.[101] Companies threatened that affiliate rules would force fragmented sectors to consolidate, promoting the very concentration of power that the legislation hoped to diffuse. If companies could not share information across the sector, they would have to merge to create self-sufficient information pools.[102]

Industry also lobbied to eliminate government oversight of private-sector enforcement. The legislative draft included a provision that required industry to appoint internal privacy officers to monitor the implementation of privacy regulations within the firm. These officers, however, in the view of industry, should not be bound by any formal regulatory obligation. Instead, privacy officers should be purely a self-regulatory strategy.

The fragmented character of several industrial sectors, which relied heavily on personal information, underpinned the intensity of industry opposition. Industries ranging from insurance to retail credit did not hold a monopoly on personal information and therefore required information exchanges to minimize fraud and promote sales. For example, the three-tiered German banking system—private banks, savings banks, and credit cooperatives—meant that few banks could rely on their own storehouse of personal information to identify risk in the retail-banking segment.[103] The savings and cooperative banks are organized around a network structure, which relies on information exchange within the networks. Following the *Regionalprinzip*, each member of the network operates in a limited territory and does not open branches in competition with other network members.[104] Members of the network rely on third-party information to prevent fraud and to market to new customers moving into their geographic area.[105] The separation between insurance firms and banks and the fragmentation of the insurance sector meant that information had to flow for the insurance industry to calculate risk. As the federal office for insurance concluded, "In order for insurance firms to fulfill their obligations to their clients they not only need extensive personal information for their own use but also require extensive transfers among firms and with the industry trade association."[106]

The business community did not see a need for private-sector data privacy legislation and feared the costs associated with burdensome centralized regulation. It believed that such rules would impinge on the data transfers needed in the fragmented financial services sector, and it supported instead internal self-regulatory efforts. The lack of personal data scandals in the private sector demonstrated industry good faith, which it promised to continue under a self-regulatory system. Rejecting government proposals to create state monitoring agencies with enforcement powers, the industry trade associations claimed that these initiatives would give government undue access to business affairs and would threaten the economic development of core economic sectors.[107]

The Legislative Dance

In light of intense industry intervention, the legislation faced many hurdles during the legislative process. After the legislation passed the German lower house (the Bundestag) by a purely partisan vote of the coalition parties in 1975, the CDU-controlled upper house (the Bundesrat) rejected the plan, citing an inadequate level of regulation for the public sector and a heavy-handed approach toward the private sector.[108] The CDU argued, in alliance with industry trade associations, that the government should not interfere with private-sector enforcement of privacy rules.[109] By the end of the spring, observers doubted that data privacy legislation would still pass before the election of a new legislature in September 1976.[110] The draft risked defeat at this bicameral veto point. Nonetheless, the government sent the legislation to a joint compromise committee in an effort to save the data privacy rules.

The inhospitable political climate for the regulation of the private sector became apparent at the final public hearing held on the issue in 1976. As the compromise committee attempted to develop a joint position on a common set of rules, the interior committee of the Bundestag held a public hearing on data privacy. At this event, industry underscored its opposition to the public-sector regulation of private-sector enforcement as well as strict rules governing the transfer of information between affiliates.[111]

Despite industry lobbying, privacy advocates led by the FDP from North Rhine Westphalia successfully strengthened the legislation in the compromise committee. The legislative draft included the protection of internal firm data, limited the categories of public data that could be processed without consent, established a federal data privacy commissioner as well as the external control of private-sector activity, and delegated state implementation to the Länder governments.[112] Industry opposition to the bill, however, found resonance in the CDU faction, which prevented the compromise committee proposal from reaching a vote in summer 1976. Despite the government acceptance of the demand that Länder governments retain control over much of the implementation, the CDU continued to oppose the bill, stressing the importance of industry self-regulation.[113] The government, unwilling to eliminate private-sector controls or strict rules for affiliates, delayed a vote on the compromise draft until after the fall elections.[114]

Upon returning after the election, the Bundestag decided to go ahead with the compromise committee draft in the face of an uncertain response by the Bundesrat. The CDU unanimously opposed the legislation in the Bundestag and threatened to block regulation in the Bundesrat. The CDU feared the overregulation of the private sector, specifically the public-sector oversight of private-sector self-regulatory efforts.[115]

The fate of the bill remained uncertain until the final vote on the floor of the Bundesrat. Given CDU opposition to the legislation in the

Bundestag and the commitment of the party to blocking regulation in the Bundesrat, many anticipated that the Bundesrat (with a majority of CDU-led Länder) would end the legislation. But, in a surprise move, two CDU-FDP–controlled Länder—Lower Saxony and Saarland—voted with the SPD-FDP government.[116] Following the September elections, the two CDU-led Länder governments were in the midst of coalition negotiations with their junior partner, the FDP. Given the nature of the German Bundesrat, which is composed of representatives from the Länder governments, smaller Länder coalition partners can leverage their interests through the Land representative in the Bundesrat. As a result of the recent election, the FDP renegotiated its political deal with the CDU in the Länder governments to guarantee the passage of strong data privacy regulations. Thus, the FDP representatives from the two Länder voted for the legislation in the final breaths of the legislature, neutralizing the Bundesrat veto point and assuring the establishment of comprehensive rules in Germany.[117]

Far from being a cultural inevitability, the form of privacy legislation was determined by political struggles in the various countries. As privacy advocates formulated a legislative strategy to guarantee individual liberties, they confronted a well-organized set of interests that fought to maintain unfettered information flows. Industry, especially the service sectors, fearing the bureaucratic costs of privacy rules, looked for allies in the legislature and the administration who hoped to realize the economic potential of technological innovation. In the United States, industry fragmentation bolstered both the logic of opposing strict privacy rules and the ability of industry to leverage political pressure. In France, both the industry and political structure favored the quick passage of comprehensive rules. The organization of business and politics, which had developed though long-term market-making and state-building processes, shaped the preferences of actors and their ability to achieve their goals.

The German case offers an interesting middle ground between those in the United States and France. The SPD-FDP coalition in Germany passed stringent rules—facing opposition from fragmented industry and resistance from regional governments—that regulated the public and private sectors, overcoming the expected institutional veto constraints. A superficial reading of the German case might cause us to conclude that it challenges the causal argument presented. The detailed narrative presented here demonstrates, however, the historical contingency of veto points. The German legislature adopted private-sector rules because the particular political constellation of federal and Länder governments neutralized the powerful veto point of bicameralism, *not* despite the presence of that veto point. Because of the FDP position in the Länder governments, the German system effectively had fewer veto points.[118] And whereas many hold that the German data privacy policy is the inevitable response to the Nazi regime, the narrative presented here highlights the precarious political fight that finally resulted in the passage of the legislation.

Although not blocking regulatory innovation, the political institutional map critically shaped the German variant of the comprehensive regime. Federalism required that public-sector oversight for Land affairs be conducted by independent regulatory agencies at the Land level, not by the federal government. Legislation created Länder data privacy commissioners alongside the federal data privacy commissioner. Similarly, oversight for the private sector was shared between the federal and Länder governments, with the requirements that firms appoint internal data privacy officers. The German legislation, heavily influenced by German federalism and the organization of the German political economy, has produced more data privacy experts than any other in the world.

In addition to explaining varying policy trajectories, the three cases presented here offer several more general insights. First, privacy typifies a set of issues in politics that blur partisan categories and expand the set of coalitional possibilities. Social libertarian issues, those concerned with the concentration of power in society, provide a prototypical example of topics that disturb traditional left-right cleavages and promote strange-bedfellow coalitions.[119] Both the progressive left and the conservative right fear the dominance of the executive branch and large corporate power. The progressive left fears that the concentration of political or economic power will weaken the position of vulnerable groups in society. The conservative right fears that such a concentration of power will limit individual liberty and economic choice.[120]

Much of the current comparative literature on party ideology is dominated by measures of left-right placement.[121] But focusing behavioral and interest-group research around continuous left-right variables blinds researchers to alternative patterns of interest formation that sit contemporaneously along multiple points of the left-right spectrum. Voters concerned with trust, the environment, and power do not easily identify with standard left-right distinctions.[122] The issue of privacy demonstrates

the need for cross-national survey research that develops measures to assess this often-overlooked set of political dynamics.[123] In such domains,
in which the old political cleavages are attenuated, political entrepreneurs are particularly important in forging alliances for policy reform
among diverse backers. In the case of data privacy, both politically activist lawyers and politicians interested in social libertarian causes emerged
as critical to the policymaking process.

Second, I highlight in this chapter the importance of patterns of information flows for preference formation in an information society. A
growing body of research in information economics demonstrates that
patterns of information flows shape firm strategy, with firms in fragmented sectors much more willing to share information than firms in
sectors where information is concentrated in the hands of a few firms.[124]
Translating these findings to the political arena, the narrative demonstrates that such patterns of information flows shape political preferences
as well. Financial services firms lobbied heavily to prevent private-sector
rules in the United States, but similar firms in France did not actively
struggle to beat back privacy legislation. This difference in position
stemmed from the distinct patterns of information needs in the two
countries. Historical regulations in the United States created a highly
fragmented financial services sector comprising many small banks, independent insurance and securities firms, credit agencies, and mortgage
brokers. These vast networks of companies relied on the free flow of personal data to overcome the information deficit imposed by their size.
This opposition contrasted sharply with the large French banks, which
depended less on external information to assess risk. The oligopolistic
structure of French banking provided financial institutions with enough
internal resources, minimizing the need to share information and in
turn the cost of privacy restrictions. The research here demonstrates the
importance of preexisting patterns of information sharing in the development of political preferences in the information age.

Third, I show the contingent nature of veto point institutions and the
ability of political actors to play veto points off one another. Veto point
variables not only change with fundamental institutional reconfigurations, such as a constitutional amendment that shifts power distribution
within the political system, but also change with the shifting constellation of political control over the various branches of government. The
George W. Bush administration, when it held Republican control of both
houses of Congress, looked a lot more like the Thatcher government

and faced fewer blocks to effecting policy change than did the Reagan administration. In the German narrative, veto points are shown to be far from merely a policy barrier; they can be deployed as a bargaining tool much like other political resources. With the powerful Bundesrat and Länder governments, the German federal government faced many barriers to legislative passage. In the case of data privacy, the CDU control over the Bundesrat could have killed private-sector rules. But the position of the FDP as both the governing party at the federal level and as a possible CDU partner in Länder governments limited the ability of the CDU to leverage the Bundesrat as a legislative veto point. In other words, the FDP mobilized the future threat of deploying a federal veto point to neutralize the effect of the bicameral legislature. Expanding the conception of veto points from being merely moments in the political process when policy may be stopped to being bargaining tools that can be traded over a certain political time horizon contributes to the debate over how political institutions facilitate policy action.[125]

Fourth, and finally, this chapter offers interesting insights into the politics of delegation. Since the turn of the twentieth century, the United States has relied on independent agencies to overcome the problems posed by the growing complexity of governing a modern society. In two waves, first with the New Deal and then with the Great Society, independent agencies were established to oversee the development of a wide range of sectors, including financial services, telecommunications, aviation, and the environment.[126] In the 1970s, just as countries such as France and Germany looked to the United States as a model for these inventive political institutions, however, the U.S. political environment for these agencies changed. Legislators became increasingly unwilling to delegate authority to such bodies, arguing that independent agencies further bloated the federal bureaucracy and lacked appropriate oversight and control.

A sizable literature has developed concerning the control dilemma posed by independent regulatory agencies.[127] In delegating authority, Congress and the president face a monitoring problem. It is difficult for the principal, in this case the Congress or president, to know exactly what the agencies do once delegation has occurred, and they have few tools to guarantee that the agencies follow orders. The principals have developed oversight mechanisms to enhance their control.

This literature has investigated the various means by which principals solve this monitoring dilemma, but the privacy case demonstrates an alternative, less well-understood outcome—no delegation. Despite a constant stream of proposals for new agencies, the U.S. government has measurably reduced the creation of independent regulatory agencies.[128] This determination to minimize delegation has held up across parties and time. The evidence from the privacy case indicates that legislators learned from previous rounds of delegation and determined that the price of delegation outweighed the potential benefits, underscoring the importance of sequencing in policymaking. It is this lack of delegation that will, in turn, hamper the ability of the United States to manage international debates that emerged in the 1990s. It will be interesting to study the European reaction to delegation over time. After a rash of delegation as part of the internal market integration process, it is unclear whether the EU national governments will support such efforts over the coming decades.[129]

Given these concerns about control and political influence, I now turn to the role that privacy agencies have played in European politics since their inception in the 1970s. Leveraging the regulatory capacity delegated to them nationally, data privacy authorities have transformed regional privacy debates in the 1990s, significantly enhancing the political viability of the comprehensive system across Europe.

CHAPTER 4

The EU Data Privacy Directive

Transgovernmental Actors as Drivers of Regional Integration

In 1995, after fifteen years of debate, the European Union[1] adopted a directive designed to regulate data privacy. The stated goal of the directive was twofold. First, regional legislation hoped to harmonize standards so as to permit the free flow of information within the European Union. Second, the directive called for a high level of protection, signaling the EU commitment to individual data privacy rights.[2] To reach these aims, the legislation required that all member states pass comprehensive data privacy legislation for the public and private sectors, establish an independent control institution, regulate the transfer of personal data to other countries, and create a working party of national regulators to oversee the implementation and enforcement of the directive. For five European nations—Belgium, Greece, Italy, Portugal, and Spain—this meant the creation of a new branch of regulatory authority. For others, it required substantial reform of their data protection systems.

In this chapter, I explore the political development of the directive and make sense of this striking expansion of pan-European civil liberties during a period typically associated with the market-conforming project embodied by the single market. Specifically, I address two fundamental questions. First, why did the European Union take on data privacy issues in the early 1990s? Second, why did it regulate in such a way as to integrate and empower the network of national data privacy authorities in the oversight and implementation of the European directive? These outcomes are particularly puzzling because the major drivers of European integration—the European Commission, large member states, the European Court of Justice, and national and pan-European industry—had either openly resisted or failed to consider a European initiative well into the 1980s. In addition to shedding light on the different mechanisms that facilitated the deeper integration within Europe, the answers to these questions underpin the ability of the region to shape regulatory debates internationally (discussed in the next chapter).

Far from simply the residue of authoritarian experience or a product imposed by powerful member states, the EU data privacy directive can be traced to its roots in the historical sequencing of national data privacy regulation and the role that the resulting independent regulatory authorities played in regional politics. As internal-market integration spilled over into data protection issues—when firms and governments across Europe began trading data with one another—data privacy officials, a product of national legislation from the 1970s, organized to resolve cross-border frictions. National data privacy authorities, acting as transgovernmental policy entrepreneurs, worked at the supranational level to not only ease transaction costs associated with market integration but also enhance individual rights. Contrary to the typical neofunctionalist arguments, data privacy authorities leveraged their extensive policy expertise, domestic authority, and network ties to overcome opposition from European industry and indifference by national governments and the European Commission. Had the internal-market project predated the institutionalization of national data privacy authorities, it is unlikely that the directive would have emerged or taken its unique institutional form. The historical narrative, then, demonstrates the power resources that transgovernmental actors have to motivate European policy and organize day-to-day operations.

At the same time, the passage of the 1995 privacy directive further institutionalized the role of data privacy authorities in regional politics, creating the Article 29 Working Party. Comprised of national data privacy authorities, the Working Party formally incorporates the network of member-state regulators into the supranational rule-making and rule-enforcing process. This unique networked structure was a compromise brokered by national data privacy authorities, which argued that it would maintain national oversight while assisting supranational policy coordination. Since its inception, the Working Party has played an active role

in the externalization of EU data privacy policy and serves as an innovative model of organizing supranational governance.

This chapter has four sections. The first section presents several alternative explanations for the evolution of the directive before previewing
my argument. The second section follows the development of the directive from the late 1980s to its passage in 1995. The third section provides
a more detailed account of the resulting document, particularly its effects on transgovernmental cooperation. And the fourth section elab-
orates several implications for theories of regulatory convergence and
transgovernmental politics. The historical narrative provides significant
evidence for arguments that identify transgovernmental actors, especially
regulatory agencies, as coalition builders capable of altering the nature
of regional integration.

National Interests or Commission Activism?

Although authoritarian legacies are often invoked to explain differences
in national privacy legislation between the United States and Europe,
the argument offers little insight into the timing of EU entry into the debate or the transgovernmental nature of the oversight of the directive.
The central explanations used to understand the expansion of privacy
protection in Europe, therefore, look to the interests of either (1) the
largest European economies or (2) the European Commission. Explanations invoking the first contend that regional initiatives resulted from
the states asserting the economic interests of their domestic interest
groups within international organizations.[3] Companies in early-adopter
countries—France, Germany, and the United Kingdom—pressured their
governments for supranational intervention to create a level regulatory
playing field with member states that lacked privacy rules.[4] In such liberal intergovernmental accounts, national executives, motivated by domestic interest groups, lobbied to incorporate their regulatory logic into
the international regime, and the most powerful states were well positioned to obtain their goals.[5] For example, several histories of the directive begin by claiming that supranational regulation resulted from
pressure by Germany and France to ease regulatory differences within
the internal market.[6]

As evidence supporting the liberal intergovernmental account, one
should expect to find in the historical narrative that powerful member
states supported supranational action; that critical industries lobbied

TABLE 5
Alternative explanations for adoption of the European Privacy Directive

Causal perspective	Expectations
Liberal intergovernmentalism	Push by powerful member states Support from national business community in these states Negotiation by national executives
Neo-functionalism	Push by supranational institutions Support from transnational business community Promotion of supranational interest groups by supranational bodies
Transgovernmental entrepreneurship	Push by sub-state public actors Agenda setting through issue expertise Leverage domestic authority to alter supranational regulatory status quo Contribute to international negotiation

their national governments to back European intervention; and that national executives, representing domestic industry, conducted policy negotiations (see table 5). But the national interest explanation does not find this empirical support. Government and business elites, as well as public opinion from the largest national economies (which were also those nations with prior legislation), did not promote EU harmonization. National governments and business spent much of the early phases of legislative developments opposing EU action. It was only after the EU Commission made it clear in the early 1990s that EU data privacy rules were critical to the completion of the internal market that national actors accepted EU action.

The second general approach is derived from the neo-functionalist tradition and argues that the central bureaucracy of the European Community, the European Commission, had the ability to expand its competencies and broaden the scope of supranational decision making. Using large community projects to expand its jurisdiction, the leadership of the Commission succeeded in promoting certain issues even against the wishes of powerful member states.[7] In other cases, civil servants in the Commission bureaucracy slowly introduced new policy ideas into regional politics.[8] Using both formal and informal mechanisms, the Commission institutionalized the supranational structure and expanded the tasks for which it is responsible. By directly funding transnational networks and interest groups, the Commission fostered a set of interests that privileges regional concerns. Transnational associations offered an important ally to Commission proposals, building a European coalition for policy action. In the case of data privacy, it has been argued that the Commission supported European rules in order to extend the European market and its authority in the emerging information society.[9]

To support the Commission-activism account, one should expect to uncover evidence of entrepreneurship from either high-ranking Commission officials or civil servants in the Internal Market Directorate. The theory predicts that supranational officials promoted the creation of and sought a coalition with transnational interest groups. Transnational business groups should then have supported and pressed for regulatory harmonization (see table 5).

Although the European Commission no doubt played an important role in the data privacy debate, it did not initially support the idea of supranational action in this area. For over a decade, the Commission argued that data privacy rules contradicted the interests of the European Community. The Commission first actively engaged data privacy debates in the late 1980s. The question then becomes: What made the Commission change its mind? Why, after a decade of resisting supranational efforts, did the Commission quickly draft data privacy legislation in 1990?

National Regulators as Actors in Regional Politics

Contrary to both the national interests and Commission activism arguments, I highlight the role of transgovernmental actors as an alternative driver of regional policymaking.[10] The literature on transgovernmentalism begins by rejecting a monolithic view of the state as a single actor in international politics and posits that governments are composed of numerous officials such as regulators, judges, and parliamentarians who seek to shape external affairs independent of their national governments.[11] While transgovernmental networks have received renewed attention in both the literature on new modes of governance within European studies and by international relations scholars, much of this work has focused on the ability of such actors to coordinate rule development and enforcement.[12] The case of data privacy suggests that in addition to overseeing and modifying existing policy, such actors may in fact be capable of policy entrepreneurship. In other words, such actors not only fulfill governance needs but may also impose their preferences on other policymakers.[13]

How and why do transgovernmental actors become policy entrepreneurs? According to Andrew Moravcsik's definition, policy entrepreneurs "aim to induce authoritative political decisions that would not otherwise occur."[14] Unlike the Commission or the European Court of Justice, however, transgovernmental actors rarely have formal authority in the supranational decision-making process. They cannot directly introduce, pass, or strike down legislation. Instead, they must rely on informal tools to shape agendas, mediate disputes, and mobilize support for their interests. Transgovernmental actors use a variety of power resources—including expertise, domestically delegated authority, and network ties—that they develop over time to lobby for their preferred policy goals. Following work on bureaucratic autonomy, it is clear that these power resources draw on different underlying processes, both material and relational.[15]

To advance the discussion about the mechanisms by which transgovernmental actors influence regional outcomes, I take each in turn.

Expertise as a Source of Power

Like epistemic communities, transgovernmental actors use technical expertise to define problem areas and offer policy solutions, playing a critical role in agenda formation and policy mediation.[16] The EU governing bodies face tight budget constraints and therefore do not have in-house technical specialists in many issue areas. Transgovernmental actors, by contrast, develop a wealth of firsthand experience in their specific policy subsystems and include individuals with a range of technical knowledge. As directives are drafted, transgovernmental actors advise the Commission on how to formulate the language of European directives, playing an active role in rule development and enforcement. These domestic officials also represent and advise member-state governments as they formulate their national policy positions and negotiate in the Council of Ministers. This means that transgovernmental actors provide the Commission and member states simultaneously with the information necessary to draft a specific policy.

Transgovernmental actors leverage this information asymmetry in several ways. During the policy formation and mediation processes, they use their information advantage in a manner commonly described in rationalist approaches to bargaining.[17] When transgovernmental actors hold scarce information, member states and the Commission rely on their technical expertise to reduce the transaction costs associated with international cooperation, as demonstrated by the reliance of the Commission on data privacy authorities in the drafting of the directive. In a

more sociological vein, transgovernmental actors frame issues to overcome objections to proposals; data privacy authorities shifted the debate
from being purely about the protection of individual citizens to the completion of the internal market. This frame facilitated the creation of new
alliances in support of regional harmonization.[18]

Domestically Delegated Authority as a Source of Power

Transgovernmental actors are not merely expert groups endowed with
information; some have the power to use domestically delegated authority to raise the cost to political elites of supranational policy inaction. Authority within the European Union is distributed simultaneously across
a number of overlapping institutional jurisdictions.[19] This structure of
the European Union opens up access points for policy entrepreneurs.
Many data privacy authorities in Europe, for example, have the domestically delegated power to block the transfer of data to firms in countries
that lack adequate data privacy standards. They leveraged this authority
to alter the cost/benefit of inaction to other European policymakers.
Transgovernmental actors within Europe include public officials that
enjoy considerable independent enforcement and implementation powers. Regional governments, national courts, and independent regulatory
agencies have delegated authority at the national or subnational level
to change the regulatory status quo. When they choose to exercise their
authority, it can cause considerable regional regulatory friction. Such
transgovernmental actors become de facto veto players in the multilevel
context. The multilevel governance system of the European Union creates this opportunity for transgovernmental actors to deploy power previously confined to the subnational level on the broader European stage.

The extent of delegated authority that a transgovernmental actor can
wield is a function of the institutional design of domestic political institutions. Constitutions provide national courts and subnational governments particular powers to enforce and implement policies. Similarly,
governments delegate statutory policy instruments to regulatory agencies, including control over market access, the power to levy administrative fines, and the power to investigate bureaucratic and firm behavior.
Differences in institutional design—such as dedicated budgets and long-
term leadership appointments—expand the ability of such agencies to
exercise policy autonomy by buffering regulatory agencies from direct
political control. The domestic institutional setting defines the scope of

authority available to transgovernmental actors and the degree of autonomy they enjoy to express their preferences in European politics. In addition to the institutional competence to regulate cross-border data flows, data privacy authorities enjoy considerable statutory buffers to direct political control.

Networks as a Source of Power

Finally, the power of transgovernmental actors is amplified by their network structure. Networks (according to the most basic definition) are a set of more than one interconnected nodes.[20] Transgovernmental networks describe the regularized interaction among substate actors.[21] Although these networks may interact with nonstate actors in larger policy networks, the transgovernmental networks themselves comprise exclusively public actors. Such networks have both horizontal and vertical dimensions.[22] Horizontal cooperation describes relationships between officials across the member states. Networks of national regulators devoted to a specific issue area demonstrate such horizontal ties. The vertical dimension consists of interactions that take place across the levels of European governance. Interconnections between national or subnational actors and supranational officials exemplify vertical ties.

Network power is derived both from patterns of information flows and delegated authority within the network and the legitimacy that the network enjoys by creating ties to constituencies and other organizations. It is inherently relational in that variation in ties across the dimensions affects the resources available to such networks to instigate policy entrepreneurship.[23] Horizontal networks amplify the effect of both information asymmetries and domestic delegation. A statement from the European network of securities and exchange commissions, for example, has a much larger framing effect than that of the Securities and Exchange Commission of Spain. Officials that lack strong enforcement authority in their home jurisdiction, for example, may serve as a tripwire, identifying regulatory breaches and then informing officials with powerful statutory authority in other jurisdictions.

Vertical ties solidify the importance of a particular information advantage. As supranational institutions build relationships with a transgovernmental network, they come to rely on the specific perspective of that network. At the same time, the network embeds itself in the rule-development and negotiation process at the supranational level. For example, data privacy authorities were integrated into the Commission drafting process and accompanied many member-state representatives in the Council of Ministers meetings. Vertical ties, then, enhance the ability of transgovernmental actors to make their preferences known and to control agenda formation.

These dynamics have been central to the progress of data privacy legislation in the European Union; data privacy authorities have formed a horizontal transgovernmental network of their peers and have forged vertical links with the Commission and the European Parliament.

As evidence supporting the transgovernmental entrepreneurship argument, then, we should expect that transgovernmental actors used their resources to alter the supranational policy process. The highly technical nature of the issue area allowed transgovernmental actors with policy expertise, such as the data privacy authorities, to formulate and lobby for a regional policy proposal. Institutions such as the Commission and member states turned to data privacy authorities for details on how to structure such proposals. In contrast to policy networks, whose role is confined to agenda formation, transgovernmental entrepreneurs use their domestically delegated authority to implement and enforce national rules and to overcome political opposition to policy change at other levels. The emergence of a horizontal network of data privacy authorities allows individual agencies to mobilize power resources available to other members, and the integration of the network vertically into multiple governance levels allows data privacy authorities to directly manage supranational deliberations (see table 5). Finally, the timing of European Union action can be explained by the lagged emergence of domestic actors with the regulatory capacity to organize and assert themselves regionally. In short, because data privacy authorities enjoy considerable expertise, delegated authority, and network ties they are able to frame an attractive policy proposal and raise the costs of policy inaction.

The Development and Passage of the Data Privacy Directive

The narrative that follows examines the development of regional data privacy regulation and evaluates the two dominant approaches to European integration. The narrative begins by providing background context on initial national regulatory developments that set the stage for regulatory fragmentation in Europe. These conditions existed from the

1970s, when initial national legislation was passed, through the late 1980s, when a pan-European initiative began. The narrative reviews early supranational policy efforts, demonstrating opposition by the Commission, member states, and industry. The second half of the narrative reveals the important role that transgovernmental policy entrepreneurs played using policy expertise, delegated authority, and network ties to force their preferences on other regional policymakers.

Early Attempts to Formulate an International Response— Expertise without Delegated Authority

As European countries considered national legislation in the early 1970s, data privacy experts from European countries met internationally to discuss the implications of cross-border data flows for personal privacy. Growing economic interdependence accompanied by mobile firms and dense intergovernmental cooperation meant that personal information increasingly moved across borders. An epistemic community composed of data privacy experts from various countries emerged that feared that, unconstrained, technology would threaten the civil liberties of European citizens. These data privacy experts lobbied European institutions for precautionary action against the dangers associated with transnational data flows.[24] They feared that if a subset of European countries did not pass data privacy rules, these underregulated nations could potentially become data havens—with organizations locating their central data banks in these countries and circumventing national rules.

Privacy experts scored some initial success with the European Parliament, which passed a series of resolutions calling for pan-European rules.[25] Despite the recommendations of the Parliament, the Commission showed little interest in data privacy during the 1970s. Rejecting the Parliament's recommendations, the Commission argued that supranational privacy rules would raise the costs of doing business in Europe. Moreover, the Commission believed that privacy rules were a public-sector issue over which the European Community did not have jurisdiction.

The Council of Europe proved to offer a more congenial platform for initial international efforts. Created in 1949 to promote collaboration within Europe, including members and nonmembers of the European Community, the Council of Europe is primarily an intergovernmental body that facilitates cooperation in the areas of human rights and legal affairs. In the early 1970s, the Council established a working group composed of national experts to examine the issue of data privacy. The working group made a set of recommendations to the Council concerning the use of personal information in the public and private sectors. These were then elaborated in the Council of Europe *Convention for the Protection of Individuals with Regard to Automatic Processing of Personal Data,* which was passed in 1981. By the end of the 1980s, nine countries had ratified the convention.[26]

Although the 1981 convention prompted legislative data privacy debates in the United Kingdom, it did not produce comprehensive coverage of data privacy within Europe. The convention, as with any intergovernmental bargain, had multiple loopholes and served primarily to reduce friction associated with transborder data flows. It was not self-enforcing (i.e., it required national implementation legislation), it did not provide for a supranational regulation of transborder data flows, and it prioritized trade over the protection of personal privacy. Most worrisome for the data privacy policy community, however, was the lack of any regulatory action by five European Community members: Belgium, Greece, Italy, Portugal, and Spain. The case of Spain proved emblematic of the shortcomings of the convention in that the country had ratified it in the early 1980s but failed to adopt national implementing legislation. As the liberal intergovernmental account predicts, the policy network of data privacy experts that helped set the agenda of the convention did not have the power to guarantee its implementation by the national governments.

Resistance from Major European Policymakers

Despite the fact that one-third of the European Community had failed to adopt national data privacy rules in response to the Council of Europe convention, the major players in European Community policymaking resisted calls for supranational action. In 1981, the European Commission rejected a recommendation by the Parliament for Community legislation. The Commission argued that governments, under the auspices of the Council of Europe convention, should adopt national legislation to address transnational frictions.[27] As always, the Commission held a range of views on the issue. But the Internal Market Directorate argued that data privacy was primarily a public-sector issue related to the regulation of member-state government data banks, and the European

Community did not have jurisdiction over public-sector issues. In matters concerning the private sector, the Internal Market Directorate resisted pan-European data privacy rules. The Commission directorate viewed data privacy harmonization as inflicting increased regulatory costs on business. Both on the political and administrative levels, the central bureaucracy of the European Union resisted engaging in the data privacy debate. Contrary to the neofunctionalist expectation that the Commission would seek to expand its task set, the Commission rejected the call to action by Parliament.[28]

Further undermining the traditional neofunctionalist explanation, there was strong opposition by pan-European industry associations to supranational action. The Union of Industrial and Employers' Confederations of Europe (UNICE), the largest cross-sector trade organization in Europe, condemned the directive as placing a huge burden on industry.[29] The European Direct Marketing Association and the European Banking Federation echoed this sentiment, declaring that the directive was unnecessary and dangerous.[30] Therefore, transnational business did not provide the impetus for supranational action.

Rather than allying with transnational industry players to promote harmonized rules, the Commission supported industry efforts to maintain national regulations through the mid-1980s. Only in 1990 did the Commission switch its position and actively back pan-European rules. And this switch occurred despite continued resistance from national and transnational industry.

The liberal intergovernmental predictions are also disconfirmed; national governments and interest groups showed little interest in supranational action during the 1980s. There is no evidence that any member state pushed for EU intervention in the area of data privacy. The British government strongly opposed such a move, arguing that it would retard economic development and increase the public administration bureaucracy; and it did not change its position, maintaining the only veto in the final vote of the Council of Ministers. Neither the German nor the French government actively promoted supranational rules.[31] The German interior minister, echoing the Commission, argued that the sensitive nature of data privacy issues for business and public security required national action.[32]

Public opinion data indicates that governments were not responding to general societal pressure for data protection. A cross-national

TABLE 6
Public opinion on EU involvement in data protection: "Protection of computer-based
information on individuals should be decided by..." (%)[a]

Countries with legislation			Countries without legislation		
	National government	Jointly with the EC		National government	Jointly with the EC
Denmark	79	21	Belgium	55	45
France	61	39	Greece	46	54
Germany	54	46	Italy	51	49
Ireland	66	34	Portugal	64	35
Luxembourg	77	23	Spain	53	46
Netherlands	59	41			
United Kingdom	66	34			
Group mean	**66**	**34**		**54**	**46**

Source: Eurobarometer 36.0, Brussels, Fall 1991 Question 26-12.
[a] EC, European Economic Community.

Eurobarometer survey conducted in fall 1991 (table 6), with over 10,000
respondents, demonstrates that the majority of citizens in the member
states hoped for national—not European Union—action to settle data
privacy problems. This generally remained the case for the citizens of
both member states that had previously enacted legislation and those
that had not. As the survey demonstrates, citizens in countries with data
privacy rules were not pressuring their governments to export their rules
throughout the European Union; on the contrary, citizens in countries
with legislation were significantly less likely to support EU regulation.[33]

Although we might anticipate that industry from high-regulatory countries would have favored pan-European rules as a means of leveling the
regulatory playing field, this was not the case. Industry groups across the
largest member states opposed European action in the 1980s. This opposition was particularly virulent in the United Kingdom and Germany,
both countries with high regulatory standards.[34]

The position of German business is perhaps the most striking. Despite the fact that Germany stood to gain considerably from upward
harmonization, business did not promote European rules. As Dr. Friedrich Kretschmer, representative of the most powerful German trade association, the Bundesverband der Deutschen Industrie (BDI), stated in
November 1989 just prior to the release of the first draft of the privacy
directive: "There is no general wish by industry for a Europeanization of
data privacy legislation.... The differences in national rules benefit our
competitors in countries with fewer regulations and result in cost savings.

German industry, however, does not view this competitive advantage as a serious problem."[35]

A survey conducted by the Gesellschaft für Datenshutz und Datensicherheit (GDD), the German private-sector data protection trade association, confirmed the BDI position. Ninety-one percent of the 255 firms that responded to the survey believed that the European initiative would exacerbate market fragmentation within Europe.[36] The results, representing a wide array of sectors and firm sizes, show the striking lack of interest of German business in harmonization. National firms had adjusted to their national regulatory systems and feared the potential costs of layering pan-European rules on top of their existing regulatory requirements. Contrary to the predictions of liberal intergovernmental theory, industry from the most powerful member states lobbied against supranational action.

By the middle of the 1980s, a consensus emerged that national—and not supranational—action should be the primary mechanism to resolve data privacy issues. Given this lack of interest by industry, member states, and the Commission, what were the origins of the directive?

Transgovernmental Policy Entrepreneurship—Expertise, Delegated Authority, and Network Ties

During the 1980s, the data privacy community underwent a transformation from a policy network comprising primarily legal experts to an institutionalized group of substate actors with domestic authority. When negotiations began in 1976 over the Council of Europe convention, only one country, Sweden, had a national data privacy authority. By the end of 1988, eleven agencies existed in Europe, of which seven were in member states of the European Union.

At the same time that their delegated authority expanded, data privacy authorities constructed a network of their peers in other member states. Transgovernmental cooperation—collaboration between substate actors—began in 1979 when the German data privacy agency organized the first conference of data privacy commissioners in Europe.[37] The group met annually to debate pressing issues, share information, discuss best practices, and release joint resolutions on political matters. In the early 1980s, the network established working groups on key issues, ranging from internal-market reform to telecommunications policy. These groups met several times per year to develop collaborative policy initiatives. Over a ten-year period, the transgovernmental network of agencies

built up their credibility as data privacy experts and formulated a coherent proposal for European Union reform.

Data privacy authorities feared that mobile capital within the European internal market might compromise national protection levels.
Firms from high-regulatory countries could relocate their operations to
nations with lax standards. These data oases would undermine the comprehensive regulatory system and threaten data privacy norms within Europe.[38] In addition, regional market integration promised to increase
the transfer of personal information across national borders and to supranational administrative units. As long as a third of Europe lacked privacy rules, these data transfers would place personal information at risk
and threaten the authority of the data privacy agencies.

By the mid-1980s, with the failure of the intergovernmental Council
of Europe convention to guarantee privacy regulations across the member states, national data privacy authorities coupled their expertise and
network ties with their newly acquired enforcement powers to motivate
supranational action.

Mobilizing Expertise to Frame the Initiative

Starting in the late 1980s, the transgovernmental network framed the issue
of supranational data privacy protection as a prerequisite to further market and administrative integration in Europe. Playing on the symbolic importance of the single market to both the Commission and the member
states, the data privacy agencies resolved in a 1989 Berlin meeting that the
European Community must take action on data privacy to guarantee the
free flow of information within the Community.[39] The privacy authorities
argued that the internal-market initiative, symbolized by the Single European Act, would increase transborder data flows. European firms would
participate in multiple national markets, and governments would share
data cross-nationally to administer the single market. The threat loomed
that firms would locate data processing in data oases such as Belgium and
Italy. Several German data processing firms had already moved operations
to the Benelux countries to avoid stringent German rules. The conference concluded with a resolution demanding supranational action.[40]

Lobbying via the transgovernmental network increased over the following months. In a March 1990 conference, the data privacy authorities threatened that if the European Union did not enact privacy rules by
1992, they would block data flows. The comments of Spiros Simitis, the

data privacy commissioner of the German state of Hesse, summarizes the position of the data authorities:

> If there are no common rules by 1992 amongst the 12 Community members then quite simply five of the countries of the European Community without such laws will have to be treated in exactly the same way as those with no rules for data privacy. Therefore, there will be no personal data transfers to those countries because data commissioners will oppose such transfers.[41]

As at the previous Berlin conference, this conference ended with an appeal to the European Community to pass a privacy directive to avoid data blockages and secure individual liberty within the emerging single market of the community.

Using Delegated Authority to Alter the Regulatory Status Quo

The transgovernmental network of data privacy authorities relied on the domestic authority granted to its members in the 1970s and 1980s to alter the preference calculation of the Commission and the member states. Using a series of threats to block transborder data flows, data privacy agencies changed the regulatory reversion point.[42] In other words, they changed the regulatory status quo, altering the costs/benefits to other European policymakers of inaction. One of the most visible attempts to raise the issue to the European Community level occurred in July 1989, when the national data privacy authority of France threatened to block data transfers between the Fiat corporate offices in France and Italy. Invoking Article 24 of the French law, the CNIL, the French data privacy authority, argued that Italy did not have adequate regulations.[43] The CNIL blocked the transfer of information about French citizens, forcing Fiat Italy to find a solution to the data impasse. After intensive negotiations with the CNIL, Fiat Italy agreed to sign a data privacy contract promising to handle personal information coming from Fiat France according to French national rules.[44] The president of the CNIL argued in a speech shortly after the Fiat case that "the Europe of trade must not take precedence over the Europe of human rights."[45]

The CNIL again leveraged its power to block data exports in September 1989, this time between France and Belgium. With support from the European Community, several member states had constructed a

European cancer registry that involved the networking of records among multiple public health institutions. The Gustave Roussay Institute, the French research center, planned to join the European Organization for Research and Treatment of Cancer (EORTC), which was based in Belgium. The CNIL argued that sensitive medical data could not be sent to Belgium because Belgium did not have national data privacy legislation. The CNIL demanded that Belgium pass privacy legislation.[46]

The controversy surrounding the Schengen agreement instigated by the data privacy authorities in the late 1980s proved even more disruptive. Initially a bilateral border control accord to permit the free movement of individuals between Germany and France, the Schengen agreement was quickly joined by Belgium, the Netherlands, and Luxemburg. Although not directly a European Community initiative, the Commission viewed the plan as an essential first step to achieving the free movement of labor within the economic area.

To create an area of free movement, the Schengen countries had to find a means to police the entry points on the emerging single border. As part of the agreement, the Schengen Information System (SIS) networked the national customs and border-control databases so as to permit mutual policing of national borders. However, Belgium did not yet have data privacy legislation. At the Tenth Annual Data Protection Commissioner Conference in 1988, the Luxembourg delegation, which had only weak domestic authority to regulate market access, used its horizontal network ties to inform the German and French groups of the planned information system and the threat it might pose to privacy.[47] French, Luxembourg, and German data privacy authorities argued that sharing sensitive police information with Belgium would violate national regulations. The agreement stalled until a data privacy solution could be found. Under pressure from the transgovernmental network, Belgium pledged to rush through legislation, and the members of the Schengen agreement developed a data privacy clause along with a data privacy–monitoring authority for the SIS.[48]

The blocking of data flows by the CNIL, the stalling of the Schengen agreement by the network, and direct appeals by data privacy authorities changed the debate for the European Commission and the member states. In contrast to the position taken by the Internal Market Directorate in the early 1980s, Commissioner Martin Bangemann concluded that data privacy was now central to the internal market and for guaranteeing the free movement of individuals within the community.[49]

The European Commission also realized that the exchange of personal information was implicated not only in business activity but also in pan-European public administration. From taxes to border controls, data blockages by national data privacy authorities threatened fundamental European Community projects and therefore fell under the purview of the Community. The European Commission adopted the frame offered by the transgovernmental network when it presented its draft of the privacy directive in 1992:

> The moves to complete the internal market have created a need to exchange personal data between private or public firms in different member states, between national authorities providing mutual assistance in areas as diverse as customs, taxation and the fight against fraud, and between associations or foundations engaged in activities relating, for instance, to medical research, social work, education or culture.[50]

Now far from being simply a policy spillover concerned with the technical details of market integration, data privacy authorities had used their domestically delegated authority to change the preference calculation of actors at other levels. A counterfactual will help to highlight the difference between the neofunctionalist argument and the sequencing argument described here. Had the single market proceeded prior to the institutionalization of independent data privacy regulators empowered to control market access, it is unlikely that the European Commission would have adopted supranational rules. The Commission had no interest in expanding its competencies into the field of privacy. The period of epistemic Community cooperation demonstrated the inability of data privacy experts to motivate European action by expertise alone. The member of the Internal Market Directorate responsible for formulating the directive argued explicitly that the Commission was being held hostage by data privacy authority demands.[51] Only when these actors had been transformed into a transgovernmental network with domestically delegated power were they able to alter the reversion point and spur international action. The timing of supranational adoption, then, corresponds to a change in the regulatory capacities available to transgovernmental actors domestically.

Leveraging Network Ties to Fix the Agenda

The Commission quickly composed a draft framework privacy directive so as to allay the concerns of the data privacy authorities. Little consultation occurred with the private sector prior to the presentation of the draft. Instead, the Commission organized a drafting committee comprising Commission officials and representatives from the data privacy authorities. A member of the CNIL was seconded to the Commission as a policy specialist, and the Commission relied heavily on the advice of national data privacy officials.[52] This drafting process established important vertical ties between the transgovernmental network and the Commission.

The release of the draft agenda in the early 1990s ushered in a round of intense lobbying by industry. After losing the agenda-setting effort, firms pushed for the inclusion of national regulatory styles in order to minimize adjustment costs. The sunk costs associated with national data protection regimes overwhelmed the advantage associated with uniform harmonization. Lobbying for the subsidiarity principle, which holds that action not required at the European level should be left to the member states, European business supported flexibility in national enforcement models.[53]

National governments also resisted complete centralization at the supranational level. Many member states feared that they would lose control over data privacy if the Commission held complete authority to shape its development and to monitor implementation. The German government joined a group of four other member states—Denmark, Ireland, the United Kingdom, and the Netherlands—that wished for more leeway in national implementation.[54] This group of states submitted a reform proposal in August 1993, whose central goal was to integrate the concept of subsidiarity into the directive.[55]

National privacy authorities did not see this push for the subsidiarity principle as a threat to their underlying agenda and built an alliance with national industries and member-state governments. To counter fears of Commission autonomy, data privacy agencies advocated the creation of the Article 29 Working Party. Consisting of national member-state regulators and housed in a Commission-sponsored secretariat, the Working Party guaranteed subsidiarity. It also guaranteed the authority of national data privacy agencies within the European regulatory system. This innovative network governance structure struck a delicate compromise between the Commission and member states.

National data privacy authorities played a pivotal role in overcoming final concerns and reaching a political deal. National governments made a series of demands in summer 1993 that, if not resolved, could have stalled negotiations.[56] Contrary to the unitary state metaphor dominant in many international relations arguments, data privacy authorities were vertically embedded in the international bargaining process. This means that alongside many national ministers sat national data privacy authorities, whose expertise in the field had tremendous sway. As Internal Market Commissioner John Mogg explained, "In these negotiations the contribution of the European Data Protection Commissioners, where it existed, has been very helpful not only in clarifying and enriching the debate but in the finding of a final compromise."[57]

In a move that highlights the importance of transgovernmental actors in mediation processes, the German delegation appointed Mr. Joachim Jacob, the German federal data privacy commissioner, to represent the German presidency during the negotiations. Given his expertise in the area, the German government felt he could best conclude the negotiations. The German data privacy authority, highly aware of the interests of the transgovernmental network, navigated the final negotiations.

The constellation of countries without privacy legislation prior to the adoption of the directive presents a final challenge to the liberal intergovernmental approach. Following the logic of the theory, firms from countries without legislation should have preferred the regulatory status quo and lobbied their governments to prevent supranational action. Given the distribution of votes within the Council of Ministers in 1994, when the directive was adopted, countries without legislation—Belgium, Greece, Italy, Portugal, and Spain—had a clear blocking minority under the qualified majority voting procedure used for the issue of data privacy. If national economic interests had dominated the push for regulation, these countries could have easily followed their self-interests and prevented the passage of the directive. Instead, all the late-adopter countries voted in favor of regional legislation.[58] In short, the liberal intergovernmental account cannot predict supranational policy.

A common position by the Council was concluded in March 1995, and the Council and the Parliament passed the directive in October 1995. As a result of the directive, five countries—Belgium, Greece, Italy, Portugal, and Spain—adopted national legislation. The remaining countries were forced to amend their preexisting laws to comply with the directive.

The Result

The 1995 directive required that member states transpose its basic mandates into national law by 1998. First, all member states adopted comprehensive national legislation coving the public and private sectors.[59]

Second, the directive required that a national, independent control institution be created with the power to implement and enforce data privacy rules. Third, non-EU countries were required to demonstrate adequate levels of data privacy for data transfers to occur.[60] Finally, a standing committee of national data privacy authorities, the Article 29 Working Party, was created to advise the European Commission on data privacy issues, to promote harmonized enforcement, and to evaluate the adequacy of privacy protection in non-EU countries.[61]

The directive enhanced the regulatory powers of the existing data privacy authorities, requiring governments to grant them both powers to investigate and sanction. This has equalized the regulatory powers among the various national agencies.[62] Generally, the directive has eased the problem of internal European data transfers, and companies within Europe no longer fear that national authorities will block information transfers, as the CNIL did in the Fiat case. Multinational firms, however, face additional scrutiny because they must demonstrate that their home markets offer adequate privacy protection to permit data exchange.

Although individual citizens in Europe, generally, enjoy a significant expansion of civil liberties, implementation and the enforcement debates are ongoing. Several member states struggled to transpose the directive into national law, in some cases taking nearly a decade. Many of the member states that had no previous regulations were the quickest. Data privacy authorities in Italy and Spain, interestingly, have reputations as strict enforcers. After all members states had adopted national legislation, the European Commission conducted an implementation study in 2004 that identified a number of areas in which further harmonization efforts were necessary. As a result, the Commission and the Working Party are engaged in a multiyear work program to minimize regulatory fragmentation. In addition to questions of compliance, there are several loopholes in the directive that establish exemptions for national security concerns. These exemptions delayed many sensitive security debates (a topic addressed at length in chapter 6). Despite these limitations, the directive extended the comprehensive regime across the growing European Union.

Consolidating the Transnational Data Privacy Community

One of the most important results of the directive has been the consolidation of transgovernmental cooperation through the formation of the Article 29 Working Party.

The Working Party has a secretariat in Brussels that is funded and staffed by the Commission. It is chaired by one of the national data privacy authorities and also includes the European data protection supervisor and a representative of the Commission. It meets five times per year and has some fifteen subgroups working on a number of specific regulatory issues such as genetic privacy, radio-frequency identification (RFID) technology, and children and privacy. The Working Party has published eight annual reports and over one hundred documents and has developed annual work plans in which it spells out its priorities for the year. The Working Party was formally granted a number of powers through the directive. These include advising the Commission on emerging data privacy issues, assessing the level of privacy protections in non-EU countries, and assisting the implementation of the directive and harmonization of enforcement.

The creation of the group at the supranational level complements the expansion of national regulatory power in domestic markets. Because it has the authority to release opinions on data privacy concerns, the group has considerable influence nationally and internationally. For example, an English judge ruled that he must consider the European directive and the Working Party recommendations when interpreting domestic data protection rules.[63] The opinions of the Working Party have forced companies to change business practices to avoid legal uncertainty. As the representative of an international telecommunications company explained, clients read the opinions of the Working Party and ask service providers to meet their requirements.[64] Notably, Google agreed to alter its data retention policy to comply with the wishes of the Working Party. In many areas of data privacy regulation, the Working Party has advocated for new regulatory initiatives, such as the electronic communications data protection regulation, initiatives for privacy-enhancing technology, employee data protection rules, and privacy standards for biometric data.[65] The status of the Working Party, as a taken-for-granted element of EU policymaking, is evident in the increasing reference to the body as an EU agency in the international press.[66]

The privacy directive also mandated the creation of an additional committee composed of representatives of the member states known as the Article 31 Committee. In contrast to the Working Party, the Article 31 Committee focuses primarily on the implementation of the privacy directive and does not give broad recommendations about emerging privacy concerns. In the area of international negotiations, however, it has provided a consistent and important source of contact between the member states and the Commission. As the United States and European Union negotiated the Safe Harbor Agreement, the Committee reviewed draft proposals and represented the member-state positions. Similarly, the Committee consults on the adequacy of regulatory policies in other countries. The Article 31 Committee, although not enjoying an independent Brussels secretariat, provides a significant coordination mechanism for the national and international implementation of European policy.

The creation of the European data protection supervisor in 2004 further strengthened regulatory capacity at the European level.[67] The 1995 directive confined the authority of the Article 29 Working Party to issues concerned with the internal market. The supervisor monitors internal data privacy efforts within the institutions of the European Union—the Commission, the Council, and the Parliament. Each of these institutions has appointed a data privacy official to oversee practices within that institution. In addition, the supervisor consults the European Union on justice and home affairs, including European police and security activity. The first appointed supervisor—a former member of the Article 29 Working Party and the Dutch data privacy authority—has worked closely with the Working Party to forge a coherent pan-European data protection strategy.

The institutionalization of the transgovernmental network at the European Union level enhances the efficacy and authority of the data privacy agencies. The European Commission–sponsored secretariat provides resources to the Working Party, such as simultaneous translation, that facilitate cross-national cooperation. The secretariat creates the space for the commissioners to develop a long-term agenda with regular meetings and a Working Party work plan. The European data protection supervisors and data privacy officials appointed to each of the institutions of the European Union bolster the efforts of the Working Party. In contrast to the relatively informal cooperation among data privacy commissioners in the 1980s, the current European regulatory infrastructure represents a robust transgovernmental network—a community that believes in the protection of individual privacy in Europe and across the globe.

The story of the EU privacy directive is embedded in the evolution of national data privacy efforts. Born from laws passed in the 1970s, the resulting independent agencies offered a breeding ground for politically powerful data privacy advocates. With the rise of transnational business activity, data privacy authorities realized the threat to personal privacy and to their regulatory power. They mobilized political opinion and controls over data flows to persuade the European Commission and powerful member states that the successful completion of a series of European projects, including the internal market, European Public Administration, and telecommunications market required European privacy rules. The development of a strong transgovernmental network prior to the completion of the single market affected the passage and content of the directive.

The product of over five years of negotiation, the directive has strengthened protection levels within Europe. Data privacy authorities have seen their regulatory autonomy reinforced as regional rules have eliminated the threat that firms would exploit data havens within Europe to force a reduction in regulatory standards. Moreover, their voice has been amplified through the creation of the Article 29 Working Party. During a period of supposed market-conforming policymaking at the supranational level, a huge expansion in political protection, specifically transnational civil liberties, occurred.

Tracing the development of the EU directive provides important insights for two literatures. First, the case examines an additional microfoundation for the trading-up of regulation.[68] In the standard trading-up story, high regulatory standards create an incentive for producers to export their rules to other jurisdictions to minimize the competitive disadvantages associated with varying regulatory regimes. In contrast to the standard producer-centered version, the case of data privacy highlights the role of independent regulatory agencies. It further complicates the story because business associations in the countries with the highest standards, Germany and the United Kingdom, did not push for harmonization. Moreover, they did not see a disadvantage in having higher regulations than other European countries. The industry interest in the directive was less about leveling the playing field or exporting regulatory burdens than about limiting the costs of regulatory change for domestic firms. Once industry recognized the commitment of the European Commission to regulation, it attempted to shape the directive so as to minimize the adjustment costs. Producer lobbying, therefore, reinforced national institutional paths.

The impetus for ratcheting up regulation in a transnational market does not always stem from business interests pushing for a level playing field. Regulatory agencies seeking to defend their authority also initiate the trading-up game. Able to pursue interests distinct from national governments and national business, data privacy authorities appealed to European institutions and the European agenda to consolidate further data privacy protections and, thus, their position in the changing economic and political environment.[69] In this effort, the critical factors that granted regulators leverage were their expert authority, their delegated authority to control market entry to large markets, and their network ties to forge coalitions to support their agenda.

Second, the case demonstrates the way in which transgovernmental actors influence the European policymaking process. The directive emerged from a convergence between domestic regulator interests seeking to bolster individual rights and the Commission aspiration to advance big European projects. National administrative and data privacy regimes flourished in the early-adopter countries, where regulators from these nations (particularly France, Germany, and the United Kingdom) had an interest in raising protection levels. During the 1970s and 1980s, data privacy specialists were transformed from an expert community that leveraged technical knowledge as its primary resource to a transgovernmental network that could back up its expertise with regulatory authority. In contradiction to integration narratives that highlight the importance of national governments or the European Commission, these transgovernmental policy entrepreneurs leveraged their political resources to motivate and influence European public policy. The narrative complements recent findings focusing on the ability of transgovernmental networks to monitor and enforce global regulations. Building on earlier research concerned with transgovernmental coalition building, it demonstrates how such actors may use their power resources to foist their preferences on other European political players. Given the rapid development of the regulatory state and new regulatory agencies over the last several decades, the case of data privacy signals a much broader transformation in European politics.

This institutional transformation—the creation of a European regulatory state—in the field of data privacy did more than alter regional politics. With the consolidation of a coherent transgovernmental network coordinated at the supranational level, European regulators shaped policy choices around the globe. The exact mechanisms by which this occurred are the subject of the next chapter.

CHAPTER 5

The Spread of Comprehensive Rules

The International Implications
of the Regulatory State

Since the 1990s, the comprehensive model has become the de facto international standard. Nations ranging from Albania to Argentina have altered their domestic regulatory policies, expanding privacy regulations in the public and private sectors. In this chapter, I explore how the European Union influenced the policy choices of other nations. The central argument here is that regulatory capacity, built at both the national and the supranational levels since the 1970s to manage domestic and regional problems, now offers Europe important tools for shaping regulatory outcomes internationally.

Common wisdom holds that market power is a crucial determinant of the ability of a jurisdiction to shape international economic governance.[1] In many of these studies, market power is operationalized either explicitly or implicitly through market size, emphasizing an economically efficient adjustment process motivated by changing market signals. Large economies leverage their market either directly through foreign firms participating in the market or indirectly by raising the production costs to those firms catering to multiple regulatory environments. Potentially excluded industries lobby their home governments to meet the demands of these large markets to avoid market exclusion and the transaction costs associated with several regulatory regimes. Scholars employ this logic to explain the growing European influence internationally under the rubric politics of scale[2]—European member states multiply their power by join-ing together into one common market. And scholars concerned with the diffusion of the comprehensive privacy regime have looked to the poli-tics of scale argument to explain European influence.[3]

Although market power has certainly played a critical role in deter-mining international regulatory influence, using market size alone to operationalize the concept fails to address several critical questions: Why are large markets not always capable of shaping international regula-tions? What explains variations in great power influence across sectors? Which mechanisms translate size into influence? The European Union enjoys a considerable internal market, but it is not dramatically bigger than the U.S. market. And in electronic commerce, in which most of the personal information is exchanged, the European market is consid-erably smaller.[4] In the field of data privacy, the three largest markets in Europe—France, Germany, and the United Kingdom—had comprehen-sive privacy rules since the early 1980s, with little effect outside of Eu-rope.[5] In short, market size is likely to be a necessary but not sufficient condition for international regulatory influence.

To better understand the dynamics of global regulatory debates, I re-formulate the discussion about market power away from arguments about material characteristics of markets and toward investigations of regu-latory capacity. The ability of a jurisdiction to shape international eco-nomic governance is a function of the political institutions that define and implement a set of market rules.[6] Jurisdictions must persuade other countries, identifying the policy reforms required for adjustment as well as creating incentives in other countries for change. The credible threat of monitoring and enforcing clearly articulated regulation plays a criti-cal role in this effort. Such regulatory sticks are complemented by efforts to minimize adjustment costs ranging from funding administrative ca-pacity building to providing legislative text. The ability of a jurisdiction to shape policy choices in other countries depends on internal regula-tory institutions that underpin diffusion mechanisms ranging from co-ercion to learning.[7]

Following the sequencing argument outlined in chapter 1, such reg-ulatory institutions are rarely created with such international problems in mind but exist (or do not exist) due to policy choices made at prior historical moments across jurisdictions. The intuition behind the argu-ment rests on the fundamental finding of historical institutionist the-ories that political institutions enable and constrain political strategies and outcomes.[8] For a policymaker to support a particular solution, she must determine whether she possesses the necessary tools to administer and enforce that policy. The Weberian administrative state is not born all at once but rather is the product of continuous institutional layering.[9] State capacity deployed at time $T = 1$ was most likely constructed at time $T = 0$, and the corresponding institutions were most likely conceived with the problem of time $T = 0$ in mind. Although states often attempt to construct new administrative capacity in the face of policy demands, existing legacies delimit the range of potential reform.[10] Within the international context, it is the sequencing of institutional change in one country as compared with another that determines the relative distribution of capacities and thus power.

To investigate the relationship between regulatory capacity and market power, I examine here the institutions of the European Union and their role in the promotion of regulation in the global economy. The explosion of regulatory capacity at the national and supranational levels, which Giandomenico Majone terms the rise of the regulatory state, provides the European Union with unprecedented tools to control the terms of competition within the European market.[11] The rise of the regulatory state internally carries a critical implication for international relations—the institution-building revolution underway regionally alters the ability of Europe to leverage its market in global regulatory debates.[12]

This influence, of course, does not guarantee that Europe can force other countries to develop exact copies of European rules. Domestic politics in those countries will interact with European pressures, producing at times unique national compromises.[13] A wide array of factors, including scandal, technological development, and subnational policy, affects interest-group preferences and levels of mobilization. These processes naturally mediate the evolution of the comprehensive privacy regime as it spreads globally; however, my focus in this chapter is not the domestic politics of adjustment, a topic examined at length in many studies of globalization.[14] Rather, I explore here the means by which the European Union shapes the policy choices and thereby the character of domestic debates in other countries.

I isolate the mechanisms available to the European Union to both intentionally and unintentionally influence global regulatory rules. In chapter 4, concerned with transgovernmental actors, I identified expertise, delegated authority, and network ties as critical components of regulatory capacity. This chapter examines how these fundamental power resources were translated into specific policy tools: control over market access, EU enlargement, centralized negotiating authority, and oversight networks. In other words, European institutions regulate market entry to stimulate domestic coalitions in other countries, tie membership accession to regulatory harmonization, integrate regulatory goals into international negotiations, and deploy regulatory capacity to refine and set the tone for global policy through soft law. These institutions did not appear overnight; they resulted from nearly a half century of regulatory policymaking at the national and regional levels.

The chapter is organized into three parts. The first describes the dominance of the European Union in setting global privacy rules. This is followed by a description of the policy tools at work in the diffusion of the comprehensive data privacy regime. The final section concludes with some theoretical implications of the argument.

The Dominance of the Comprehensive Model

The comprehensive model found early support in the democracies of western Europe. Seven nations, including Sweden, Germany, and France, adopted sweeping rules in the 1970s. Despite the western European commitment to stringent data privacy rules, the model motivated little international action. By 1990, the year that the first draft of the EU privacy directive was introduced, Israel was the only non–western European nation to pass comprehensive legislation. Not only did the comprehensive model seem relegated to the quirky politics of Europe, but many non-European countries adopted limited regimes. After the passage of the U.S. Privacy Act in 1974, the other largest economies of the world, including Japan, Canada, and Australia, followed suit in the 1980s with limited models of their own.

The future of the comprehensive model took an upward turn, however, in the early 1990s when the European Union introduced its data privacy directive. As described in chapter 4, the directive required member states to implement comprehensive privacy legislation by 1998. In addition, the directive contained an extraterritorial provision, known as Article 25, which permitted the European Union to ban transfers of information to countries that failed to maintain adequate protection standards. Unlike most product regulations that affect the character of goods entering the European market, Article 25 imposed a regulation that affected how personal information was handled outside the

European market.[15] Just as national data privacy authorities had threatened to block data transfers between European countries in the late 1980s, under the directive the European Union now had the authority to stop cross-border exchanges between Europe and other nations.

Since the early 1990s, over thirty countries from five continents have moved toward adopting comprehensive regulations. Most members of the OECD—with the exception of the United States—have adopted or are considering comprehensive rules in their legislatures. The global debate has clearly shifted, elevating the stature of comprehensive privacy rules in the international regulatory scene.[16]

In addition to a rise in the number of countries adopting comprehensive data privacy regulations, a transformation has occurred whereby nations that previously regulated only the public sector have adopted private-sector legislation. Since the introduction of the draft directive, eight countries—Australia, Canada, the Czech Republic, Japan, Lithuania, New Zealand, Slovakia, and Switzerland—have reformed their privacy policies.[17] This does not mean that the limited regime has been entirely abandoned. A few countries—notably South Korea, Thailand, and the United States—have maintained limited regimes. And a group of countries under the auspices of the Asia-Pacific Economic Cooperation (APEC) have attempted to develop an alternative privacy framework to that of the European Union.[18] The APEC framework might eventually emerge as a counterweight to European efforts, but as of 2007, it remained essentially a policy document with little implication for cross-border regulation. As figure 2 in chapter 2 demonstrates, the limited regime is quickly being squeezed out as a viable regulatory model in the international political economy.

Even the United States, which invented the limited regime, has come under pressure to adjust. In contrast to trading nations such as Canada, the large internal market in the United States buffers many domestic firms from the extraterritorial provisions of the European Union. Nevertheless, U.S. multinationals faced the same threat of market exclusion as any other internationally interdependent firms.[19] EU demands raised ire across the Atlantic, and the U.S. government vigorously promoted self-regulatory solutions for the governance of electronic commerce.[20] This produced posturing at a fever pitch between the United States and Europe, which threatened to spark the first trade war of the digital era.[21]

After nearly two years of negotiations, however, in fall 2000 the two sides constructed a novel compromise, the Safe Harbor Agreement. As discussed in more detail in chapter 2, the agreement permits U.S. companies to transfer data between the United States and Europe as long as they comply with European regulations. Firms that enter into the agreement commit themselves to following European regulatory standards when processing personal information covering EU citizens.

The spread of comprehensive rules, however, does not mean that countries have adopted identical national regulatory systems. As in Europe, enforcement and implementation mechanisms vary. Some countries, including many in central and eastern Europe have constructed centralized regulatory structures, whereas other nations, such as Australia and Canada, have privileged decentralized structures. As explained in chapter 2, these differences have important implications for business compliance and interest-group development at the national level.

Although national rules vary in terms of some implementation and enforcement practices, alternatives to the comprehensive regulatory regime have been squeezed out as viable regulatory options at the international level. With the notable exception of U.S. citizens, consumers across the globe increasingly enjoy enforceable rights of consent, notice, and access to personal information collected in the public and the private sectors. There exists a distinct trend internationally for privacy protection through the comprehensive model.

The Mechanisms of Effective Market Power

Political institutions provide the backbone for regulatory export. Although market size matters, its effect depends on the regulatory institutions that translate economic clout into international influence. The international effect derived from market size depends on the regulatory capacity of a jurisdiction—the ability to formulate, monitor, and enforce market rules.

As discussed in chapter 4, regulatory capacity includes both informal and formal resources, such as the technical expertise over a specific domain, the statutory authority to implement a given set of regulations, and network ties to promote such rules. According to work on bureaucratic autonomy, these power resources draw on different underlying processes, both material and relational, and include the production of information, coercive sanctions, and the construction of norms governing appropriate behavior.[22] Bureaucrats rely on combinations of these resources to influence the behavior of others, exploiting their greater knowledge of an issue to persuade or their enforcement tools to coerce.

Regulators have the ability to shift the cost/benefit calculation associated with policy inaction and therefore have the power to shape the policy choices of other actors and, in turn, political outcomes. In other words, for EU policy to affect other nations, the European Union must have the regulatory capacity to define a clear EU regulatory policy along with the capacity to implement those rules.

The comprehensive regime poses real costs to companies that previously had enjoyed few restrictions on their collection and use of personal information. International resistance to the regime, especially in the information-intensive sectors, was strong and vocal. The widespread diffusion of comprehensive rules resulted, in large part, from the continuous political pressure exerted by European regulatory institutions on other jurisdictions. Specifically, four policy mechanisms that drew on different elements of regulatory capacity proved critical: control over market access, EU enlargement, centralized negotiating authority, and oversight networks. These mechanisms did not guarantee a perfect replication of the European system, but they changed the arguments available to interest groups in other countries. In the sections that follow, I consider each mechanism in turn, highlighting the importance of regulatory institutions for expanding European influence.

Controlling Market Access

The extraterritorial provision of the EU directive lies at the core of the global diffusion of the comprehensive model. Article 25 of the directive provides the European Commission with the authority to ban the transfer of personal information from the European internal market to nations that fail to enforce adequate privacy rules. Firms that transfer data to countries deemed inadequate may be fined by the national data privacy authorities. Even though the size of the European market creates a rational incentive for firms to naturally change their behavior, the adjustment process was often highly politicized. The size of the market only highlights the potential costs of nonadjustment. Regulatory capacity underscores the probability that penalties will be enforced. Skilled European officials actively monitored the regulatory behavior of other nations and engaged with those countries to reform their privacy rules. The threat, for example, of an inadequacy ruling by the Commission or of individual fines to firms provided clearly defined and powerful instruments based in statutory authority.

The Article 29 Working Party, an EU advisory body composed of representatives from the national data privacy authorities, has the authority to make recommendations to the Commission on the adequacy of rules in other countries and, thus, on whether information should be exchanged. The European Union permits personal information to flow only to countries that maintain adequate levels of protection. Countries such as Canada, Hungary, and Switzerland that have reformed their data privacy rules have been given a positive adequacy status at the recommendation of the Working Party.[23] Normal data flows between the European Union and these nations cannot be challenged. Firms from nations that have failed to obtain an adequacy ruling, on the other hand, face the uncertainty of sanctions from national regulators for cross-border data transfers. Determining the adequacy status of a country depends on a robust institutional apparatus that has the expertise and ability to evaluate foreign regulatory regimes and whose decisions are respected by the political institutions of the European Union.

Control over market access has played an important role in exerting international influence. The Australian adjustment process provides a valuable example of how the European Union employed regulatory capacity to shape regulatory reform in another country. Australia first confronted the issue of data privacy in the 1970s. A multiyear study commissioned by the attorney general and conducted by a group of legal scholars called for the adoption of comprehensive rules for the public and private sectors, enforced by an independent regulatory agency. After several years of political jockeying, industry and the state governments exploited political fragmentation within the Australian system to block the adoption of comprehensive rules. The Commonwealth government enacted a limited privacy regime in 1988.[24]

Despite a series of privacy scandals and some flirting with the idea of regulating the private sector, Australia firmly committed itself to the limited regime and private-sector self-regulation through the mid-1990s. In 1996, however, the extraterritorial provision of the EU directive began to destabilize the status quo in the domestic Australian debate.[25] The attorney general released a discussion document concerned with private-sector privacy relations, citing emerging technological and international pressure. Observers believed that this heralded a new era in Australian privacy regulation.[26] In a surprise reversal, however, Prime Minister John Howard rejected the attorney general's effort in 1997, arguing that private-sector rules would, "further increase compliance costs for all

Australian businesses, large and small."[27] Motivated by intense pressure from the Australian Chamber of Commerce and Industry against formal legislation, the government ordered the public-sector privacy commissioner to work with industry to develop self-regulatory standards.[28] The government hoped that this industry-led effort would mollify European demands while minimizing national adjustment.

Despite the government position, the EU privacy directive altered the political landscape in the Australian privacy debate, bolstering the arguments of privacy advocates. As the European Union prepared to bring the directive into force in summer 1998, the Commission prepared a document that outlined the requirements for other countries to obtain an adequacy ruling. The limited self-regulatory regime in Australia would have had difficulty meeting adequacy requirements for the private sector.[29] Some industry groups and parts of the Australian government recognized the threat posed by the extraterritorial provision. The Australian Computer Society, for example, warned the government that the reliance on self-regulation and the lack of private-sector legislation would isolate Australian business, particularly the information technology sector, from the European market.[30] The Department of Industry, Science and Tourism concurred, arguing that the EU privacy directive required that the government take action for the continued growth of e-commerce in Australia.[31] The government, however, still faced intense political pressure from a coalition of industry, including the Australian Chamber of Commerce and Industry, the Australian Direct Marketing Association, and the National Insurers Association, that supported self-regulatory efforts and the limited extension of private-sector legislation, especially to small business.[32] Privacy advocates and internationally competitive firms, particularly in the high-tech sector, faced off against smaller companies that served local markets and were less affected by European trade.

In 1999, bowing to concerns that the self-regulatory strategy failed to comply with the EU directive and threatened highly innovative, internationally competitive firms, the government reluctantly introduced legislation that enacted private-sector privacy rules.[33] The Explanatory Memorandum that accompanied the bill singled out the EU directive for shifting the legislative debate:

> Businesses engaging in trade with European Union Member States are likely to experience difficulties under the current self-regulatory approach. There are serious questions surrounding the ability of Australia to meet

the requirements for continued trade with EU Members under the European Union Directive on the Protection of Individuals with Regard to the Processing of Personal Data and on the Free Movement of Such Data ("the EU Directive"). The need to meet the requirements of the Directive will result in ongoing costs to business associated with European Commission negotiations and will also affect the extent to which electronic commerce opportunities across borders can be fully utilised.... The extent to which a flow-on effect from the requirements of trading with EU Member States will result in other countries moving to restrict transborder data flows is not clear, but should not be discounted as a potential trade barrier in the future.[34]

The Explanatory Memorandum goes on to address how EU regulations directly affect the cost/benefit calculations to industry of shifting from a purely self-regulatory system to a comprehensive regime, citing the conclusion of Nigel Waters, a privacy advocate:

> even if some sectors or jurisdictions are able to pass the EU "adequacy protection" test, this would still leave most Australian businesses, and governments, in the situation of having to demonstrate on a case by case basis that they ensured adequate protection for particular transfers of personal data from Europe. The cost, and cost of uncertainty, involved will potentially massively outweigh the modest compliance costs associated with a sensible, light handed statutory privacy scheme.[35]

The final legislation established a comprehensive regulatory regime based on co-regulation. Under co-regulation, similar to regulations in European countries such as the Netherlands, firms comply with a set of national privacy principles based on the FIPPs that are monitored and enforced by the federal data privacy commissioner. Industry associations may opt to develop their own sector-specific codes of conduct and establish independent arbitration mechanisms that, when approved by the data privacy commissioner, supersede the national privacy principles. The co-regulation system offered industry a choice between a centralized or decentralized regulatory structure. If industry took no action, it would be governed by national rules enforced by the data privacy commissioner; if, however, industry took it upon itself to tailor privacy regulation to its needs, the private sector would oversee the day-to-day management of enforcement and implementation. Industry codes of conduct must get approval from the privacy commissioner, and this approval may be revoked (thus co-regulation).[36] Despite continued insistence by members of the Australian government that their privacy regulation emphasizes industry participation, the majority of firms continue to comply with the national rules. The privacy commissioner has approved only three industry codes and, of those, the insurance industry withdrew its code. In a 2005 review of the private-sector privacy legislation, the privacy commissioner concluded that industry had little incentive to cover the costs of running an enforcement system that the government would otherwise bear. Co-regulation in Australia has relied much more on direct government oversight than was originally envisioned.[37]

Even after Australia introduced comprehensive rules, the European Union continued to use its regulatory capacity to shape the details of national rules. As the result of considerable industry lobbying, the Australian system introduced a series of exemptions; the legislation excluded small business and foreign nationals, and it limited the privacy commissioner's oversight powers to Australian citizens.[38] Representatives from the European Commission traveled to Australia and testified to the legislature that the exemptions, particularly the small-business exemption and the limited enforcement powers of the privacy commissioner, undermined the Commission's confidence in reaching an adequacy ruling for Australia.[39]

Because of these problems, the Article 29 Working Party recommended that the European Union deem Australian legislation inadequate, creating an important bargaining chip for the Commission and point of argumentation for domestic privacy advocates.[40] The Commission has not yet made an official decision on the adequacy of the Australian system, choosing instead to use the conclusions of the Working Party as a basis from which to negotiate with the Australian government. Although the Australian attorney general initially lambasted the European Union for being ignorant of Australian law, the Australian government has moved to reform various pieces of its legislation to address the concerns of the Working Party.[41] The government extended protection to non-Australian citizens in 2004, and in 2006 it redirected additional resources to the privacy commissioner to support enforcement efforts, particularly the review of complaints. The European

Commission has commissioned an expert study to evaluate these reforms and to determine whether they resolve the concerns of the Article 29 Working Party.[42]

Privacy advocates in Australia have leveraged the threat of EU sanction to motivate further reform, particularly in the case of the small-
business exemption.[43] Industry has argued that the lack of adequacy
has not caused any serious economic disruption. Despite vocal industry resistance to its elimination, the Australian Senate in a review of the
legislation affirmed the position of privacy advocates and called for the
elimination of the small-business exemption so as to comply with EU
adequacy requirements.[44] The final outcome of this debate is still uncertain. The Australian government convened the Australian Law Reform
Commission to conduct a multiyear study on the reform of Australian
privacy laws to assess existing legislation and examine the recommendations of recent reform proposals. The initial discussion paper of the
Commission, released in fall 2007, recommended that the government
attempt to meet the EU adequacy demands, placing additional pressure
on the government.[45]

Even though market access control did not produce an exact replica
of European rules in Australia, it proved critical in moving the national
regime from the limited to comprehensive regime camp. Australian
industry and the Australian government did not rise quickly to meet
the European demands, casting doubt on causal arguments that stress
efficiency and the natural adjustment bought on by reform in large markets. Concerns about the regulatory burden of a comprehensive regime
dominated the debate for several years, threatening to derail policy
change. The extraterritorial provision regulating market access, backed
by expert European negotiators and regulators who could evaluate Australian efforts, proved critical in shaping the policy choices in Australia.
By evaluating draft proposals and condemning the final results, the European Union offered domestic interest groups important arguments
to support their cause. Similarly, other countries—from Argentina to
Japan—have felt the European influence as they attempt to reform their
privacy policies in keeping with the comprehensive model.

Europe not only has the institutional capacity to monitor the adequacy of other national privacy regimes but also has the institutional resources to enforce its regulations on firms within Europe. National data
privacy authorities have the power to fine companies conducting business within their borders that process personal information in countries

without adequate regulations. Control over market access does not just affect national policy decisions in other countries but also shapes the behavior of multinational firms active in the European market.

After the directive came into force in 1998, European privacy officials initiated a series of enforcement actions against large companies participating in the European market. In 1999, the Spanish data privacy authority investigated the exchange of personal information between Microsoft US and Microsoft Iberia. The Spanish authority found that the company had illegally transferred data concerning Spanish citizens from the corporate office in the United States to the Spanish affiliate without obtaining consent from the individuals involved. The authority fined the company approximately $60,000.[46] Similar instances of enforcement followed in several sectors, including telecommunications and aviation. In a dramatic case, the Spanish data privacy authority fined the Spanish telephone company, Telefónica, over $600,000 for opening up its customer database to direct marketers. Since the turn of the twenty-first century, data privacy authorities have enforced privacy rules against a host of private-sector companies across Europe.[47]

Compliance with the Safe Harbor Agreement further demonstrates the importance of regulatory capacity. Although the United States and Europe concluded the agreement in June 2000, European regulators agreed to suspend enforcement actions until July 2001. In the first four months of the agreement, no companies signed. But after the July 2001 deadline, firms rapidly joined. The timing of firm decisions to join underscores the importance of regulatory capacity for the perceived costs of noncompliance. The ability of European regulators to sanction individual violators, such as Microsoft, proved vital to activating the potential threat of market exclusion.[48] Figure 4 illustrates the expansion in the number of firms joining the agreement after the July 2001 enforcement deadline.

With the development of regulatory institutions that have control over market entry and access, Europe has built the regulatory capacity to project its rules in the global economy. By combining expertise and statutory authority, the European Union can identify and sanction noncompliance. Control over market access does not guarantee that countries will directly copy the comprehensive regime, but it alters the costs to national governments of inaction. Countries such as the United States and Australia have adapted to European rules in unique ways, and there can be no doubt that European regulatory institutions have reshaped

Comprehensive legislation has been introduced from the top down by governments hoping to meet accession requirements. This runs counter to arguments that emphasize market size, which would lead us to expect, instead, domestic firm pressure to limit regulatory transaction costs. I found no evidence that industry groups promoted comprehensive legislation in central Europe;[55] the new member states adopted data privacy legislation as a bureaucratic condition of entry, not as a means to help their firms compete in the enlarged Europe.

Another group of countries—including Albania, Bosnia and Herzegovina, and Serbia—are not applicant countries but aspire to eventual entry; these countries have also adopted data privacy rules. Given their relative socioeconomic conditions, it is unlikely that these countries would have passed such legislation without the bureaucratic signaling of the European Union. In many cases, countries have adopted data privacy rules before they have confronted the private-sector problems that data privacy legislation is intended to combat.[56] In addition to formal membership negotiations, the European Union employs association agreements to promote its rules.[57] Making regulatory adjustment a condition of regional cooperation extends EU influence beyond formal enlargement to include a range of external relations.

In addition to these peer-pressure tactics, the European Union actively promotes its standards through twinning procedures.[58] Possible accession countries are matched with member-state experts, who assist the accession countries to adjust their domestic regulatory environments. Thus, the European Union not only requires that these candidate countries emulate EU regulations but also sends European experts to monitor and advise on the specifics of policy reform and policy implementation.[59] And in addition to formal twinning programs, civil servants from current EU members take on informal twinning responsibilities by advising, holding seminars, and exchanging experiences with accession countries. Twinning activities, therefore, elevate the role of the national data privacy authorities to trans-European policy advisors, who have been instrumental in formulating and revising legislation in accession countries.

For example, starting in 1999, national data privacy officials went to central European countries to provide advice on legislative reform. The most extensive collaboration occurred between the Czech Republic and Spain. During the negotiation of the accession partnership, the European delegation made it clear that the Czech privacy law was inadequate. The Czech government then applied to the Twinning Program for a multiyear grant to build the administrative capacity necessary for a functioning data protection regime. The European Union funded a 400,000-euro project that worked toward consolidating an independent regulatory agency, harmonizing the Czech data privacy law, and building relationships among data privacy authorities from various member countries.[60] Similar projects have been carried out in Latvia, Lithuania, and Malta, bringing the EU investment in data privacy through twinning projects to over 3 million euros.[61]

The adoption of national legislation transposing EU directives never guarantees real on-the-ground implementation. Initial evidence, however, does suggest that the new member states are actively enforcing their data privacy laws. In a study conducted by Privacy International in 2006 and 2007, new member states generally received high marks for enforcement.[62] This finding is especially remarkable given that many of these countries recently transitioned to democracy and had no previous experience with overseeing data privacy regimes.

As a result of the EU enlargement process, countries have adopted data privacy legislation far in advance of any domestic economic need for personal information rules. Because of the relative immaturity of information-intensive industries in these countries, opposition from the private sector has been minimal. Governments have emulated EU regulations to receive favorable accession reviews. EU regulators have the expertise and training to monitor implementation efforts and advise the accession countries, significantly shaping the resulting regulatory reforms. The EU deploys its regulatory capacity in the EU enlargement process as both a carrot and a stick, rewarding reforms and punishing failures to adjust.

Centralized Negotiation Authority

In a number of issue areas, the European Union enjoys international negotiating authority. This is most clearly the case in trade policy, in which the European Union has the jurisdiction to negotiate trade agreements on behalf of the entire Community.[63] But, increasingly, the European Union is represented at international negotiations ranging from the environment to security.[64] International organizations as well as the economic great powers such as the United States and Japan recognize that EU officials are often the appropriate contacts for negotiating bilateral and international agreements.[65] With the European Court of Justice decision on Open Skies, which ruled that existing bilateral air-traffic agreements between member states and nonmember states must be re-negotiated by European negotiators, the role of centralized negotiating authority in areas of the internal market will expand in the decades to come.[66]

Whenever negotiating authority is centralized, the European Union has the ability to link its negotiating and substantive policy expertise. In so doing, European negotiators make demands at international negoti-ations that make sense in the context of the European agenda but that previously would not have been viewed by a national government as a priority. Defending EU policies and the integrity of the internal market are elevated in international discussions when EU negotiators enter in-ternational deals. The regulatory capacity to define and defend a set of market rules has been translated into a potentially powerful negotiating advantage internationally.

European officials learned about privacy issues during the develop-ment of the European directive and have applied this expertise in in-ternational negotiations. After the Schengen debacle, when national data privacy officials threatened to block the creation of a single mar-ket for labor within Europe, the European Commission realized that it needed to develop European data privacy legislation for the successful completion of the internal market. Just as the Commission had been unwilling to take on data privacy rules in the 1980s because it viewed European privacy laws as a nontariff barrier to trade, Commission offi-cials expected other countries to raise similar objections to European rules in the 1990s. The Commission correctly feared that countries such as the United States would protest the extraterritorial implications of European rules at the World Trade Organization (WTO).

Elevating European interests in creating the single market, Commis-sion negotiators went to world trade negotiations over services with the goal of exempting privacy rules. Trade in services was added to interna-tional trade liberalization efforts in 1986 as part of the Uruguay Round under the General Agreement on Trade in Services (GATS). The agree-ment applied conventional trade liberalization norms, including most-favored-nation status and national treatment, to the area of services. This meant that countries would not be permitted to discriminate among for-eign trade partners or between foreign and national firms.[67] Privacy rules that banned data transfers to countries deemed to have inadequate reg-ulations potentially violated such norms. The GATS negotiations moved into their final phase during the mid-1990s, running parallel to the development of the European privacy initiative.[68]

The Commission realized that if it wanted to guarantee European privacy rules, it would have to remove them from the trade debate. The United States, however, did not yet understand the implications of the privacy exemption. The trade negotiations occurred prior to the release of the final data privacy draft, and the United States had no major official working on privacy rules.[69] So, the European Union, with its clear grasp of the implications of the directive, easily pushed through a privacy exemption. The final exemption in Article XIV c ii of the GATS states:

> nothing in this Agreement shall be construed to prevent the adoption or enforcement by any Member of measures...necessary to secure compliance with laws or regulations which are not inconsistent with the provisions of this Agreement including those relating to...the protection of the privacy of individuals in relation to the processing and dissemination or personal data and the protection of confidentiality of individual records and accounts.

Only after the passage of European rules did the United States understand the significance of the privacy exemption contained in GATS.[70] With the implementation of the directive in 1998, U.S. firms feared that data privacy rules would be used to block transfers of information between U.S. businesses and their European affiliates. International business turned to the U.S. government to limit the extraterritorial application of European rules, and the U.S. government responded by threatening to turn to the WTO to strike down European regulations.[71] The U.S. government argued initially that privacy rules hindered international trade in services and therefore should be subject to international trade-dispute-settlement mechanisms.[72] Unfortunately for the United States, it soon became apparent that the GATS exemption negotiated by the European Commission limited this claim.[73] The inability of the United States to weaken the EU privacy rules through the GATS process forced U.S. officials to move toward a conciliatory position in transatlantic privacy debates. By cutting off the multilateral trade strategy, the European Union forced the United States into direct negotiations.[74]

In consolidating negotiating authority, the European Union is able to elevate European interests in international debates. In the case of data privacy, EU officials responsible for the internal market connected the internal regulatory process to the external trade environment. They used their regulatory expertise concerning privacy issues and world trade to circumvent a potential threat to the EU rules. European institutions (and the lack of corresponding institutions in the United States) became essential to the long-term viability of stringent privacy rules in a liberal trading regime and, more generally, demonstrate the power of clear regulatory delegation in international negotiations.

Oversight Networks

The expansion of regulatory capacity within Europe has also enhanced the ability of regulatory institutions to frame and define the terms of appropriate behavior in world markets. Through informal and formalized networks of experts, EU officials rely heavily on the opinions of national regulators. In a number of issue areas, such as telecommunications, finance, and energy, consultation with national regulators has been formally integrated into the policymaking process. These transgovernmental networks receive the authority to monitor and enforce the implementation of directives, highlight emerging problems in their issue area, and offer recommendations to the Commission on possible policy solutions.[75] The Article 29 Working Party fulfills this role in the area of privacy, offering interpretations and recommendations concerning the further evolution of European law. Because these opinions have been used in the national courts, firms view them as de facto rules and integrate them into their cognitive maps of acceptable behavior. The export of European regulations transpires through informal mechanisms, whereby regulators release opinions concerning acceptable business practices.

The case of data privacy clearly demonstrates this new soft law capacity.[76] The 1995 directive created the Article 29 Working Party, which is housed by a Commission-sponsored secretariat and releases opinions on a range of issues, including recommendations on the adequacy of privacy rule in other countries, interpretations of the directive for emerging telecommunications technology, and recommendations for potential future privacy challenges such as genetic privacy. So far, the Working Party has released over one hundred opinions.[77]

Although the opinions of the Working Party are nonbinding, they send a signal to national regulators, the Commission, and national courts.

Their statements, therefore, have a quasi-regulatory effect that diffuses through networks ties with other public officials and representatives of industry.

Growing enforcement cooperation through the Working Party coordinates national regulatory activity regionally, while relying on national delegated authority to enforce agreed upon standards. This began informally as national regulators learned from the group and then went back to their home jurisdiction and implemented best practices. Since 2004, the Working Party has begun to formalize joint enforcement practices. In these joint enforcement efforts, the Working Party identifies an issue area and then national regulators agree to investigate it at the national level. The results of the investigation are then reported back to the Working Party. The first such initiative focused on the health insurance sector and was conducted in the twenty-five member states plus Norway and Iceland. A survey was developed jointly by the data privacy agencies and took the better part of a year to construct. Each national regulator conducted the survey of implementation in their respective markets. The results of the survey form the basis for a comprehensive compliance report in the sector and give notice about the key components of regulatory oversight to firms active in health insurance.[78]

The global importance of opinions of the Working Party is best demonstrated in the debate over online authentication services. More and more online services require consumers to log into virtual stores. This allows companies to charge for services, monitor customer behavior, and enhance marketing. Major technology companies have begun to explore ways to help consumers manage the explosion of logins and centralize customer-behavior profiling across online stores. One solution, favored by Microsoft, would have consumers log into a single trusted service, known as .NET Passport, which would authenticate its customer across a range of service providers. Microsoft would then provide profiling data to the various companies that participate in its program. Such a system naturally involves a tremendous amount of data transfers containing personal data.[79]

In July 2002, the Working Party released a preliminary opinion concerning online authentication in which it raised several objections to the Microsoft system. The Working Party was particularly concerned with the lack of information given to consumers about how their personal information would be used as well as the lack of input given to consumers over which profiling data could be exchanged and under what conditions. The Working Party developed over a six-month period a more detailed framework for considering data privacy concerns for such authentication systems.[80] After the release of the nonbinding opinion, Microsoft agreed to change its program to address the privacy concerns of the Working Party and to avoid any public relations scandal. The Microsoft decision to integrate the new privacy-enhancing features globally demonstrates the far-reaching effects of the opinions of European regulators.[81]

In a similar case in 2007, the Working Party worked with Google to shorten its data-retention policy. Search engines record search patterns, which indicate interests and tastes, to develop marketing applications. Google announced in spring 2007 that it would retain such data for twenty-four months before annonimizing it. In May 2007, the Article 29 Working Party sent a letter to Google asking the company to explain this retention policy.[82] Although the Working Party applauded the decision to annonimize the archived data, they feared that the period of data retention still was in violation of European law. After consultation with the Working Party, Google reduced its retention period to eighteen months. Other major search-engine companies, including Yahoo and Microsoft, followed suit over the following months.

Multinational firms monitor the statements of the Working Party to determine how national regulators and courts might implement the directive and to identify future directions in regulatory policy. Because national courts employ the decisions of the Working Party to determine legislative intent, businesses look to law firms to interpret the implications of its recommendations.[83] Law firms examine the opinions and offer compliance advice. Professional services that seek to protect their clients from uncertainty bolster the authority of the decisions of the Working Party. Firms often conclude that it is in their best interest to comply with the opinions of the Working Party and avoid litigation in the national courts or regulatory penalties, even though the opinions have no direct regulatory application.[84] Multinational firms integrate the opinions of such advisory bodies into their global best practices, limiting the costs of maintaining multiple policy standards across their interdependent affiliates.

After building considerable regulatory competence, the European Union can deploy expert knowledge to shape international markets. European regulators interpret and implement EU law, fleshing out the implications for firms hoping to compete within the European market.

This soft-law power allows the European Union to evolve regulations by working directly with firms and without the passage of new legislation. Bypassing the complex and slow institutional processes of the European Union, regulation through recommendation offers an appealing alternative for Community officials. Thus, transgovernmental networks can leverage the cost of regulatory uncertainty and potential national judicial intervention to shape private-sector behavior.

Over the last decade, Europe has proven that it has the capacity to shape international economic governance across a host of regulatory domains.[85] In contrast to arguments that focus on the material measures of markets to determine influence, the evidence in this chapter points to the importance played by the *institutions* that permit a jurisdiction to leverage its economic might. Such regulatory capacity draws on a variety of power resources, including technical expertise, delegated authority, and network ties, which are then used in a number of specific policy tools: control over market access, EU enlargement, centralized negotiating authority, and oversight networks. The greater the regulatory capacity to define, monitor, and enforce a set of market rules internally, the greater the ability of a jurisdiction to influence international market regulation.

Although research in international relations identifies market power as an important variable related to international influence, little work has really scrutinized this concept. In this chapter, I identify regulatory capacity as an independent factor distinct from (albeit related to) market size and contributing to market power. As such, changes in relative power arise even when relative market size remains constant. The size of the European market did not change dramatically either before or after the adoption of the privacy directive, and the European market in electronic commerce was much smaller than its U.S. competitor. Moreover, the biggest economies within the European Union—France, Germany, and the United Kingdom—had already had independent comprehensive rules for twenty years, with no noticeable international diffusion. So, although market size provides an important precondition, it alone cannot make sense of the rising European influence in the late 1990s.

This chapter also extends my sequencing arguments into the international realm. Although comparative political analyses have long stressed the importance of timing, they do so within specific cases; the emergence of an independent civil service prior to the expansion of the franchise, for example, moderated clientalistic tendencies in a polity compared with other societies that delayed the creation of an independent civil service.[86] Similarly, work on foreign economic policy has used differences in domestic institutions to explain individual national decision making.[87] The argument here notes the relational aspect of sequencing that arises in the international context. The construction of regulatory capacity in the European Union (compared with the weak institutional environment in the United States) offered the European Union an important advantage in international negotiations over GATS. Emphasizing the relational aspect of timing and sequencing expands systemically the ways in which domestic institutions can be integrated into international relations debates.[88]

Reconsidering the role of authority, specifically of regulatory capacity, in international economic governance helps reveal an additional mechanism driving change. By expanding the boundaries of jurisdictional authority—from national to supranational—market power may increase even without a change in market size.[89] National markets for electronic commerce within Europe, for example, are still largely national and distinct. But due to the privacy directive, other countries outside Europe face a common regulatory regime. In elevating authority to the EU level, power vis-à-vis other nations was aggregated. This leads to the startling conclusion that policymakers can augment market power through regulatory—and not necessarily market—integration.

The question then becomes whether these findings in the realm of economic governance are applicable to other issue areas. In the next chapter, I address the generalizability of the importance of regulatory capacity for international influence by examining cases dealing with national security—an area in which European capacities are still in considerable flux. I continue this exercise in the concluding chapter, which examines several cases dealing with internal-market issues other than privacy.

CHAPTER 6

The Struggle over
Transnational Civil Liberties

In chapters 4 and 5, I explain the adoption of comprehensive regulations regionally in Europe and the subsequent spread of these rules globally. I isolate institutional developments—specifically transgovernmental networks and regulatory capacity—within Europe as critical drivers of the outcomes. Because the focus of this investigation centers primarily on the market integration and information technology innovations of the 1990s, the legislative debates emphasized political economy issues. The passage of the EU privacy directive and the diffusion of the comprehensive model have greatly enhanced the protection of personal information in the private sector. The global war on terror, however, has presented new challenges and has resulted in policy actions that often privilege security interests over privacy concerns. In this chapter, I take the theoretical claims developed previously and scrutinize them in this emerging national security environment, addressing, on the one hand, how the European Union balances internally questions of privacy and security and, on the other, the ability of the European Union to influence global privacy debates in this policy domain. Because of the unique separation of powers among the institutions of the European Union, Europe confronts distinctive constraints on its regulatory capacity in the area of police and judicial cooperation. The cases presented here, therefore, offer particularly important points of comparison to the previous two chapters (which focus on economic issues dealing primarily with the European internal market) and help identify boundary conditions for the theoretical argument.

The terrorist attacks in the United States, Spain, and the United Kingdom since 2001 motivated governments across the advanced industrial democracies to step up surveillance and the monitoring of personal data. These moves have often transcended national borders as governments expand transnational police cooperation and monitor activity in digital space. Long viewed as a core domestic policy concern, civil liberties have taken on a critical international dimension, with individuals increasingly finding themselves subject to multiple civil liberties regimes simultaneously. Traditional notions of sovereignty based on territory are strained when citizens residing in one country can view Internet postings on servers housed in other countries.[1] Speech or content determined to be illegal in one jurisdiction becomes freely available through the network. Similarly, cooperative police efforts within Europe, such as the European Arrest Warrant or the growing transatlantic partnership between the Federal Bureau of Investigation (FBI) and Europol, obscure the separation between domestic and international security. Distinct from traditional human rights concerns, in which nations agree to abide domestically by basic standards concerning human dignity, *transnational civil liberties* involve overlapping jurisdictions and conflicting interpretations of how these basic principles should be carried out; the international and national blur.

To understand the role of transgovernmental actors and regulatory capacity in this area of transnational civil liberties, I examine here two additional narratives. The first centers on an intra-European debate over the collection and sharing of telecommunications data, which resulted in supranational legislation requiring telecommunications and Internet operators to retain customer data for a period between six months and two years. The second narrative examines a highly contested transatlantic debate over the transmission of airline passenger data from Europe to the United States. I do not attempt to provide a comprehensive policy review of national security challenges to privacy, and I largely ignore new domestic surveillance initiatives; rather I use these two cases as a check on the argument developed in the previous chapters.

Because of the institutional structure of the European Union, the decision-making and legislative process differs considerably across issue areas. As a result of these institutional differences, EU regulatory capacity is much more limited in police and judicial cooperation than in areas directly tied to the management of the internal market.[2] The Commission, the European Parliament, and the European Court of Justice all have less authority in police and judicial cooperation, with member states retaining primary responsibility. Within the highly intergovernmental environment of internal security, national government preferences play a more dominant role. With regard to the role of transgovernmental actors within European politics, the narratives suggest that, as politics becomes more intergovernmental and less technical, such players are less able to dictate debates and are more likely to provide information and credibility to other actors that have formal authority in the policy-making process. More specifically, as the power resources available to transgovernmental actors in such policy domains are constrained, their influence becomes limited. In terms of international regulatory power, the cases suggest that Europe is on a much surer footing when it negotiates under the auspices of the internal market, in which it enjoys substantial regulatory capacity, than in police and judicial affairs. On a policy level, the examples demonstrate that comprehensive privacy regimes are not incompatible with the new security environment but are in a constant dialogue, attempting to balance surveillance and civil liberties concerns.[3]

Data Retention and the Move to Monitor Communication

Data networks and cellular phones have radically altered the way people communicate with one another. This poses challenges and opportunities for law enforcement officials. The expanded communications options require more complicated surveillance techniques to uncover the digital trails left by suspects. National security agencies have pushed for wider monitoring of communications as a means of tracking and catching criminals and terrorists. Law enforcement agencies, especially within Europe, cooperate across borders to make use of information generated in other states. As part of these efforts, the national governments have called for data retention laws, which guarantee that telecommunications data will be saved for a specified amount of time. Because this challenges many long-held assumptions about data privacy policy, such as the principle that data retention should be minimized, data privacy authorities were forced to delicately navigate an intense debate between those advocating for the protection of civil liberties and those interested in bolstering national security. The question then arises: Can data privacy authorities exert the same kind of influence as they did in the case of the 1995 privacy directive?

To understand the data retention debate, it is first important to recognize that laws adopted during the market-making initiatives of the 1990s limited the amount and type of data that telecommunications companies could collect. The European Union passed a set of directives to facilitate the liberalization of the telecommunications sector. As this liberalization process advanced, the European data privacy authorities lobbied extensively and successfully to include specific data protection provisions for the telecommunications sector, realizing demands dating back to early efforts by the transgovernmental network.[4] Data privacy authorities convinced the European Commission that data privacy was an integral part of an internal market in telecommunications services and that the emerging information society required a set of guarantees to assure consumer confidence in the new technology.[5] The 1997 telecommunications directive, which passed within the first pillar of the European Union (dealing with the internal market), required operators to erase consumer data after billing. In some countries, such as Germany, telecommunications operators erased most traffic data after three months. It also limited marketing practices to an opt-in procedure, which meant that firms could use customer information for marketing only if the customer had consented to such data use.[6]

As digital technologies expanded in the late 1990s, the Commission drafted an additional directive that applied these telecommunications rules to electronic communications companies. This directive on electronic communications sought to consolidate consumer protection in the information age generally, but national law enforcement agencies feared that a sweeping data protection requirement would impede their ability to fight crime. Motivated by these concerns, the Council of Ministers sought to integrate a data retention clause into the reform. This clause permitted national parliaments to adopt legislation that would require telecommunications operators to retain information on customers for law enforcement purposes. This voluntary retention clause reiterated the legal status quo in that under the 1997 directive national legislatures had the right to make exceptions for national security issues. Responding to concerns raised by industry and data privacy authorities, however, the European Parliament added language to the directive that required national data retention regimes to prove that they were "necessary, appropriate, and proportionate" and held data for a "limited time."[7]

Despite the 2002 directive, which explicitly permitted national retention, only a handful of member states passed legislation, and some, such as Germany, maintained strict erasure requirements. Pressure intensified from national securities agencies to eliminate erasure rules. If companies did not store customer data for long periods of time, law enforcement feared that insufficient data would exist to track suspects. The first hint of a more far-reaching reform came in August 2002 when the Belgian government floated a document calling for mandatory data retention. Mandatory data retention requires communications operators, such as telecommunications companies and Internet service providers, to retain traffic data on all consumers for a specified time period (some proposals called for four years). This would have been a radical departure from the original 1997 directive and would have set a unique precedent in the industrial world. Even the United States, which many consider active in expanding surveillance power, did not have mandatory data retention. The United States, along with most countries, used a system of data preservation in which law enforcement officials request data on specific suspects. Telecommunications companies preserve data concerning those individuals instead of maintaining sweeping data banks covering the whole society.[8] The Belgian effort was quickly and rather decisively condemned. European civil rights organizations leaked the proposal to the press, raising concern in the member states.[9] The European data privacy authorities met and released a statement opposing the plan.[10] The Article 29 Working Party concurred, finding long-term data retention efforts in violation of European data privacy norms. The Working Party concluded that retention efforts should not exceed six months.[11] If retention was to occur for this limited period of time, data collection and transfers must occur within the realm of existing privacy laws.

Industry lined up with the data privacy authorities. Because of previous data privacy laws, companies faced many restrictions on using consumer data and therefore would be forced under a retention system to store data but be limited in their ability to use such data for their own purposes. Law enforcement, in a sense, wanted to outsource data warehousing without conferring any business advantage to industry. Given the lack of data retention in other nations, industry feared that the cost associated with retention could hamper the international competitiveness of the sector. A broad coalition of industry, including the International Chamber of Commerce, international and European telecommunications associations, and the European business association, opposed mandatory retention.[12] Faced with opposition from data privacy authorities and business, the Dutch, who held the rotating presidency of the European Union at the time, downplayed the effort, claiming that no formal proposal had been submitted.

After the Madrid terrorist attack in spring 2004, data retention again rose to the forefront of policy debates. France, Sweden, the United Kingdom, and Ireland presented a formal draft for a Framework Decision on data retention to the Council of Ministers.[13] These countries called for mandatory data retention for up to three years and looked to pass the proposal in the third pillar of the European Union (responsible for police and judicial cooperation). Because of the intergovernmental nature of decision making in police and judicial cooperation, pursuing a legislative strategy under the third pillar weakened the ability of several European institutions to oppose the measure. The European Parliament (the only directly elected body of the European Union) has only an advisory role in third-pillar issues rather than the full codecision rights it enjoys in the first pillar of the European Communities; similarly, because the 1995 privacy directive was passed under the first pillar, the Article 29 Working Party does not have any formal jurisdiction in third-pillar matters. Although this third-pillar strategy avoided some institutional hurdles, third-pillar rules require unanimity within the Council of Ministers (comprising representatives from the various member states).

Once again, a similar opposition lined up. Industry feared the costs of such proposals and claimed that the national governments had not demonstrated a need for such a plan. Industry estimated that the creation of a retention system would cost in the hundreds of millions of euros and would threaten the international competitiveness of the sector.[14] The Article 29 Working Party released a recommendation that warned that blanket mandatory retention for more than one year would violate the European Charter on Human Rights, raising the specter of a judicial challenge to any EU effort.[15] The conference of German data privacy officials quickly pressed for resistance by the German government, and the federal data privacy commissioner condemned German Interior Minister Otto Schily's interest in EU retention proposals.[16] Despite the interior minister's general support of retention, the German parliament came out in opposition to such efforts.[17] And given the unanimity rule regarding third-pillar issues, German opposition would be enough to block the Council proposal.

The concerns raised by industry and the data privacy authorities quickly found their way into hearings held by the European Parliament.[18] Picking up on the argument of the Article 29 Working Party, the parliamentarians responsible for reviewing the retention framework decision argued that it violated the European Charter on Human Rights. The parliamentarians cited the effect of such legislation on industry as a reason to shift the issue from a third-pillar to a first-pillar decision, calling for a review of the legality of the draft.[19]

Despite continued support from a majority of the Council, the retention proposal stalled as summer arrived. Opposition on privacy grounds from a few member states, particularly Austria, Germany, and Finland, blocked unanimity in the Council. A challenge by both the Parliament and the Commission as to the legality of proceeding with the third-pillar process cast doubt on the proposal. The Commission went so far as to announce that it would introduce its own first-pillar retention directive as an alternative to the Council effort.[20] A first-pillar directive fully engaged the parliamentary codecision process and provided a greater voice to the concerns raised by the Article 29 Working Party. After over two years of negotiations, the efforts of industry and the privacy authorities stalled the Council effort.

With the terrorist attacks in the United Kingdom in summer 2005, however, the retention proposal was viewed with renewed urgency. The United Kingdom, which held the rotating presidency of the European Union, integrated retention legislation into a broader set of terrorism proposals.[21] The Commission responded by calling for retention in its response to the attacks. The Commission then developed a draft directive under the first pillar that required uniform retention of one year for telecommunications and six months for Internet data. Recognizing the concerns of industry and privacy authorities, the Commission proposal reflected an effort to harmonize retention times and minimize collection periods.[22]

Over the fall, the European institutions negotiated about critical pieces of the legislation. Data privacy authorities continued to call for limited retention periods and adequate safeguards, but it was clear that the London attacks had shifted the debate. This is most clearly seen in the opinion of the European Data Protection Supervisor (EDPS), which argued that there was now some evidence that a twelve-month retention period was justified.[23] Likewise, the Article 29 Working Party, although reiterating their demand to limit retention periods and to integrate data privacy safeguards into the proposal, acknowledged the changing domestic security circumstances.[24] The German election also weakened a critical impediment to retention legislation. The newly appointed Christian Democratic Interior Minister Wolfgang Schäuble enjoyed the support of the new coalition government in Germany when he argued strongly in favor of data retention.[25]

In the final days of the 2005 session of the European Parliament a compromise bill was adopted.[26] The bill scaled back the retention period to between six months and two years from initial proposals calling for up to four years. Data maintained by companies under a retention regime continued to fall under European data privacy laws and data privacy authority oversight. Regulations limited the use of the retained data to issues directly related to international criminality. According to data privacy authorities, however, the bill lacked many important privacy safeguards. The Working Party called on the member states to address these concerns in the national implementation of the directive and spelled out eight specific measures that would bolster data privacy.[27] Both the EDPS and national data privacy authorities raised the possibility that a failure to address these deficiencies would result in a judicial challenge to the legislation (and in March 2008, the German constitutional court handed down a preliminary ruling that sharply curtailed the German transposition of the law). The Commission call for uniform rules that would reduce the economic burden on the private sector was ignored. The absence of any requirement for governments to reimburse companies for retention further frustrated industry. In short, the European Union and the member states could claim that they had struck a legislative victory against terrorism but not without upsetting most of the key players involved, including the data privacy authorities and industry.

While the issue of data retention is far from settled, the history of this policy illuminates the many mechanisms by which data privacy authorities continue to engage EU politics. By integrating data privacy into Community law through the 1995 general privacy directive and the 1997 telecommunications data privacy directive, the transgovernmental network had critically altered industry interests. The opt-in requirements for marketing put in place in the 1990s limited the economic benefits of retention for firms, and retention programs placed a new burden on firms, which had to store, sort, and deliver the requested data to security officials. Under the European telecommunications privacy regime, industry viewed retention as a cost that has no benefits. Once again, transgovernmental actors were able to use the unsettled nature of politics during the market-making process to forge a coalition supporting change.[28] The role of the transgovernmental network was augmented by its formalization within the European Union as the Article 29 Working Party and through the creation of the EDPS. The opinions of the Working Party provided the framework and argumentation for the other political actors, including the European Parliament, which resisted retention efforts and for civil liberties organizations. Simultaneously, national data privacy authorities lobbied their home governments. At the national level, these privacy concerns seem to have influenced policy as even the most pro-retention governments—in the United Kingdom and Spain— have drafted laws that limit retention to one year (not the two-year maximum allowed by the law) and apply only to telecommunications data.

The importance of the data privacy authorities in regional politics is best demonstrated by the fact that their very participation was taken for granted.[29] None of the major European actors—the Council, the Commission, the Parliament, or the interest groups—questioned their involvement in European policy discussions. Whether through the Working Party, the EDPS, or national agencies, the data privacy authorities are part of the European policy environment.

The final compromise, however, disappointed many, including the data privacy authorities.[30] When assessing the role of transgovernmental actors in European politics, therefore, the metric must be stated explicitly. Rather than asking whether these networks can define and achieve a specific policy outcome, it is important to identify whether and how they can disturb the policymaking process. The data privacy authorities did not universally reject retention but lobbied for the inclusion of basic privacy principles in the legislation. They had limited regulatory capacity to back up their position; retention laws redefined legal behavior and thereby removed any immediate threat that the data privacy authorities could sanction or block data flows. Instead, the data privacy agencies relied on their expertise, ties to national and European parliamentarians, and the delayed threat of a judicial challenge. It follows that the data privacy authorities should have had less influence than in the 1995 privacy directive, in which they enjoyed considerably more delegated authority.

Because the retention legislation was long debated under the auspices of the third pillar (concerned with judicial cooperation), the debate took on an intergovernmental tone. This put many supranational bodies on the sidelines, not just the transgovernmental network. Because

of the institutional configuration of the European Union in these matters, national governments could minimize the input of groups such as
the European Parliament and the Working Party. This highly political
atmosphere, with the clearly defined national interests of the security
community, circumscribed the room for transgovernmental coalition
building. It was only after the Commission threatened to introduce its
own legislation under the first pillar that the Council integrated wider
voices. The data retention debate says as much about the internal institutional power struggles within European Union as it does about the EU
response to new national security threats.

Nevertheless, the European data privacy authorities offered an important counterweight to national law enforcement agencies hoping to
expand surveillance at the regional level. It is readily apparent that their
argumentation influenced the policy debate. The final bill scaled back
the retention period, included the specification of the purpose of the
data, and empowered data privacy authorities to implement and monitor data privacy requirements in the telecommunications sector. In the
end, European retention legislation is embedded within the comprehensive privacy regime, which stands in sharp contrast to similar proposals in
the United States, which lack privacy guarantees.[31] Far from demanding
the absolute protection of privacy in the face of new security concerns,
data privacy authorities adjusted their position and worked within the
institutions of the European Union to produce legislation that balanced
national and individual interests.

Watching the Friendly Skies

In addition to the intra-European debate spurred by the retention legislation, national security issues have also sparked controversy between
the transatlantic partners. Responding to the 2001 terrorist attacks, the
U.S. government created a host of new security measures aimed at identifying and tracking terrorists attempting to enter U.S. territory. Among
these, the Aviation and Transportation Security Act of 2001 required
international airlines to report extensive passenger information to the
U.S. Customs Bureau before permitting entry. The initial list of required
information included meal options, credit card numbers, and previous
flight data. The U.S. government requested that the Customs Bureau
have direct online access to European airline databases to pull the required data as the need arose. This information could be retained for

a period of fifty years without individual's having the right to review or correct the stored data. The U.S. government asked foreign governments to comply with these demands in late 2002 and threatened to levy fines of thousands of dollars per passenger per flight against noncompliant European carriers and to possibly limit landing rights.

The government backed up its demands with considerable regulatory capacity. The Federal Aviation Administration and the U.S. Customs Bureau have the authorities to regulate landing rights and border entry, respectively. The Department of Homeland Security appointed a chief privacy officer in 2003 who is responsible for monitoring the privacy implications of U.S. security policy. In contrast to the negotiations discussed in chapter 5, the United States entered into these debates with a considerable amount of expertise and delegated authority.

Concerned that European carriers were stuck between EU privacy laws and U.S. security requirements, the Commission entered into negotiations with the U.S. Customs Bureau under the auspices of the first pillar in an effort to avoid any negative economic impact on European airlines. These talks produced a Joint Statement in February 2003, in which the Commission agreed as a stop-gap measure to delay the enforcement of European privacy laws and permit data transfers until a more robust agreement could be negotiated. The Joint Statement detailed that the United States would limit the exchange of sensitive data and the scope of agencies with access to the data. The Commission indicated that data privacy authorities might accept the Joint Statement as sufficient to permit the data transfers.[32]

Unfortunately for the Commission, both the national data privacy authorities and the European Parliament came down hard on the Joint Statement. The Article 29 Working Party offered a recommendation in October 2002, stating that such transfers were in direct violation of the 1995 privacy directive and breached Community law. The Working Party was particularly concerned with direct access of U.S. agencies to the databases of European firms, the sharing of sensitive data such as meal choices that might indicate religious affiliation, the extended retention period, the vague standard for collecting and transferring the information to other agencies, and the lack of a formal control mechanism to monitor use.[33] In March, contradicting the Commission statement, Stefano Rodota, the chair of the Working Party, warned the European Parliament that continued transfers might result in regulatory or judicial intervention; given the requirements of the European privacy directive, data privacy authorities might be forced to sanction carriers that transferred data under the Joint Statement.[34] Compared with the case of data retention, data privacy authorities at that moment in the dispute had considerable regulatory capacity beyond mere expertise to bolster their position.

The Parliament concurred with the data privacy authorities and argued that the demands placed by the United States were unacceptable, especially the request for direct access to carrier databases. European parliamentarian Sarah Ludford (United Kingdom-Liberal), citing the argumentation of Article 29 Working Party Chair Rodota, summarized the dispute: "This is a stunning rebuff to the Commission. He [Chairman Rodota] said in essence that National Data Protection Commissioners and courts were not free to suspend application of relevant laws just on the say-so of the Commission. That must be right. It is a reminder to the Commission that if it will not be the guardian of Community law, then others have to be."[35]

The concerns of the Working Party and the Parliament forced the Commission to reengage the negotiation process. Although neither the Working Party nor the Parliament could veto a transatlantic agreement, they could make the task of the Commission extremely difficult. The data privacy authorities had two main channels to constrain the Commission. First, they could directly enforce their national privacy laws. This happened in 2003 when the Italian data privacy commissioner limited the data transfers from Alitalia to the United States to information contained in a passport; similarly, the Belgian authority ruled in late 2003 that U.S.-EU transfers violated data privacy laws. Second, the data privacy authorities in the Working Party had the expertise to evaluate the adequacy of the data protection regimes of other countries. For the Commission to achieve a legally stable long-term deal, the Working Party would have to determine that the U.S. airline data protection system met EU adequacy standards. If the Working Party found the U.S. system inadequate, the Article 29 Working Party opinion would bolster a case in the European Court of Justice that the Commission had overreached its authority. The threat of a negative adequacy ruling by the Working Party imposed an important constraint on Commission behavior.

The position of the Working Party set the terms of negotiation for the Commission in that it spelled out the barriers to achieving a positive adequacy opinion.[36] The importance of the Working Party to the Commission can be seen in a letter sent from Frits Bolkestein, of the Internal

Market Directorate to Tom Ridge, head of Homeland Security: "Data protection authorities here take the view that PNR [passenger name record] data is [sic] flowing to the US in breach of our Data Privacy Directive. It is thus urgent to establish a framework which is more legally secure.... The centerpiece would be a decision by the Commission finding that the protection provided for PNR data in the US meets our 'adequacy' requirements."[37] Mirroring the arguments of the data privacy authorities, Bolkestein went on to ask that the United States limit the purposes for which such data could be used, the amount of data collected, and the retention period and that it create a monitoring system to guard against potential abuse.

The Article 29 Working Party and the European Parliament kept up the pressure on the Commission through fall 2003. In September, at the International Conference for Data Protection Commissioners in Sydney, the world data privacy authorities released a recommendation calling for a clear legal framework protecting privacy before transferring airline passenger records. Referencing this resolution, the European Parliament passed a series of resolutions skeptical of any agreement with the United States.[38] Far from taking an absolutist position, the Working Party determined that such transfers could be permitted to Canada because that country had an adequate protection system in place. Still, as Chairman Rodota argued in an address to the European Parliament, the concessions made by the United States were not sufficient to satisfy the Working Party.[39]

After a long negotiation with the United States, the Commission agreed in December 2003 to the transfer of data from European airlines to the U.S. Customs Bureau. This transfer would not include access to carrier databases, and sensitive information would be filtered out. The compromise solution included the reduction of the number of categories of data collected from thirty-nine to thirty-four, the deletion of sensitive data, that the purposes of collection be limited to terrorism and transnational crime, a retention period of three and one-half years, a sunset clause that forced renegotiation after three and one-half years, and annual joint audits of the program.[40]

The Commission argued that the pressure imposed by the Parliament and the Working Party helped force the United States to make these concessions.[41] They placed an important constraint on the Commission, which the Commission could then leverage in negotiations with the United States. Arguing that data privacy concerns had tied its hands, the Commission then pressed for concessions. At the same time that the European Union was negotiating with the United States, the European Union concluded similar agreements with Canada and Australia. The Working Party declared these adequate, demonstrating that the Working Party was not opposed to all such agreements but required that such efforts contain sufficient privacy safeguards.[42]

Since the conclusion of the first agreement, data privacy authorities were actively involved in monitoring its implementation. During fall 2005, for example, a contingent of European Community officials, including several representatives from data privacy agencies, went to the United States to conduct the first joint review of the system.

Despite the various concessions and safeguards, the Parliament and data privacy authorities continued to oppose the agreement with the United States. In a dramatic turn, the Parliament filed a suit with the European Court of Justice in summer 2004.[43] The complaint rested on two basic arguments. First, the Commission had overstepped its authority by concluding the agreement under the first pillar of the European Union (dealing with the internal market) when the transfer of airline data was clearly a security concern governed by the third pillar. Second, following the logic of argumentation presented by the Working Party, the Parliament argued that the agreement was in violation of Article 8 of the European convention on Human Rights, which protects the private life of European citizens.[44] Specifically, data in the United States were not monitored by an independent regulatory agency and the limitation on the purpose the data could be used for was weak, allowing security agencies to use the information for unspecified transnational crimes.

In an important institutional evolution, the European Court of Justice granted the EDPS the right to intervene in the case. Concerned that the Commission had overstepped its jurisdiction and failed to integrate sufficient privacy safeguards, the EDPS developed a brief for the court.[45] The European Court of Justice accepted the EDPS call and concluded that the EDPS has the authority to intervene in cases concerned with data privacy and is not limited to those dealing directly with the use of personal data by European institutions. The EDPS submitted an intervention and made oral arguments before the Court on the PNR agreement supporting the position of the Parliament.[46]

In a blow to coordinated supranational regulatory capacity, the European Court of Justice sided with the Parliament and the EDPS, arguing that the Commission did not have the authority under the first pillar to negotiate the agreement. Sidestepping the more fundamental debate about privacy, however, the Court found that the transfer of airline data between the United States and Europe was clearly a security issue. As such, procedures for a third-pillar decision (for police and judicial cooperation) would have to be followed as the agreement was renegotiated.[47] In short, there was no basis for supranational action.

Ironically, this ruling effectively put the transgovernmental network and the European Parliament on the sidelines regarding the future evolution of the PNR regime. Under the third pillar, the Council of Ministers, comprising national executives, negotiates external relations. In these issue areas, the Parliament has no formal role in the legislative process and the Working Party has no formal jurisdiction. The Council, led by Interior Minister Schäuble from Germany, was much more predisposed to the U.S. position and reluctant to privilege privacy over security. After signing a temporary agreement in October 2006, the Council and the Department of Homeland Security worked to find a lasting agreement during spring 2007.

During this final phase of negotiations, the United States leveraged an additional powerful regulatory tool—the U.S. Visa Waiver Program. A select group of countries, including most of those in western Europe, have an agreement with the United States that allows their citizens to travel to the United States without a visa. The original EU-15[48] are parties to the program, but the newer EU member states were negotiating with the United States to be admitted. In November 2006, the Department of Homeland Security added the transfer of PNR data to the requirements for new candidates.[49] This placed added pressure on the Council representatives from many new member states.

The transgovernmental network, however, continued to press for more data privacy protection during these negotiations. The Working Party released a recommendation in February detailing a standard format for privacy notices that should be distributed to passengers flying on transatlantic routes.[50] Although the Working Party did not have any formal authority at the supranational level, they used their national authority to structure on-the-ground implementation. Noting that he was not party to the negotiations, the EDPS wrote a letter to Minister Schäuble calling for increased data protection in the proposed agreement.[51] Specifically, he noted his concern regarding the retention period and the potential transfer of data from the Customs Bureau to other agencies.

These concerns were once again taken up by the European Parliament, which vocally opposed the terms of the new agreement. Citing the letter of the EDPS, the Parliament passed a strong resolution and called on the national parliaments to evaluate the legality of the agreement.[52] It also called on the EDPS and the Working Party to conduct comprehensive reviews. Despite the harsh words and condemnations, neither the transgovernmental network nor the European Parliament had any real institutional levers to use in the negotiations.

The final agreement was reached in July 2007 between the Council and the Department of Homeland Security.[53] In terms of data privacy, it is rather a mixed bag. It specifies the transfer of types of data similar to those in the earlier agreement. The agreement also calls for the use of a push system, as opposed to the original pull system. Under the push system, U.S. agencies do not receive access to European airline databases, but are sent relevant data. This had long been a demand of the transgovernmental network and nongovernmental-organization data privacy advocates. In an important move, the Department of Homeland Security extended the protections of the Privacy Act to data transferred under the agreement. This mitigated the concerns about access and redress that often arise in transatlantic privacy debates. European citizens could request to see their collected data and could call for the correction of incorrect entries.[54] In a blow to data privacy protection, the agreement included an extended data retention period of seven years. In addition to this, a dormant period of eight years was created; this new classification of data allows information to be kept but not used in active searches. The agreement does not prohibit the further transfer of data from the Customs Bureau to other agencies or to third-party countries. Theoretically, data could be shared with a large number of U.S. agencies and foreign security services. Most advocates of strong data privacy rules have concluded that despite a number of protections, the new agreement offers fewer safeguards than the compromise struck down by the European Court of Justice.

The future of the agreements is still uncertain. Although the European Court of Justice ruled on the institutional jurisdiction of the previous compromise, it did not examine its legality with regards to fundamental privacy protections. The Court, therefore, could find the July 2007 agreement lacking and nullify its provisions. In addition, legal cases testing it could be brought before national constitutional courts. Given the strong constitutional protection of data privacy in some countries, such as Germany, it is possible that the new agreement could be struck down on privacy grounds by these courts. This has happened in other areas of the third pillar, such as the European Arrest Warrant (and the

Constitutional Court is currently reviewing a case about data retention). At least one national parliament (in the Czech Republic) has already expressed concern regarding the level of data privacy protection in the agreement.[55] And the European Parliament has actively called on other national parliaments, the Working Party, and the EDPS to review the legality of the agreement under European and national laws.[56]

In terms of my theoretical argument, the case offers important evidence for the role of regulatory capacity in international affairs. European data privacy authorities had the expertise to define a specific set of negotiation parameters. Although they did not achieve their ideal outcome—which would have involved the United States adopting a European regulatory system for airline data—the series of compromises prevented the wholesale access of foreign security agencies to European airline databases. When the debate occurred under the auspices of the first pillar (for the internal market), the data privacy authorities placed an important constraint on the Commission and in turn shaped the bargaining process. This must be viewed as a considerable victory given the power that the U.S. security apparatus currently projects internationally. On the U.S. side, the case further reinforces the role of regulatory capacity. In contrast to the diffusion of the EU comprehensive privacy regime, in which the United States had no comparable institution to define and defend its limited regime, the United States has substantial regulatory capacity in the area of border control and airline regulation. The threat of fines on European carriers by the U.S. Customs Bureau was backed up by the Federal Aviation Administration, an independent regulatory agency with real monitoring and enforcement powers. Leveraging the Visa Waiver Program and newfound expertise housed in the Department of Homeland Security Chief Privacy Officer, the United States used a wide array of institutional tools.

With the 2006 European Court of Justice decision moving negotiations to the third pillar, the regulatory capacity of those advocating enhanced data privacy protections was severely constrained. Both the European Parliament and the Working Party were effectively removed from the debate. Their delegated authority eliminated, the Parliament and the Working Party had few bargaining tools to leverage in political conversations.

The negotiations over the transatlantic transmission of financial data by the European database organization the Society for Worldwide Interbank Financial Telecommunication (SWIFT), by contrast, demonstrate the difference between issues debated under the first and the third pillars.

SWIFT is an industry-owned cooperative established in the 1970s in Belgium to facilitate international financial transfers. Reports emerged in winter 2006 that millions of financial data routed by SWIFT were monitored after September 11, 2001, by the U.S. Treasury. Some of that data pertained to EU citizens. Because financial services are covered by the EU directive and Belgian privacy law, the transgovernmental network had strong oversight responsibilities. The Belgian data privacy authority and then the Working Party ruled the transfers illegal.[57] This forced the Commission and U.S. Treasury into delicate negotiations. The final agreement signed between the United States and the Commission limits the use of data exclusively to combating terrorism, specifies those with access to the data, and constrains the sharing of data with other countries and other U.S. agencies outside the U.S. Treasury. The retention period is five years and an eminent European is to review the data transfers annually.

Looking to the future, I anticipate that the ability of Europe to shape international regulatory debates will be weakened by the European Court of Justice decision, which pared back the ability of the Commission to negotiate collectively for the European Union in the area of internal police and security affairs. As the early negotiations over the transfer of PNRs and the SWIFT case suggest, EU authority is much clearer under the first pillar. Despite the continued uncertainty brought on by the European Court of Justice ruling, however, the narratives bolster the claim that regulatory capacity is critical for international regulatory influence.

In this chapter, I have presented cases involving national security to scrutinize the continued role of transgovernmental actors in regional politics and regulatory capacity for international influence. The intra-European debate over data retention demonstrates that the data privacy agencies created in the 1970s and further empowered by the 1995 privacy directive retain a vital—and very much accepted—role in policy issues concerned with the new security environment. Their interests compete with those of many actors, including national security forces, industry, elected officials, and European institutions. The case of data retention demonstrates both the difficulties and the opportunities data privacy authorities face as they attempt to promote a balance between individual privacy and national security within Europe. And it underscores the argument that the ability of transgovernmental actors to influence regional politics is conditioned by the extent of their regulatory capacity in an issue area.

In addition, when preferences are certain and there are fewer actors available for new alliances, transgovernmental coalition building will be more difficult.

Internationally, the ability of Europe to shape global policy in the area of security and police cooperation has become increasingly constrained. Although the European Commission used the concerns of the Parliament and the Working Party to obtain concessions from the United States in the early negotiations over airline passenger data, the European Court of Justice decision has far-reaching implications, curtailing Commission authority to coordinate and negotiate pan-European positions in the field of internal security more generally. At the same time, the United States is far better positioned in terms of regulatory capacity to challenge Europe when it comes to issues of border control and immigration. The case of PNR underscores the importance of regulatory capacity in international governance, particularly how changing levels of authority across sectors can account for variations in outcomes.

In the final chapter, I build on this causal reasoning, scrutinizing the generalizability of the claim that regulatory capacity bolsters international influence and exploring the implications of my argument for international relations more broadly.

CHAPTER 7

Regulatory Power in the Global Economy

Starting with the adoption of the mainframe computer in the 1970s, societies confronted the difficult question of how to regulate the mounting collection and processing of personal information. As we have seen, in response, governments have established one of the two basic types of regulatory systems to manage data privacy concerns: a limited regime that focuses legislative attention on the public sector and a few sensitive industries or a comprehensive regime that covers the public and private sectors and is monitored and enforced by independent regulatory agencies.

These two regulatory regimes long coexisted internationally, but beginning in the 1990s, the comprehensive system spread globally, coming to dominate international data privacy efforts. By 2005, only a few nations continued to follow a limited regime, whereas over forty countries, including the majority of OECD countries, had comprehensive rules. Of course, this is not to say that the convergence to a comprehensive regime has been identical. National enforcement and implementation mechanisms within the comprehensive regime vary, with some countries privileging centralized regulatory bodies and others emphasizing codes of conduct and internal data privacy officers. Nevertheless, there has been a noticeable shift across countries toward rules that cover both the public and private sectors. This shift toward the comprehensive system has occurred despite considerable resistance from both governments and industry the world over. Given the widespread dominance of U.S. preferences in regulating most international issues associated with information technology and the general concern that international interdependence has placed downward pressure on regulatory standards, the case of data privacy is quite startling. In this book, I have attempted to answer these questions: Why did the European Union pass stringent regulations in 1995, forcing all its members to adopt comprehensive rules? And why has the comprehensive system become the de facto international model?

As I have shown, the core explanation lies in the stepwise, sequenced construction of regulatory capacity in Europe that began in the 1970s with the passage of the initial comprehensive legislation in nations such as France and Germany and that was amplified by the market integration process in the 1990s. Regulatory actors—the data privacy authorities—established through national legislation worked together to lobby governments and the European Commission. Initially the Commission, powerful member states, and industry resisted taking action. But relying on their power resources—domestically delegated authority, expertise, and diverse network ties—data privacy authorities successfully persuaded the various actors that a failure to enact high levels of privacy protection across the European Union endangered larger political and economic objectives. Data privacy authorities effectively held the European integration process hostage to their demands for greater protection within Europe by threatening to block data flows between EU companies and governments. Far more than simply implementing and enforcing national privacy rules, these protectors of privacy became political players in the integration process capable of bolstering European rules. Through institutionalization in bodies such as the Article 29 Working Group and the EDPS, data privacy has become a taken-for-granted issue in European debates. Despite the new challenges raised by security concerns and the rebalancing of domestic preferences toward privacy, data privacy authorities continue to participate in and shape European policy.

Globally, the power of the European Union to persuade other countries to adjust their national rules toward a comprehensive regime is deeply tied to its regulatory capacity internally. When Europe adopts a regulatory position with extraterritorial implications, interest groups in other countries assess the costs and benefits of changing their domestic rules. Whereas the European market size determines the extent of the potential damages of nonadjustment, regulatory capacity determines the probability that Europe will be able to enforce its rules. Europe deploys its regulatory institutions to ease or emphasize the costs of adjustment. These regulatory tools did not guarantee convergence around a single outcome; rather, they mixed with the domestic policy setting in other countries to produce national responses.

In the remainder of this chapter, I examine the implications of my arguments for international relations more generally. In the next section, I extend the argument that regulatory capacity plays a critical role in the global influence of a jurisdiction, looking at the European regulatory state in sectors other than privacy: financial services regulation and airline safety. Although in no way an exhaustive test of my claim, these examples demonstrate the importance of regulatory capacity in different sectors, institutional settings, and regulatory outcomes. The final section examines the implications of the stepwise argument for issues of agency, policy diffusion, and power in the global political economy.

International Implications of the European Regulatory Revolution

Over the last thirty years, Europe has undergone an institutional revolution at the national and regional levels. At the core of the effort to liberalize and integrate the European market, the European Union and its member states have created a host of market rules enforced by independent regulatory agencies, greatly increasing European regulatory capacity. In sectors ranging from telecommunications to financial services, governments privatized nationalized firms and established arms-length controls. At the same time, EU institutions have been constructed to manage regulatory decisions directly or to coordinate national regulatory activity. This has led many observers of European politics to identify the emergence of a regulatory state in Europe.[1]

The expansion of regulatory authority at the national and regional levels and the formalization of European cooperative efforts have significant international implications.[2] I do not expect, however, this expansion to cause a universal increase in EU power internationally; rather, influence should vary by sector according to differences in regulatory capacity. Here, I focus on financial services regulation and airline safety.

Let us start with an area with varying levels of regulatory capacity over time—financial services. Europe long stood on the receiving end of U.S. regulatory export in this sector. Starting in the 1980s, for example, the

Securities and Exchange Commission (SEC) actively promoted strict insider-trading rules internationally, monitored and enforced by independent regulatory agencies. The complex system of overlapping board memberships in many continental varieties of capitalism, with self-enforced governance structures, made the adoption of such rules quite costly. Nevertheless the SEC persisted, threatening to deny market access to the U.S. stock market to nations that failed to meet SEC insider trading requirements. Following the relative sequencing argument outlined in chapter 1, the early development of regulatory state institutions in the United States, compared with the lack of corresponding actors in Europe, bolstered U.S. extraterritorial efforts. The perceived threat of exclusion forced European countries to rethink their position, and over the course of the next ten years, they adopted insider-trading laws modeled on U.S. demands and monitored and enforced by new SEC-like regulatory agencies.[3]

As market integration progressed in Europe, these national regulators, along with EU officials, looked for means to coordinate activity. European securities regulators began meetings in 1997 as part of the Forum of European Securities Commission (FESCO). This network attempted to smooth regulator frictions among member states arising from the internal market. As the integration of the financial services sector progressed, EU officials sought to bind this cooperative arrangement directly into the EU policymaking apparatus. As a result of a review chaired by Alexandre Lamfalussy, an agreement was reached to formalize the transgovernmental coordination of FESCO in the Committee of European Securities Regulators (CESR) and to link this network directly with EU initiatives. CESR was given the authority to monitor the enforcement and implementation of European financial services reforms at the national level as well as to advise the Commission on emerging directives. In 2003, the Lamfalussy process was extended, and similar networks were formalized in the banking and insurance sectors.[4]

It is not surprising, following the regulatory capacity argument presented in this book, that the European Union has become increasingly assertive on international financial services regulation. In a series of moves, the European Union has forced U.S. regulators to adjust.[5] This adjustment occurred even though the EU financial market was smaller than the U.S. market, again casting doubt on the market size argument. For example, in 2002 the European Union adopted a consolidation of regulation rule that required that a single national regulator be responsible for all operations of a conglomerate across all types of financial services. The hydra-headed regulatory structure in the United States, with distinct regulators for securities, insurance, and banking, failed to meet this new EU rule, and member-state regulators threatened to exclude a host of powerful multinational firms based in the United States from the European markets. The United States then adapted its financial regulations to comply with European demands. This revision occurred despite the fact that the United States had just undergone a major regulatory reform process.[6]

Similarly, facing demands by the European Union, the United States has eased the extraterritorial applications of its financial services rules. In the wake of a series of major corporate scandals, in 2002 the United States adopted the Sarbanes-Oxley Act, which was intended to enhance accounting oversight. The legislation applied to all public companies and accounting firms, regardless of their national origin, and required these firms to register with a new agency, the Public Company Accounting Oversight Board. But European regulators under the auspices of CESR argued that they should be responsible for such oversight. CESR and the SEC working together reached a compromise whereby European regulators maintain regulatory authority over auditing questions.[7] Similarly, the European Union has forced the United States to reconsider its requirement that all firms listed on a U.S. stock exchange follow U.S. accounting standards. This requirement had proven quite costly for European multinational companies, forcing them to maintain duplicate accounting practices. Following a period of convergence negotiations, the United States agreed that European firms may in the future use international accounting standards in the United States.[8] The European Union, supported by CESR, has been a key driver in the promotion of international accounting standards. In short, the expansion of regulatory capacity in Europe has severely weakened U.S. dominance in finance and has elevated the European Union from a policytaker to a policymaker at the international level.[9] Research indicates that the European internal regulatory reforms have had far-reaching consequences for transatlantic economic governance in areas of regulatory policy as diverse as antitrust, pharmaceutical approval, industrial chemicals, and telecommunications.[10]

The area of food safety, however, offers an instructive counterpoint. For over two decades, European countries and the European Union have worked to regulate the quality of their food in areas ranging from the hormones used in beef production to the labeling of agricultural products. Until the turn of the twenty-first century, however, European national food safety policy was not typically monitored and enforced by a single independent regulatory agency parallel to the U.S. Food and Drug Administration. Instead, ministries of agriculture tended to dominate food safety debates. The European Food Safety Agency, the supranational agency created in 2002, had mainly an advisory role. Lacking delegation to independent regulatory agencies at the national level, food safety remained highly politicized and contentious.[11] Parties hoping to capitalize on the spoils associated with agricultural policy and to win the prized farmer vote resisted removing such issues from partisan government ministries. Scholars have identified this weak regulatory capacity as hindering the international effects of extensive national and EU policy efforts.[12] The transition to a regulatory state in the area of food safety over the last five years, with the creation of national independent food safety authorities in some countries and the expansion of the authority of the European Food Safety Agency, could substantially strengthen the European position.[13]

The international effects of European regulatory capacity are not limited to the transatlantic relationship. In the area of aviation safety, for example, a transgovernmental network of regulatory agencies has played a critical role in promoting European safety regulations globally. With the continued expansion of passenger air transport, national governments have worked to guarantee aviation safety. Since the 1950s, and then accelerating with the liberalization of the sector in the 1970s and 1980s, governments established regulatory agencies—civilian aviation authorities—to oversee the industry. Responsible for a variety of tasks ranging from product safety standards to in-flight protocols, the civilian aviation authorities monitor and enforce national legislation. In 1990, national authorities in Europe forged a transgovernmental network called the Joint Aviation Authorities (JAA). The JAA, although not grounded in an intergovernmental agreement or international law, became the de facto European counterpart of the Federal Aviation Administration, issuing safety standards and investigating complaints.

After its inception, the European Union increasingly relied on the JAA as a coordinating body for pan-European aviation safety rules. Starting in the early 1990s, the European Union recognized the safety recommendations of this body as binding European standards.[14] The European Union formalized the work of the JAA with the creation of the European Aviation Safety Agency (EASA) in 2003; the EASA has an independent

secretariat and is distinct from the JAA process, but its board is composed primarily of national aviation authorities.[15] Following a pattern
similar to that in data privacy, the European Union slowly incorporated
transgovernmental cooperation directly into the supranational legislative process.

Long concerned with aviation safety internationally, European aviation authorities and the EASA received renewed attention in the last
several years with the publication of airline safety blacklists. Following
a series of international crashes in 2005 that killed European citizens,
European governments—most notably Belgium and France—published
the results of national aviation authority safety studies. These blacklists
detail the airlines that are considered by the aviation authority to be
unsafe for travel by national citizens and that are banned from landing at European airports and from flying over European territory. The
European Union, fearing regulatory fragmentation, passed legislation
that required the publication of a pan-European list. In 2007, over 150
airlines were placed on the list. The European Union updates the list
every few months, drawing on reports from national aviation authorities
and the EASA. In addition to conducting on-the-ground safety inspec-
tions, the European Union provides technical and economic assistance
to countries whose airlines are on the list. Although the program has
only a short track record so far, the Commission reports that European
security audits combined with the blacklist have produced safety reforms
in other countries.[16] The EU regulatory capacity to control market access, name and shame foreign air carriers with poor safety records, and
provide technical support has improved safety procedures. This policy
strategy has transformed the large European travel market into a powerful tool for shaping industry performance globally. These brief examples highlight the importance of regulatory capacity for international
affairs and underscore the variation across sectors that such an account
provides.

Broader Implications and Conclusions

The historical narrative describing the evolution of data privacy policies
nationally, regionally, and globally portends dramatic developments in
international politics. So far the specific relevance of transgovernmental networks for European integration and regulatory capacity for policy

diffusion have been examined; but it is also vital to cast a wider net. Here I consider how these developments implicate decision making and power in the international arena. I conclude by examining three topics: regulators as drivers of regional integration, the historical institutional roots of diffusion, and regulatory power in the global political economy.

Regulators as Drivers of Regional Integration

Groups of regulators, bureaucrats, and judges are increasingly linking up and cooperating across borders.[17] Recent research has focused on how these networks serve to supplement or supplant traditional forms of international governance.[18] Such networks share best practices with one another or enter into collaborative enforcement efforts. Although this research has produced valuable findings, following the argument developed here we can also view these regulators as important agents of change capable of driving regional politics. Transgovernmental actors rely on their power resources—expertise, delegated authority, and reputation—to assert their preferences and to lobby supranational institutions. This is all the more exciting given that transgovernmental networks may form organically without pressure from international organizations or national governments. Regulators, perceiving a threat to their mission and their authority, organize and mobilize politically.

Driven both by their professional mandate—say, to protect the environment or to safeguard personal privacy—and their interest in sustaining their political authority, bureaucrats leverage their regulatory capacity to shape political outcomes. As Daniel Carpenter argues, "Bureaucratic autonomy occurs when bureaucrats take actions consistent with their own wishes, actions to which politicians and organized interest defer even though they would prefer that other actions (or no action at all) be taken."[19]

As discussed in the previous section, the rise of the regulatory state in Europe is far from limited to the area of data privacy. The European Union and its member states have reorganized market and social regulation, spawning a new armada of regulatory agencies.[20] The simultaneous emergence of numerous regulatory agencies at the national level has created an incubator for regulatory cooperation across European borders. Officials from national agencies engage their European colleagues to discuss national policy, share regulatory strategies, and examine challenges posed by integration.[21]

To extend its limited resources, the Commission has formally integrated the transgovernmental groups into the regional policymaking process. Just as the 1995 privacy directive formalized the cooperative efforts of the European data privacy authorities, similar institutional arrangements have been constructed in financial services, telecommunications, energy, and transportation. Previously informal associations of national regulators now have been explicitly written into EU directives to serve vital governance tasks.[22] National regulators have gained prominence in policy circles at the supranational level as well as nationally.

In contrast to the expectation forwarded by principal-agent theory, which focuses on agent behavior given a static zone of discretion, transgovernmental actors use their resources to promote new policy action and often re-create their own mandate.[23] By participating in transgovernmental networks, regulators augment the resources at their disposal to build coalitions of support regionally for their policy goals. Regulators leverage the complementary assets of their neighbors, multiplying their ability to monitor compliance and regulatory developments. Agencies with weak enforcement powers, for example, may provide needed technical expertise and information to those with powerful statutory authority. In addition, transgovernmental coordination amplifies lobbying efforts. Transgovernmental groups have not only their domestically derived formal authority and expertise but also a myriad of relationships in their national setting, which can be leveraged to achieve political ends.[24]

Given the complex nature of global governance, many of the monitoring and control mechanisms devised by government officials to rein in agency autonomy domestically become attenuated in the transgovernmental setting.[25] Transgovernmental networks, such as the Working Party, were often constructed to help member-state governments monitor the behavior of international organizations such as the Commission. But the national executives did not devise institutions to watch the watchers. Transgovernmental networks at the European Union level rarely have to formally report back to the national parliaments and, given the weakness of civil society oversight at the pan-European level, few private-sector actors exist to protest network autonomy. A logical corollary of research on the regulatory state and bureaucratic autonomy, then, is that, as independent regulators establish themselves in a wide range of sectors and collaborate with their counterparts across borders, they have the potential to become drivers of regional integration, redefining the very dynamics of European politics.[26]

The ability of well-resourced transgovernmental actors to foist their preferences on others or to forge new political coalitions is naturally shaped by several factors. The case of data privacy highlights the technical nature of the issue area and the uncertainty of the political setting as important conditions for transgovernmental influence. In those areas where policymakers are unclear about the nature of the problem or the solution, they are more likely to turn to transgovernmental actors, who may then influence agenda setting.[27] In terms of coalitional entrepreneurship, however, broader environmental uncertainty is critical. Market-making and state-building unsettle established interests and raise the possibility of new political deals. Entrepreneurs, such as transgovernmental actors, may use their resources to forge innovative coalitions and bring together previously disparate interests.[28] The single market initiative of the 1980s and 1990s provided fertile ground for such efforts. It will be interesting to study similar processes as Europe attempts sweeping changes such as the integration of its services market and police and judicial affairs.

The entrepreneurial activity of regulatory bodies has, of course, raised concerns about democratic accountability and legitimacy.[29] As unelected national bureaucrats oversee an increasing number of international issue areas, questions emerge as to whether these efforts comport with the wishes of the electorate. The very autonomy that such agencies enjoy when they act transnationally accentuates the threat of technocratic, antidemocratic decision making.

On a different level, the distribution of power within regulatory networks poses an important challenge to legitimacy. It is naïve to think that all regulators are equally represented or have equal clout in the transgovernmental setting. Rather, the representatives of the four or five great powers in Europe will benefit disproportionately from their ability to influence network decisions. This does not mean that smaller players might not enjoy some new power by linking up regionally, but in general, these networks affect the distribution of influence among the great powers. An underexamined question for those concerned with issues of representation is not whether regulators listen to their home electorates but how French or German regulatory dominance in transgovernmental networks shapes the legitimacy of regional cooperation. Next I develop the implications of this discussion for power more generally.

Historical Institutional Roots of Convergence

Over the last two decades, political science has paid considerable attention to the effect of globalization—the expansion of international trade and communication—on national policymaking. Two broad images have emerged. The first relies on efficiency arguments to explain the growing similarity of policy across countries. That is, as technology has facilitated international business and national markets grow increasingly interdependent, regulatory decisions are mimicked across countries. This has occurred because business interests lobby national governments to standardize rules to reduce the transaction costs faced by firms playing in multiple jurisdictions. The logic that multiple regulatory rulebooks create inefficiencies that then spur harmonization has been used to explain both the ratcheting up and down of regulation.[30]

The second image in the literature, by contrast, emphasizes the importance of domestic politics in the national adjustment process. Political parties and institutional legacies filter the effects of globalization. Rather than easing the adjustment process, domestic politics feature centrally in the debate and promote diverse national outcomes.[31] From the comparative politics perspective, examining each country in isolation, historical institutional developments prevent policy convergence.

The analytic narrative I have presented here grapples with these two contradictory images to derive an argument that highlights the historical and political roots of international policy convergence. Far from relying on a simple process of osmosis whereby efficiency drives policy change, jurisdictions have to deploy political institutions to alter the policy choices of foreign jurisdictions. Naturally, jurisdictions endowed with larger markets are better positioned to exert pressure on others. But market size alone does not ensure an automatic response. As shown in the findings of the national diversity literature, domestic politics mediate international pressure. Jurisdictions attempting to promote their regulations internationally rely on regulatory capacity to affect the domestic political game in foreign jurisdictions. A political struggle ensues at the systemic level, which is in large part defined by the historical legacy of institution building nationally. Jurisdictions that in earlier periods constructed comparatively more capable institutions to monitor and enforce market rules are better positioned to shape international outcomes in future periods.

This relative sequencing approach offers a nuanced explanation for diffusion processes. Instead of arguing that economic integration forces convergence or that national institutions result in national diversity, the historically rooted institutional argument anticipates that the extent of convergence varies with the regulatory capacity of the promoting jurisdiction and the domestic political configurations in the receiving jurisdiction. Far from being merely the result of efficiency, convergence outcomes are integrally linked to domestic institutional diversity.

Regulatory Power in the Global Political Economy

This brings me to the final and potentially most provocative point of this book. The historical analysis of international data privacy suggests that a new form of power has emerged on the international scene. Whereas much of the research of the postwar period focused on military and economic might as the sources of international influence, this study suggests that regulatory authority is a new locus of power.[32]

The intuition behind the argument rests on the fundamental finding of historical institutionalist theories that political institutions enable and constrain political strategies and outcomes.[33] As Peter Evans, Dietrich Rueschemeyer, and Theda Skocpol explain, there are

> specific organizational structures the presence (or absence) of which seems critical to the ability of the state authorities to undertake given tasks. In turn, the presence or absence of organizational structures is connected to past state policies, thus underlining the need for historical as well as structural analysis if specific state capacities and incapacities are to be understood.[34]

Politics is significantly shaped by the administrative instruments available to implement the demands of policymakers. And by extension, international politics is conditioned by the development of regulatory institutions in one market relative to developments in another. The argument bridges work from comparative politics and international relations, emphasizing the interaction among national, regional, and international developments.

In addition to guns and factories, nations must have the expertise and centralized coordination capacity to develop and define political and market rules. The ability to set and enforce such rules often determines the allocation of resources internationally.[35] This account provides unique expectations concerning major international political economy debates. Mysterious phenomenon shaping global trade such as border effects, in which national borders, not tariffs, determine levels of trade, become predictable.[36] In contradiction to those expecting the inevitable and unstoppable rise of China, for example, the regulatory power argument anticipates variation based on internal regulatory developments. The advances of China in a number of international technology standards debates, an area in which it has invested heavily in political institutional development, contrast sharply with its international embarrassments regarding food safety, an area in which it has a decapitated regulatory state.[37] Obviously, the chances are slim that poor countries with feeble militaries can rely on regulatory power to play in this game, but among the five or six great powers of the coming century, regulatory capacity will be a critical complement to powerful militaries and economies.

The fundamental insight presented here is to acknowledge that power is in large part derived from the internal political institutions that activate military or economic resources. Nations rely on regulatory capacity to develop, coordinate, and implement market rules. This capacity relies on the expertise to define and defend a set of regulations and on the authority to sanction noncompliance. Jurisdictions use regulatory capacity to shape the cost/benefit analyses of other countries, using both carrots and sticks to coax adjustment. The use of these carrots and sticks alters the configuration of domestic interests regarding particular policy choices in the receiving country. These internal institutions do not develop in isolation but relative to similar processes in other countries. Regulatory power is derived from the distribution of such institutions globally.

Europe has spent the last three decades developing its regulatory capacity. This has occurred through national liberalization efforts, regional integration, and participation in world trade negotiations. Although still facing considerable ambiguity in the area of police and judicial cooperation, Europe now has a full complement of political institutions trained and focused on economic regulatory matters. Europe employs this regulatory capacity to produce and maintain the rules that govern international markets in a wide range of sectors including product standards, chemical regulations, and telecommunications.[38] This led Rockwell Schnabel, the former U.S. ambassador to Brussels, to conclude that Europe is "increasingly seeking to act as the world's economic regulator."[39]

Some scholars of European external relations emphasize the civilian or normative power that Europe wields internationally.[40] Far from being solely a discursive effect whereby regulators convince others of appropriate norms, regulatory power includes coercive tools to shape international outcomes. I do not intend here to impugn the importance of soft power, the ability to convince rather than coerce, in international affairs. The regulations of a jurisdiction are fundamentally an expression of political values. My argument does, however, emphasize the equally critical hard edge of regulatory power and acknowledges that the persuasive appeal of many regulatory solutions depends on the looming threats that motivate negotiations.[41] Regulatory power, then, is not merely an extension of either norms or economic size. It is rooted in the institutions and in the expertise and authority they enjoy to govern markets and society.

Although Europe has committed increasing resources to such institutions, the United States has slowed its delegation of authority to independent regulatory agencies. Skepticism concerning bureaucratic accountability amplified by domestic political pressure to reduce government intervention in the economy has circumscribed regulatory resources and authority. This focus on accountability and small government has unintentionally undermined the power resources available to the United States to promote its interests globally.

Europe long played second fiddle to the United States in international economic affairs, but its ongoing institution building has repositioned Europe in the world economy. The United States now faces mounting challenges to develop, set, and enforce the rules of global markets from one of its strongest allies, the European Union.

Notes

Chapter 1. Data Privacy and the Global Economy

1. See *New York Times,* "Size of Military Data Theft Grows to Affect Millions of Troops," June 7, 2006 [online]. The British Government lost records on twenty-five million individuals, accounting for nearly half the population of the country, in 2007.

2. See Rubina Johannes, *Identity Fraud Survey Report* (Pleasanton: Javelin Strategy Group, 2006).

3. Data privacy deals with an individual's ability to control the use and dissemination of personal information. This definition is derived from the work of Alan Westin, *Privacy and Freedom* (New York: Atheneum, 1967). The terms *data privacy* and *data protection* are used interchangeably in the following chapters. *Data protection* gained prominence with the passage of the German data protection law in the 1970s, but the term has been controversial since its inception. *Data privacy* has increasingly been used to refer to European efforts and is preferred in many English-language texts. It is important to note that data privacy is distinct from both bodily privacy issues, such as the right to have an abortion, and constitutional privacy, which encompasses an individual's right to be free from unwarranted search and seizure. For a detailed discussion of privacy in its many varieties, see Fred Cate, *Privacy in the Information Age* (Washington, D.C.: Brookings Institution, 1997); European Parliament and the Council of the European Union, *Directive 95/46/EC on the Protection of Individuals with Regard to the Processing of Personal Data and on the Free Movement of Such Data, Official Journal of the European Communities* L281, Brussels, November 23, 1995, 31 [hereafter: Directive 95/46/EC].

4. A study by Privacy International notes both the generally higher level of protection in countries with comprehensive rules and the recent increase in surveillance across countries. See http://www.privacyinternational.org/article.shtml?cmd[347]= x-347-559597 (accessed January 2008).

5. See for example, Ron Lieber, "Banks Now Get Daily Reports on Their Customers," *San Francisco Chronicle*, August 4, 2003, E5. The new security environment has amplified this problem. See Anjan Sundaram, "The Fiasco of Wiring Money to 'Ahmed'," *Philadelphia Inquirer*, July 7, 2006, C6.

6. See Tara Lemmey, "Your Next Identity Crisis," *Business 2.0*, September 2000 [online].

7. See Linda Koontz, *Personal Information: Agencies and Resellers Vary in Providing Privacy Protections* (Washington, D.C.: Government Accountability Office, 2006).

8. See Robert O'Harrow, *No Place to Hide* (New York: Free Press, 2005).

9. During 2002, JetBlue secretly released some 5 million passenger records concerning over 1 million passengers to Torch Concepts, a Defense Department contractor. Torch Concepts networked the personal information with other databases to establish personal profiles of the passengers, including social security numbers and employment status. See *New York Times*, "Two US Agencies Investigate JetBlue over Privacy Issues," September 23, 2003, C4. In 2006, it was revealed that telecommunications companies provided the National Security Agency with tens of millions of consumer telephone records. See Leslie Cauley, "NSA Has Massive Database of Americans' Phone Calls," *USA Today*, May 11, 2006, 1.

10. Peter Swire and Robert Litan, *None of Your Business: World Data Flows, Electronic Communication, and the European Privacy Directive* (Washington, D.C.: Brookings Institution, 1998).

11. See Henry Farrell, "Constructing the International Foundations of E-Commerce: The EU-US Safe Harbor Arrangement," *International Organization* 2 (2003): 277–306.

12. For a recent attempt to legislate privacy in the realm of offshore outsourcing, see Kim Zetter, "Outsourcing: Danger to Privacy," *Wired*, February 20, 2004 [online].

13. See Kristin Archick, *US-EU Cooperation against Terrorism* (Washington, D.C.: Congressional Research Service, 2005).

14. See *New York Times*, "Europe Fights U.S. Over Passenger Data," September 23, 2003, C4.

15. See *New York Times*, "Europe Panel Faults Sifting of Bank Data," September 26, 2006 [online].

16. See Solveig Singleton, *Privacy as a Trade Issue: Guidelines for US Trade Negotiators* (Washington, D.C.: Heritage Foundation, 2002).

17. See Samuel Warren and Louis Brandeis, "The Right to Privacy," *Harvard Law Review* (1890): 193–220.

18. See Nick Platten, "Background to and History of the Directive," in *EC Data Protection Directive*, edited by David Bainbridge, 13–32 (London: Butterworths, 1996).

19. See Andrew Moravcsik, *The Choice for Europe: Social Purpose and State Power from Messina to Maastricht* (Ithaca: Cornell University Press, 1998).

20. See Scott James and David Lake, "The Second Face of Hegemony: Britain's Repeal of the Corn Laws and the American Walker Tariff of 1846," *International Organization* 43 (1989): 1–29.

21. See Gregory Shaffer, "Globalization and Social Protection: The Impact of EU and International Rules in the Ratcheting Up of US Privacy Standards," *Yale Journal of International Law* 25 (winter 2000): 1–88.

22. See David Vogel, *Trading Up: Consumer and Environmental Regulation in a Global Economy* (Cambridge, Mass.: Harvard University Press, 1995).

23. See Alan Tonnelson, *The Race to the Bottom* (Boulder: Westview Press, 2000); Janos Kovacs, "Approaching the EU and Reaching the US? Rival Narratives on Transforming Welfare Regimes in East-Central Europe," *West European Politics* 25 (2002): 175–208.

24. Henry Laurence, "Spawning the SEC," *Indiana Journal of Global Legal Studies* 6 (1999): 647–83.

25. These figures are based on work conducted by Forrester Research and are available from the author. By all measures, the United States leads Europe in electronic commerce. For example, in 1999 there were twenty-eight personal computers per one hundred inhabitants in Europe, compared with fifty-one in the United States. Similarly, the average number of secure servers, which is the technology required for the safe transmission of credit card data, per 1 million inhabitants in 2000 was thirty-two in Europe, compared with 170 in the United States. See Mark Uncapher, "Global E-Data: Continental Divide—Will Europe Lag behind the US?" (2000) Available from: http://www.emarketer.com/enews/20000920_cdivide.html (accessed June 28, 2004).

26. The argument builds on the fundamental insights of historical institutional research, which emphasizes the importance of time in causal arguments. See, for example, Tim Büthe, "Taking Temporality Seriously: Modeling History and the Use of Narratives as Evidence," *American Political Science Review* 96 (2002): 481–93; Paul Pierson, *Politics in Time: History, Institutions, and Social Analysis* (Princeton: Princeton University Press, 2004).

27. For further development of this concept, see David Bach and Abraham Newman, "The European Regulatory State and Global Public Policy: Micro-Institutions and Macro-Influence," *Journal of European Public Policy* 14, no. 6 (2007): 827–46.

28. For an examination of the sequencing argument in the comparative politics field, see Paul Pierson, *Politics in Time.*

29. Colin Bennett, *Regulating Privacy: Data Protection and Public Policy in Europe and the United States* (Ithaca: Cornell University Press, 1992).

30. See Ellen Immergut, "The Rules of the Game: The Logic of Health Policy-Making in France, Switzerland, and Sweden," in *Structuring Politics,* edited by Kathleen Thelen, Sven Steinmo, and Frank Longstreth, 57–89 (Cambridge, UK: Cambridge University Press, 1992).

31. *Policy feedbacks* are mechanisms that result from institutional change and that reinforce that change. For example, social policies often create client populations that lobby to maintain these social policies. See Paul Pierson, "When Effect Becomes Cause: Policy Feedback and Political Change," *World Politics* 45 (1993): 595–628. It is helpful to distinguish between client feedbacks, like those often described in the welfare state literature, and administrative feedbacks. In contrast to client feedbacks, in which client groups demand the expansion of entitlements, in administrative feedbacks administrators work to expand protection. See Abraham Newman, "Protecting Privacy in Europe: Administrative Feedbacks and Regional Politics," in *Making History: European Integration and Institutional Change at Fifty,* edited by Sophie Meunier and Kathleen McNamara, 123–39 (New York: Oxford University Press, 2007).

32. See Robert Keohane and Joseph Nye, "Transgovernmental Relations and International Organizations," *International Organization* 27 (1974): 39–62.

33. The argument builds on the concept of transgovernmental coalition-builders developed originally by Keohane and Nye. Ibid. Whereas the policy entrepreneur literature in EU studies often focuses on the role of the European Commission and the European Court of Justice as actors, my claim borrows from a critical insight of the transgovernmental literature that substate actors such as regulators have become important international actors. For the policy entrepreneurs argument, see Wayne Sandholtz and John Zysman, "1992: Recasting the European Bargain," *World Politics* 42 (1989): 95–128; Neil Fligstein and Iona Mara Drita, "How to Make a Market: Reflections on the European Union's Single Market Program," *American Journal of Sociology*

102 (1996): 1–33. For the transgovernmental actors debates, see Ann-Marie Slaughter, *A New World Order* (Princeton: Princeton University Press, 2004); Abraham Newman, "Building Transnational Civil Liberties: Transgovernmental Enterpreneurs and the European Data Privacy Directive," *International Organization* 62 (2008): 103–130.

34. For a similar argument in the domestic context, see John Goodman, "The Politics of Central Bank Independence," *Comparative Politics* 23 (1991): 329–49; Daniel Carpenter, *Forging of Bureaucratic Autonomy: Reputations, Networks, and Policy Innovation in Executive Agencies* (Princeton: Princeton University Press, 2001). For the ability of epistemic communities to shape international policy agendas, see Peter Haas, "Introduction: Epistemic Communities and International Policy Coordination," *International Organization* 46 (1992): 1–35.

35. For a detailed analysis of the spillover argument, see Alec Stone Sweet, Wayne Sandholtz, and Niel Fligstein, *The Institutionalization of Europe* (Oxford: Oxford University Press, 2001).

36. Rather than a natural alignment between substate and supranational actors (such as the European Commission), as has been identified in neofunctionalist arguments focusing on the judicial realm, transgovernmental actors exercise their authority to block cross-border data exchange in order to alter the preferences of other international actors. For neofunctional work in the judicial realm, see Joseph Weiler, "The Transformation of Europe," *Yale Law Journal* 100 (1991): 2403–83; Ann-Marie Burley and Walter Mattli, "Europe before the Court: A Political Theory of Legal Integration," *International Organization* 47 (1993): 41–76; Karen Alter, "Who Are the 'Masters of the Treaty'? European Governments and the European Court of Justice," *International Organization* 52 (1998): 121–47.

37. See Fritz Scharpf, *Governing in Europe: Effective and Democratic?* (Oxford: Oxford University Press, 1999).

38. For a review of diffusion mechanisms ranging from coercion to learning, see Colin Bennett, "What Is Policy Convergence and What Causes It?" *British Journal of Political Science* 21 (1991): 215–33; Zachary Elkins and Beth Simmons, "On Waves, Clusters, and Diffusion: A Conceptual Framework," *Annals of the American Academy of Political and Social Science* 598 (2005): 33–51.

39. See Beth Simmons, "The International Politics of Harmonization: The Case of Capital Market Regulation," *International Organization* 55 (2001): 589–620.

40. Wade Jacoby, *The Enlargement of the EU and NATO: Ordering from the Menu in Central Europe* (New York: Cambridge University Press, 2006).

41. See Giandomenico Majone, *Regulating Europe* (New York: Routledge, 1996).

42. See Adrienne Heritier, "Public Interest Services Revisited," *Journal of European Public Policy* 9, no. 6 (2002): 995–1019.

43. See Steve Vogel, *Freer Markets, More Rules: Regulatory Reform in Advanced Industrial Countries* (Ithaca: Cornell University Press, 1996).

44. See Fabrizio Gilardi, "The Institutional Foundations of Regulatory Capitalism: The Diffusion of Independent Regulatory Agencies in Western Europe," *Annals of the American Academy of Political and Social Science* 598 (2005): 84–101.

45. For more on international market regulation see Henry Farrell and Abraham Newman, "The Domestic Institutional Determinants of International Market Regulation," paper presented at the 103rd American Political Science Association, Chicago, September 2, 2007.

46. See Youri Devuyst, "Transatlantic Competition Relations," in *Transatlantic Governance in the Global Economy,* edited by Mark A. Pollack and Gregory C. Shaffer, 127–52 (Lanham: Rowman and Littlefield, 2001).

47. The former U.S. ambassador to Brussels, Rockwell Schnabel, argued that Europe is "increasingly seeking to act as the world's economic regulator." These comments were seconded by the current U.S. ambassador, Boyden Gray, who claimed that "from a US perspective, the main problem is less that our regulations differ than a general sense that Europe is overregulated." Quoted in George Parker and Tobias Buck, "Washington Bridles at EU's Urge to Regulate," *Financial Times*, May 12, 2006 [online].

48. See Brandon Mitchener, "Increasingly, Rules of Global Economy Are Set in Brussels," *Wall Street Journal*, April 23, 2002 [online].

49. See Charlotte Bretherton and John Vogler, *The European Union as a Global Actor* (London: Routledge, 1999); Michael E. Smith, *Europe's Foreign and Security Policy* (Cambridge, UK: Cambridge University Press, 2003).

50. See Sophie Meunier and Kalypso Nicolaidis, "Who Speaks for Europe? The Delegation of Trade Authority in the EU," *Journal of Common Market Studies* 37, no. 3 (1999): 477–501; Sophie Meunier, *Trading Voices: The European Union in International Commercial Negotiations* (Princeton: Princeton University Press, 2005).

51. See Liesbet Hooghe and Gary Marks, *Multi-Level Governance and European Integration* (Lanham: Rowan & Littlefield, 2000).

52. See Ann-Marie Slaughter, "Agencies on the Loose? Holding Government Networks Accountable," in *Transatlantic Regulatory Cooperation*, edited by George A. Bermann, Matthias Herdegen, and Peter L. Lindseth, 521–46 (Oxford: Oxford University Press, 2001).

53. See Helen Milner, "Rationalizing Politics: The Emerging Synthesis of International, American, and Comparative Politics," *International Organization* 52 (1998): 759–86. Notable exceptions include G. John Ikenberry, *Reasons of State: Oil Politics and the Capacities of American Government* (Ithaca: Cornell University Press, 1988); Peter Katzenstein, "International Relations and Domestic Structures: Foreign Economic Policies of Advanced Industrial States," *International Organization* 30 (winter 1976): 1–45.

54. See Kathleen Thelen and Sven Steinmo, "Historical Institutionalism in Comparative Politics," in *Structuring Politics: Historical Institutionalism in Comparative Analysis*, edited by Kathleen Thelen, Sven Steinmo, and Frank Longstreth, 1–32 (Cambridge, UK: Cambridge University Press, 1992); John Zysman, "How Institutions Create Historically Rooted Trajectories of Growth," *Industrial and Corporate Change* 3 (1994): 243–83.

55. See Martin Shefter, "Party and Patronage: Germany, England, and Italy," *Politics and Society* 7 (1977): 403–51.

56. See Simmons, "International Politics of Harmonization."

57. See Bach and Newman, "European Regulatory State."

58. This argument is inspired by the work of Alexander Gerschenkron; see *Economic Backwardness in Historical Perspective* (Cambridge, Mass.: Belknap, 1962).

59. See Steve Bellman, Eric J. Johnson, Stephen J. Kobrin, and Gerald L. Lohse, "International Differences in Information Privacy Concerns: A Global Survey of Consumers," *Information Society* 20 (2004): 313–24; Henry Farrell, "Governing Information Flows: States, Private Actors, and E-Commerce," *Annual Review of Political Science* 6 (2006): 353–74; Abraham Newman and John Zysman, "Transforming Politics," in *How Revolutionary was the Digital Revolution: National Responses, Market Transitions, and Global Technology*, edited by John Zysman and Abraham Newman, 391–411 (Palo Alto: Stanford University Press, 2006).

60. See James Mahoney, "Strategies of Causal Assessment in Comparative Historical Analysis," in *Comparative Historical Analysis in the Social Sciences*, edited by James

Mahoney and Dietrich Rueschemeyer (Cambridge, UK: Cambridge University Press, 2003); Tim Büthe, "Taking Temporality Seriously: Modeling History and the Use of Narratives as Evidence."

61. For examples from comparative research, see Margaret Weir and Theda Skocpol, "State Structures and the Possibility for 'Keynesian' Responses to the Great Depression in Sweden, Britain and the United States," in *Bringing the State Back In*, edited by Peter Evans, Dietrich Rueschemeyer, and Theda Skocpol, 107–63 (Cambridge, UK: Cambridge University Press, 1985); Peter Hall and David Soskice, *Varieties of Capitalism* (Oxford: Oxford University Press, 2001).

62. See Pierson, *Politics in Time*.

63. Some one hundred interviews were conducted between 2000 and 2007 with national and European experts, such as politicians, regulators, industry representatives, civil servants, and members of nongovernmental organizations.

Chapter 2. Privacy Regimes

1. Both regimes include numerous exemptions for internal security measures and police activities.

2. I focus in the book on formal legal structures that shape privacy regulation as these are at the center of international debates. There are naturally other governance strategies to manage privacy concerns that emphasize technology or civil society. I address these as they interact with the formal regimes.

3. See Fritz Hondius, *Emerging Data Protection in Europe* (New York: Elsevier, 1975).

4. See Bennett, *Regulating Privacy*.

5. Bennett finds a similar result in his examination focusing on public-sector regulations; ibid.

6. Others have distinguished between omnibus and sectoral regulation. See Paul Schwartz and Joel Reidenberg, *Data Privacy Law: A Study of United States Data Protection* (Charlottesville, Va.: Michie, 1996); Bellman et al., "Information Differences in Information Privacy Concerns."

7. The rules do not have to be exactly the same across the private sector or between the private sector and the public sector. Germany, among others, passed additional privacy rules for the telecommunications sector above and beyond the general rules governing the private sector.

8. The German data privacy commissioner in 2007, for example, was a member of the Green Party and was appointed under the coalition between the Social Democrats and the Greens that ended in 2005. Despite the formation of the Grand Coalition between the Social Democrats and the Christian Democrats, the commissioner retains his five-year appointment. Under German law, a call for dismissal must be affirmed by a judge and be based in employment law.

9. See David Flaherty, *Protecting Privacy in Surveillance Societies* (Chapel Hill: University of North Carolina Press, 1989).

10. See Information Commissioner, *Annual Report 2005*, London, 2006, 8.

11. See Commission Nationale de l'Informatique et des Libertés, *Press Conference on Annual Report 2003*, Paris, 2004, 2–3; Commission Nationale de l'Informatique et des Libertés, *Press Conference on Annual Report 2002*, Paris, 2003, 2–3.

12. This figure does not include the staff or budget of the seventeen state-level data privacy commissioners. The 2007 budget and staffing size are available at: http://www.bmi.bund.de/cln_012/nn_148122/Internet/Content/Behoerden/

bfd__einzel__engl.html. The figure for 1987 comes from Flaherty, *Protecting Privacy in Surveillance Societies,* 55.

13. By *comodification,* I mean the ability to assign personal information a value that can be traded in a market. See Oscar Gandy, *Panoptic Sort: A Political Economy of Personal Information* (Boulder: Westview Press, 1999).

14. Representatives from the Bundesverband Deutscher Banken (the trade association for banks in Germany) and the trade association that represents the savings banks confirmed that consent rules facing the banking sector hinder cross-selling strategies with life insurance companies. A representative from the savings bank association argued in an interview with the author, "the exchange between savings banks and third-parties like Provinzal is hindered by data protection. It is still not always the case that consent forms are signed during the opening of a new account. And to retroactively acquire consent is expensive and difficult. It costs money and image." Berlin, 2002.

15. Data retention legislation has been adopted by the European Union and has been proposed several times in the United States. See The European Parliament and the Council of the European Union, *Directive on the Retention of Data Generated or Processed in Connection with the Provision of Publicly Available Electronic Communications Services or of Public Communications Networks and Amending Directive 2002/58/EC, Official Journal of the European Communities* L105, Brussels 2002, 54.

16. For a general description of information commodification in the U.S. market, see Federal Trade Commission, *The Information Marketplace: Merging and Exchanging Consumer Data* (Washington, D.C.: Government Printing Office, 2001).

17. See Cynthia Glassman, *Customer Benefits from Current Information Sharing by Financial Services Companies* (New York: Ernst & Young, 2000).

18. See Michael Turner and Lawrence Buc, *The Impact of Data Restrictions on Fundraising for Charitable and Nonprofit Institutions* (New York: Privacy Leadership Initiative, 2002). Similarly, tough privacy standards could cost the online marketing sector $1 billion. See Michael Turner, *The Impact of Data Restrictions on Consumer Distance Shopping* (New York: Privacy Leadership Initiative, 2001).

19. The most well known of these firms are Experian, TRW, Equafax, Acxiom, and Donnelly Marketing. Experian, TRW, and Equafax are simultaneously the largest credit-reporting agencies in the United States, but have developed independent data-compiling operations to circumvent credit-reporting regulations that may limit data transfers.

20. See Experian, *Corporate Fact Sheet,* Costa Mesa, 2004.

21. See Koontz, *Personal Information.*

22. MBNA estimates that 66 percent of doctors hold an affinity card as well as 3.5 million alumni and students from over six hundred colleges and universities that endorse MBNA products. MBNA customers carry balances that are 50 percent higher than the industry average and have a delinquency rate below the industry average. A 2002 industry-sponsored study claims that restrictions in information flows could hobble the MBNA business model and raise direct marketing costs nearly 20 percent. See Michael Staten and Fred Cate, *The Adverse Impact of Opt-In Privacy Rules on Consumers: A Case Study of Retail Credit* (New York: Privacy Leadership Initiative, 2002).

23. See, for example, Ron Lieber "Banks Now Get Daily Reports on Their Customers," *San Francisco Chronicle,* August 4, 2003, E5.

24. A 2005 scandal involving ChoicePoint highlights this tendency in the limited regime. A hacker broke into the data banks of ChoicePoint, a data aggregator that holds some 19 billion records on nearly the entire adult population of the United

States. Roughly 150,000 records were stolen, leading to calls for new regulations. See, for example, John Schwartz, "Some Sympathy for Paris Hilton: A Grim Week for Privacy," *New York Times*, February 27, 2005, 1; Tom Zeller, "Breach Points Up Flaws in Privacy Laws," *New York Times*, February 24, 2005, C1.

25. For differences in national implementation structures, I focus on the distribution of authority between a centralized regulator and other actors. Others have focused on the type of sanction authority available to regulators. See Sandra Milberg, H. Jeff Smith, and Sandra Burke, "Information Privacy: Corporate Management and National Regulation." *Organization Science* 11, no. 1 (2000): 35–57.

26. For the difference between self-regulatory regimes in the two systems, see Abraham Newman and David Bach, "Self-Regulatory Trajectories in the Shadow of Public Power: Resolving Digital Dilemmas in Europe and the United States." *Governance* 17 (2004): 387–414.

27. For a review of a variety of privacy protection strategies, see Colin Bennett and Charles Raab, *The Governance of Privacy: Policy Instruments in Global Perspective.* (Boston: MIT Press, 2006).

28. The data privacy agency of the German state of Schleswig-Holstein has been particularly active in this effort; see http://www.datenschutzzentrum.de/.

29. Although some have argued that the comprehensive approach creates a human right to privacy, these accounts can be misleading. Data privacy regulations create a framework under which information may be exchanged. Some more cynical interpretations even argue that data privacy laws legitimize surveillance efforts. See Reg Whitaker, *The End of Privacy* (New York: New Press, 2000).

30. For an assessment of the UK initiative, with its implications for individual privacy, see Simon Davies, Gus Hosein, and Edgar Whitley, *The LSE Identity Project Report* (London: London School of Economics, 2005).

31. See European Parliament and the Council of the European Union, Directive 95/46/EC. Personal data are defined as any information relating to an identified or identifiable natural person (data subject). An identifiable person is one who can be identified, directly or indirectly, in particular by reference to an identification number or to one or more factors specific to his or her physical, physiological, mental, economic, cultural, or social identity.

32. The independence and regulatory powers of the national supervisory authorities are spelled out in Article 28 of the 1995 EU directive. All agencies must have the power to investigate, intervene, and engage legal proceedings and these functions shall be conducted "with complete independence."

33. For an overview of national data protection laws, see Electronic Privacy Information Center, *Privacy and Human Rights 2005* (Washington, D.C.: EPIC, 2006).

34. The role of enlargement in emulation in central Europe is directly addressed in chapter 5.

35. The Canadian Privacy Commissioner explains,

Personal Information Protection and Electronic Documents Act (*PIPEDA*) came into force in stages, beginning January 1, 2001. At that time, it covered personal information about customers that was collected, used or disclosed in the course of commercial activities by federal works, undertakings an businesses— organizations such as banks, airlines, and telecommunications companies. The personal information of employees of such federal works, undertakings and businesses was also covered. The Act was extended to cover personal health information for these organizations and activities in 2002. *PIPEDA* was fully implemented by January 2004. As of 2004, under the Trade and Commerce power in section 91 of the Constitution, the Act was extended to cover organizations engaged in commercial activities, including those that for other purposes (for example, employment) are regulated by the provinces. *PIPEDA* therefore covers the retail sector, publishing and insurance companies, the service industry, manufacturers and other organizations, such as those in the health sector.

PIPEDA Review Discussion Document, Ottawa, 2006, available at: http://www.privcom. gc.ca/information/pub/pipeda_review_060718_e.asp.

36. The European Union has been engaged in ongoing negotiations with Australia over, for example, the independence of its regulatory authority and the protection of noncitizens under the Australian regime. This issue is taken up in greater detail in chapter 5.

37. Jacoby, *Enlargement of the EU and NATO.*

38. See Asia-Pacific Economic Cooperation, *APEC Privacy Framework* (Singapore: APEC Secretariat, 2005).

39. The federal attorney general of Australia pressed for the self-certification requirement in initial negotiations over the APEC standard. See John McGinness, *What's Up in the Asia Pacific? APEC Privacy Initiatives.* (Privacy Issues Forum: Wellington, New Zealand, 2003).

40. The list is available at: http://www.export.gov/safeharbor/doc_safeharbor_ index.asp.

41. See Commission of the European Communities, *The Implementation of Commission Decision 520/2000/EC on the Adequate Protection of Personal Data Provided by the Safe Harbour Privacy Principles and Related Frequently Asked Questions Issued by the US Department of Commerce,* Brussels, October 20, 2004.

42. Generally, see the work of the Ponemon Institute (http://www.ponemon.org), which has conducted several benchmarking studies on corporate privacy practices.

43. Indian firms active in software development and call center operations have adopted European standards as they press for domestic legislation to be passed. See *Asia Pulse,* "India's Business Process Outsourcing Industry Pushing Government for Data Security Laws," June 9, 2005 [online].

44. See Dorothee Heisenberg, *Negotiating Privacy: The European Union, the United States, and Personal Data Protection* (Boulder: Lynne Rienner, 2005).

45. See Global Business Dialogue, *Paris Recommendations 1999* (Paris: Global Business Dialogue, 1999); Virginia Haufler, *A Public Role for the Private Sector: Industry Self-Regulation in a Global Economy* (Washington, D.C.: Carnegie Endowment for International Peace, 2001).

46. See Swire and Litan, *None of Your Business.*

Chapter 3. The Computer Age

1. In this chapter, I focus attention on policy developments in France and Germany, instead of other early adopters such as Sweden, because of their central roles in later European Community efforts.

2. By focusing on the scope of regulation, the chapter differs from many past studies that concentrated on efforts targeted at the public sector. See, for example, Flaherty, *Protecting Privacy;* Bennett, *Regulating Privacy;* Priscilla Regan, *Legislating Privacy: Technology, Social Values, and Public Policy* (Chapel Hill: University of North Carolina Press, 1995).

3. See John Zysman, *Governments, Markets, and Growth* (Ithaca: Cornell University Press, 1983); Robert Kagan, *Adversarial Legalism: The American Way of Law* (Cambridge, Mass.: Harvard University Press, 2001).

4. See Office of Management and Budget, *Historical Tables* (Washington, D.C.: U.S. Government Printing Office, 2004).

5. See Gosta Esping-Andersen, *The Three Worlds of Welfare Capitalism* (Princeton: Princeton University Press, 1990).

6. These figures were provided by Lewis Branscomb, IBM vice president, see U.S. Senate, *Privacy: The Collection, Use, and Computerization of Personal Data, Joint Hearings before the Ad Hoc Subcommittee on Privacy of the Committee on Government Operations and Information Systems and Subcommittee on Constitutional Rights of the Committee on the Judiciary* (Washington, D.C.: Government Printing Office, 1974), 673.

7. See U.S. Senate, *Federal Data Banks, Computers, and the Bill of Rights,* Committee on the Judiciary, Subcommittee on Constitutional Rights (Washington, D.C.: Government Printing Office, 1971); Sam Ervin, "The First Amendment: A Living Thought in the Computer Age," *Columbia Human Rights Law Review* 4 (1972): 13–47.

8. Gerhart Baum, "Auszug aus der Rede am 10.6.1976," in *Datenschutz* (Bonn: Friedrich Naumann Stiftung, 1980), 14.

9. See Organisation for Economic Cooperation and Development, *Inventory of Data Banks in the Public Sector* (Paris: OECD, 1971).

10. See Priscilla Regan, *Legislating Privacy.*

11. See Hessischer Ministerpraesident, *Der Grosse Hessenplan,* Wiesbaden, 1968.

12. For a history of data processing in the Hess administration, see Datenschutzbeauftragte, *Ersten Tätigkeitsbericht* (Wiesbaden: Hessischer Landtag, 1972).

13. See Werner Liedtke, *Das Bundesdatenschutzgesetz: Fallstudie zum Gesetzgebungsprozess* (Düsseldorf: Mannhold, 1980).

14. See, for example, *New York Times,* "To Preserve Privacy," August 9, 1966, 36; Nan Robertson, "Data Center Held Peril to Privacy," *New York Times,* July 27, 1966, 41; *Die Welt* "Benutzung von Datenbänken darf Privatsphäre nicht gefährden," November 8, 1972, 7.

15. See *Congressional Quarterly Almanac,* "Senate Hearings on Invasion of Privacy," 27 (1971): 772–79.

16. Although not solely responsible for privacy legislation, Watergate catalyzed interest in the issue and raised its policy salience. See Richard Cohen, "Protection of Citizens' Privacy Becomes Major Federal Concern," *National Journal* 6, October 12 1974, 1521–30.

17. See Philippe Boucher, "Safari ou la chase aux français," *Le Monde,* March 21, 1974 CNIL Archive.

18. See Herbert Burkard, "Privacy—Data Protection," in *Governance of Global Networks in the Light of Different Local Values,* edited by Christoph Engel and Kenneth H. Keller, 43–70 (Baden-Baden, 2000).

19. See Bernard Tricot, *Rapport de la Commission Informatique et Libertes* (Paris: La Documentation Francaise, 1975). For background on the Commission, see the interview with Bernard Tricot in *Informatique,* "Bernard Tricot," December 1975, 85–89.

20. Commissions were established across the industrialized world to examine the relationship between the new technology and individual privacy, for example, the Royal Commission on Publicity and Secrecy (Sweden, 1969), The Younger Committee on Privacy (United Kingdom, 1970), Arbeitsgruppe Datenschutz im Bundeskanzleramt (Austria, 1971), Norwegian Research Center for Computers and Law (Norway, 1971), and The Privacy Report (Australia, 1972).

21. See Organisation for Economic Cooperation and Development, *Guidelines on the Protection of Privacy and Transborder Flows of Personal Data* (Paris: OECD, 1980).

22. Recall that the first data privacy legislation was passed in the German state of Hess in 1970. This was followed by the first national legislation in Sweden in 1973 and in the United States in 1974.

23. The report included five basic principles:

1. Secrecy—There must be no personal record-keeping system whose very existence is secret.
2. Notice—There must be a way for an individual to find out what information about him or her is in a record and how it is used.
3. Consent—There must be a way for an individual to prevent information about him or her that was obtained for one purpose from being used or made available for other purposes without his or her consent.
4. Correction—There must be a way for an individual to correct or amend a record of identifiable information about him or her.
5. Security—All organizations creating, maintaining, using, or disseminating records of identifiable personal data must assure the reliability of the data for their intended use and must take precautions to prevent misuse of the data.

See U.S. Department of Health, Education, and Welfare Secretary's Advisory Committee on Automated Personal Data Systems, *Records, Computers, and the Rights of Citizens* (Washington, D.C.: Government Printing Office, 1973). For background on the HEW Report, see *US News and World Report*, "A Secret Dossier on Every American," August 27, 1973, 54.

24. This followed the passage of subnational legislation for the public sector in the German state of Hess in 1970.

25. As quoted in Flaherty, *Protecting Privacy*, 166.

26. See Hondius, *Emerging Data Protection in Europe*.

27. Ervin long opposed government constraints on individual liberty, championing privacy and free speech. Ironically, he was one of the leading opponents of civil rights legislation geared toward integrating the South. For Ervin's philosophy, see Jon Herbers, "Senator Ervin Thinks the Constitution Should Be Taken like Mountain Whiskey—Undiluted and Untaxed," *New York Times*, November 15, 1970, 25.

28. Ervin explains his position on privacy:

vast network of intelligence-oriented systems which are being developed willy-nilly throughout our land, by government and private industries....I believe that in these systems, where they contain the record of the individual's thoughts, beliefs, habits, attitudes, and personal activities, there may well rest a potential for political control and for intimidation which is alien to a society of free men.

Quoted in ibid, 25. See also David Anderson, "Senator Ervin vs. 'Information Power'," *Wall Street Journal*, February 8, 1971, 12; Sam Ervin "The Most Precious Freedom," *New York Times*, June 21, 1971, 29.

29. Koch and Goldwater's initial legislation covered the public and private sectors and established an oversight board to monitor implementation; see *Washington Post*, "New Bill on Privacy Introduced," April 11, 1974, A20. Koch's interest in privacy grew out of a negative personal experience he had with an insurance company, which

denied him coverage based on an interview with a neighbor. As he states, "the right to privacy remains threatened as long as there are no effective legal constraints on the understandable but dangerous appetite of public servants who have forgotten whom they serve." Quoted in Richard Lyons, "'Right to Privacy' Backed at a Hearing," *New York Times,* June 19, 1974, 35. Goldwater formed the Republican Privacy Initiative, which released a statement calling for the strict regulation of personal information in the public and private sectors. See Cohen, "Protection of Citizens' Privacy."

30. In following legislative sessions, the team introduced Bill 1984, which proposed extending protection to the private sector. See Constance Holden, "Privacy: Congressional Efforts Are Coming to Fruition," *Science,* May 16, 1975, 713.

31. See Gerard Grunberg, "Liberal Parties in Europe: The Case of France," in *Liberalism and Liberal Parties in the European Union,* edited by Lieven De Winter, 201–17 (Barcelona: ICPS, 2000).

32. Giscard d'Estaing quoted in John Frears, "Liberalism in France," in *Liberal Parties in Western Europe,* edited by Emil Kirchner, 146 (Cambridge, UK: Cambridge University Press, 1988).

33. David Cameron, "The Dynamics of Presidential Coalition Formation in France," *Comparative Politics* 5 (1977): 253–79.

34. A copy of the proposal is on file with the author.

35. In September 1974, Poniatowski organized a conference on information technology. In his opening address, he stressed the importance of data privacy laws and the protection of individual liberty for the successful diffusion of information technology. A copy of the speech is on file with the author.

36. For a description of Joinet's role, see *Transnational Data Report,* "Louis Joinet: France's Astute Legal Expert and Diplomat," March 1978, 2.

37. The term *liberal* is used here in the European sense.

38. Culminating in the failed 1848 Revolution, German liberalism has long consisted of two core strains. This first, known historically as the conservative wing, promoted German unification and laissez-faire economic policy; the other, known as the social-liberal wing, focused on anchoring liberal political rights such as self-government in the German Constitution. In the post–World War II period, these two elements of German liberalism were fused for the first time in the FDP. Given its financial and organizational resources, the conservative wing dominated FDP politics in the postwar period through the mid-1960s. For the party history, see Karl Bracher, Wolfgang Jaeger, and Werner Link, eds., *Republik im Wandel 1969–1974* (Mannheim: Deutsche Verlags-Anstalt, 1986); Emil Kirchner and David Broughton, "The FDP in the Federal Republic of Germany: The Requirements of Survival and Success," in *Liberal Parties in Western Europe,* edited by Emil Kirchner, 62–92 (Cambridge, UK: Cambridge University Press, 1988).

39. As a result of the desire of the Sozialdemokratische Partei Deutschlands (SPD) to court the FDP, the FDP received control over the Interior Ministry between 1969 and 1980. During the height of social-liberal power in the mid-1970s, the FDP led a series of social reforms, including decriminalizing homosexuality, equalizing the position of women in divorce proceedings, and reducing penalties for political demonstrations. The goal of these legal reforms, much like that of the data protection legislation, was to democratize society. For a discussion of the FDP domestic agenda in the 1970s, see Bracher, Jeager, and Link, *Republik im Wandel 1969–1974.*

40. Facing electoral decline and the role of opposition to the two larger parties, younger left-oriented party members attempted to reshape the party in the late 1960s.

This effort proved successful, in that Walter Scheel, a pragmatist, replaced the conservative Erich Mende as party chair. With this shift, the possibility of creating a coalition with the SPD became possible. The power of the social-liberal wing culminated in the presentation of the Freiburger Theses at the Party Congress in 1971. Written in large part by Werner Maihofer, a socially active law professor, the Freiburger Theses called for the democratization of society and the protection of human dignity and self-determination. For a discussion of the rise of the social-liberals in the party, see Peter Loesche and Franz Walter, *Die FDP: Richtungsstreit und Zukunftszweifel.* (Darmstadt: Wissenschaftliche Buchgesellschaft, 1996); Ferdinand Mueller-Rommel, "The FDP: Small but Beautiful," in *Liberalism and Liberal Parties in the European Union,* edited by Lieven De Winter, 85–118 (Barcelona: ICPS, 2000).

41. The FDP first recognized the problems associated with computerization in its 1970 Party Congress Resolution to Prevent the Misuse of the Computer. The role of the social-liberal wing in promoting data protection issues within the government was confirmed by interviews with Frank Haenschke, SPD parliamentarian responsible for the legislative process, as well as with Burkhart Hirsch, member of the FDP and former interior minister for the state of Nord Rhine Westphalia, Cologne and Düsseldorf 2003. Baum's commitment to the issue can be seen in his passionate speech before the Bundestag, "Auszug aus der Rede." Although individual SPD party members played a significant role in the passage of the legislation, the party itself was not decisive in bringing the issue to the table. The weak links between data protection and the SPD were expressed in interviews with both current and former members of the party.

42. The Interior Ministry repeatedly made note of public pressure to act. One ministry civil servant warned in a ministry letter, "The topic 'databanks' has taken on a lively echo in the public." See Egon Hoelder, *Bericht der interministeriellen Arbeitsgruppe Datenbanksystem* (Bonn: M. Rottmann, 1971). All quotations from German texts in this chapter were translated by the author.

43. In addition to the previously cited engagement of high-level social-liberal party officials, local officials actively pushed the data protection agenda. Note the FDP Nuernberg position at the Land Party Congress of 1975:

> The possession of data creates a one-sided information monopoly that without a proper data protection law weakens the position of the citizen. Already the current public sector data processing systems provide comprehensive summaries of individuals. Fortunately, these efforts remain independent and separate. The voters will not understand if the FDP does not become active in this issue area.

FDP Kreisverband Nuerberger Land, *25 Ordentlicher Landesparteitag,* Augsburg, 1975.

44. The following statement by Sears, Roebuck captures the position held by industry with regard to private-sector regulation:

> It is our judgment that the cost factors necessary to meet the requirements of the legislation before the joint subcommittee as applied to private industry are completely out of proportion to any gain or benefit to be achieved by the public. Also the inequality of such a cost would be magnified if forced on industry without a clear showing of abusive or damaging practices which would require such broad and sweeping legislation. Sears has never been and will never be insensitive to the needs and demands of the consumers, including

his right to privacy. We believe that the manner in which our record keeping systems are operated is fair to our customers and that the general public can place their trust and reliance on the integrity of our policies involving personal data systems.

We believe that Congress should carefully examine each and every provision of the proposed legislation to insure that any potential social benefits will fully offset the disruption of private industry and the prohibitive costs to both industry and the consumer. If Congress finds that such legislation is necessary it should then adopt only such measures that will penalize those who violate the law through the implementation of a Federal preemptive statute which identifies specific violations and provides specific individual remedies. We believe this is a more sound approach than creating another Federal Agency with broad and sweeping powers to be imposed on every organization using personal data processing systems.

U.S. Senate, *Privacy*, 658. Business raised similar protests about further efforts by Koch and Goldwater to regulate the private sector. See *Privacy Journal*, "Private Business on HR 1984," 2 (1975): 3.

45. See Solveig Singleton, "Privacy and Human Rights: Comparing the United States to Europe," in *The Future of Financial Privacy*, edited by Competitive Enterprise Institute, 186–203 (Washington, D.C.: Competitive Enterprise Institute, 2000); Lucas Bergkamp, "EU Data Protection Policy: The Privacy Fallacy," *Computer Law and Security Report* 18 (2002): 31–47.

46. See Warren and Brandeis, "Right to Privacy"; William Prosser, "Privacy," *California Law Review* 48 (1960): 383–423.

47. See Cate, *Privacy in the Information Age*.

48. See David Vogel, "The Power of Business in America: A Re-appraisal," *British Journal of Political Science* 13 (1983): 19–43; Vogel, *Trading Up;* Kagan, *Adversarial Legalism*.

49. See William Howell and David Lewis, "Agencies by Presidential Design," *Journal of Politics* 64, no. 4 (2002): 1095–114.

50. As explained to the author in interviews with German and French officials, Frankfurt 2002 and Paris 2003.

51. See, for example, Arthur Miller, *The Assault on Privacy: Computers, Data Banks, and Dossiers* (Ann Arbor: University of Michigan Press, 1971); Hans Peter Bull, *Datenschutz oder Die Angst vor dem Computer* (Muenchen: Piper, 1984).

52. Interview with the author, Frankfurt 2002 and Paris 2003.

53. See Spiros Simitis, "Die informationelle Selbstbestimmung—Grundbedingung einer verfassungskonformen Informationsordnung," *Neue Juristische Wochenschrift* 37 (1984): 398–405.

54. See Immergut, "Rules of the Game"; Evelyne Huber, Charles Ragin, and John Stephens, "Social Democracy, Christian Democracy, Constitutional Structure, and the Welfare State," *American Journal of Sociology* 99 (1993): 711–49; Jonah Levy, Robert Kagan, and John Zysman, "The Twin Restorations: The Political Economy of the Reagan and Thatcher 'Revolutions'," in *Ten Paradigms of Market Economies*, edited by Lee-Jay Cho and Yoon Hyung Kim, 3–58 (Seoul: Korea Research Institute for Human Settlements, 1997).

55. The year 1990 is used as the cut-off in order to minimize the affect of EU activities, which mandated private-sector action for EU members. The first EU draft directive was published in September 1990.

56. A score of 1 indicates that a country adopted a comprehensive regime; a score of 0 indicates a limited regime. The data were taken from Electronic Privacy Information Center, *Privacy and Human Rights 2005;* Council of Europe, *National Laws, 2007,* available at: http://www.coe.int/t/e/legal_affairs/legal_co%2Doperation/data_pro tection/documents/national_laws/NATIONAILAWS_en.asp#TopOfPage. Although many cite Switzerland as adopting privacy rules in 1992, limited rules were actually first adopted by the Swiss senate in 1981. See Otto Stich, *Botschaft zum Bundesgesetz über den Datenschutz,* Bern, Swiss Bundesrat, 1988.

57. Fascist legacy is recorded as a dichotomous variable, where 1 indicates a significant fascist experience. The following countries are coded as having had a significant fascist experience: Austria, Denmark, France, Germany, Israel, Japan, Netherlands, and Norway. Israel is coded as having a fascist experience because the establishment of the Israeli state is directly tied to the legacy of German fascism.

58. The composite veto-point measure includes a measure of presidentialism, electoral system, bicameralism, referendum, and judicial review. Higher scores represent more veto points. An equivalent measure for Israel was constructed by the author. In contrast to the Huber, Ragin, and Stephens measure, federalism is not counted as an additional indicator; federalism was excluded because the measure of bicameralism covers the most important veto path inspired by federalist issues in the regulatory area of data privacy. Substituting Huber, Ragin, and Stephens's measure also produces a statistically significant result. See Evelyne Huber, Charles Ragin, and John Stephens, *Comparative Welfare States Data Set* (Chicago: Northwestern University and University of North Carolina, 1997).

59. Given the binary nature of the dependent variable, it would be appropriate to use techniques such as logit and probit, which are suited for analyzing binary outcomes. These techniques, however, do not guarantee accurate estimates given such a small sample size. See J. Scott Long, *Regression Models for Categorical Dependent Variables Using STATA* (College Station, Tex.: STATA Press, 2003). The ordinary least squares (OLS) estimator provides a useful second-best approach. Nevertheless, I also conducted probit regressions for the three models; the results confirmed the OLS findings.

60. Industry positions became interesting only when legislation overcame resistance by the public sector; in many countries, administrative offices blocked the legislation. So, I am looking here at countries that passed some form of legislation to minimize this debate. In the countries under investigation, industry was forced to defend its interests because the bureaucratic lobbies failed to block regulation.

61. See Richard Clarke, "Collusion and the Incentives for Information Sharing," *Bell Journal of Economics* 14 (21983): 383–94; Tullio Jappelli and Marco Pagano, "Information Sharing in Credit Markets," *Journal of Finance* 48 (1993): 1693–718.

62. Departments such as Commerce and Treasury and the Office for Management and Budget rejected plans for an independent regulatory agency, objecting to external oversight by an independent authority. The following statement by Chase Manhattan summarizes the industry position:

> We suggest that the burdens set by 301(b)(6) are unreasonable. If the modern world is to function, computers are essential tools. Yet, to require "appropriate...safeguards...to protect against embarrassment (or) inconvenience" is to mandate a zero error computer environment, which is not attainable.
>
> We feel that the inquisitorial powers given to the Commission under Section 104 and 105, with regard to the Study of the Private Sector mandated by Section 107, are unprecedented, exceed to the probable need, and inequitably

balance the national interests involved: the Study, as opposed to the need of the private sector for continuity of operations unhindered by thorough and meddlesome interposition by the Commission, not to mention the concomitant potential violation of our customer's privacy. Even a minimal intercession by the Commission with, say our demand Deposit (check) information system will cause untold dislocation and hardship in the check clearing system and conceivably place us in violation of the banking laws.

U.S. Senate, *Privacy,* 528.

63. See ibid., 525, 515, 629. A similar coalition was successful in bringing down private-sector legislation in the Ohio legislature, as explained by state Senator Stanley Aronoff:

The Ohio bill was killed by a coalition of government and special interests that lobbied feverishly against its passage as soon as the bill became calendarized for actual senate floor debate. The Governor's office, which had appeared as a proponent in committee activity lobbied against its passage claiming that it would curtail some of its government information gathering practices. Probably the most active opponent was the Ohio Council of Retail Merchants which included credit bureaus, department stores, and mail order houses and so forth, in its membership. The Ohio Council organized a barrage of telegrams and acted as a coordinating unit for some of the other lobbies. (214)

64. See Michael Moran, "The State and the Financial Services Revolution: A Comparative Analysis," *European Politics* 17 (1994): 158–77.

65. Statements from the life insurance, publishing, retail, and bank trade associations demonstrate the importance of information flows to the various sectors. The American Life Insurance Association argued:

The effect of these measures on life insurance companies could be extremely burdensome. The approximately 1,800 life insurance companies—both large and small—in the United States have many millions of policyholders in the aggregate, and an even greater number of beneficiaries. In addition, they have over one million employees.

U.S. Senate, *Privacy,* 515. The Association of Publishers contended:

If literally construed, this would prevent the normal practice of transferring mailing lists between affiliated and successor businesses and between the professional developers of mailing lists and their customers. For example, small specialized book clubs, lacking the financial strength to finance their own lists, buy or rent from those in the business of building various types of market lists. Unless the operation of mail order book clubs were explicitly exempted from the application of this section, we feel that the impact on the publishing industry could be devastating. (524)

The National Retail Merchants Association claimed, "There can be no doubt that personal data information systems are both necessary and vital components of retail operations" (629). Similarly, the American Bankers Association argued that the inclusion of the private sector would bring down the entire legislation: "It seems to us likely, on the other hand, that an effort to solve the problems of both public and private data banks in one bill might well result in such controversy and confusion as to make it more difficult to bring about enactment of any legislation in this field during the present Congress" (525).

66. Ibid., 606.

67. For the general power of the financial services industry in congressional politics, see Larry Makinson *Open Secrets: The Encyclopedia of Congressional Money and Politics* (Washington, D.C.: Congressional Quarterly, 1972). The historical influence provided to small banks is explained in Nicholas Economides, R. Glenn Hubbard, and Darius Palia, "The Political Economy of Branching Restrictions and Deposit Insurance," *Journal of Law and Economics* 39 (1996): 667–704.

68. Consumer groups, on the other hand, might have lobbied effectively, but they were unconvinced that strong privacy protections were in the best interests of the consumer movement. A critical feature of the public-interest landscape during the 1970s was the rise of Ralph Nader and his collection of public-interest lobbies. Nader's network of consumer advocates attempted to deploy political institutions to turn the tables on powerful private-sector interests. Best known for suits over car safety, the Nader strategy entailed uncovering insider documents and information to leverage media attention and the courtroom. This consumer movement believed that enhanced transparency was the cornerstone to better protection and lobbied extensively to change the procedures of government. See David Vogel, "The Public-Interest Movement and the American Reform Tradition," *Political Science Quarterly* 95 (1981): 607–27. This deep-seated belief in the primacy of transparency, however, did not bode well for privacy issues. Nader's consumer movement could not be persuaded to pursue privacy legislation because it fundamentally did not agree that privacy rules were in the best interests of the movement. As Douglas Lea, director of the ACLU Privacy Project, argued, "There are organizations we thought would have lined up with us—Common Cause and Ralph Nader—but they are wary of the issue. They want more disclosure (by government and business), and they seem to think there would be a conflict." *Congressional Quarterly*, "Privacy: Congress Expected to Vote Controls," 32 (1974), 2613. Similarly, Koch reflects on the lack of public interest support for private-sector privacy legislation, "There is no indication that there is a strong consumer movement requesting or seeking further legislation to control information practices of private business." *Privacy Journal*, "1984," May (1975), 7.

69. The Privacy Project began in 1972 as a nonprofit association geared toward examining the effect of information technology on individual liberties. Funded through grants from industry, including IBM and Polaroid, the Privacy Project developed best practices suggestions and legislative proposals but was not permitted to lobby.

70. The interest of the ACLU in public-sector abuse was made clear by Hope Eastman, the associate director, during the government hearings: "Our experience at the ACLU is directed primarily against the Government because we deal with the Bill of Rights. So I do not have a long list of cases to give you that the ACLU has brought against private business. But I have no reason to think that the abuses do not exist." U.S Senate, *Privacy*, 155.

71. *Congressional Quarterly*. "Committees Probe Ways to Curb Data Use," March 16 (1974): 683.

72. Ervin's staff argued that despite Ervin's desire to regulate the private sector, the only realistic option at the time was public-sector rules. See *US News and World Report*, "A Curb on Prying," July 1, 1974, 42.

73. See *New York Times*, "Privacy: A Year-End Report," December 26, 1974, A24.

74. Speaking on behalf of the Ford administration, Senator Roman Hruska (R-Neb.) argued: "it would create another layer of federal officials...would be far

flung in its organization...would be armed with money and with penetrating powers...and will tend to result in confusion and conflict and indecision." *Congressional Quarterly Almanac,* "Privacy Act," 293. The president himself in a letter to Congress threatened to veto the bill if it contained provisions for a regulatory board. For a discussion of Ford's general weakness on privacy issues, see Warren Weaver, "ACLU Official Criticizes Ford on Privacy Bills," *New York Times,* January 8, 1975, 23.

75. Senator Percy, a cosponsor of the bill in the Senate, explains his concerns:

> Now, in your statement you indicate that Congress "should establish an 'independent' agency subject to joint Presidential and congressional control." How much real control does the President or the Congress really have over such an independent agency, given all their other responsibilities? How much control would that agency have over its own policies? Couldn't it very quickly become captured by the very agencies it is supposed to regulate? Once the members are appointed, where does the control really lie? Since hundreds of these agencies are already in existence, doesn't your proposal really call for creating an agency over which there are no effective Presidential or congressional controls?

U.S. Senate, *Privacy,* 100.

76. For a discussion of the executive threat to use an executive order, see Cohen, "Protection of Citizens' Privacy."

77. The final-hour compromise is described in Richard Cohen, "New Privacy Law to Have Major Impact on Government Data," *National Journal,* January 4, 1975: in U.S. Senate, *Legislative History of the Privacy Act* (Washington, D.C.: Government Printing Office, 1976): 1208. For the results of the study commission, see Privacy Protection Study Commission, *Personal Privacy in an Information Society,* Washington, D.C., 1977. After the publication of the report, the commission was dissolved.

78. See *E'chos,* "La chasse aux français est toujours ouverte," September 11, 1974, Commission Nationale de l'Informatique et des Libertés (CNIL) archive.

79. See Richard Mooney, "Paris Promises Not to Use Equipment for Atomic Weapons," *New York Times,* October 22, 1966, 40.

80. Quoted in Richard Mooney, "France Entering Computer Battle," *New York Times,* April 14, 1967, 55.

81. Simon Nora and Alain Minc, *L'Informatisation de la Société* (Paris: La Documentation Française, 1978).

82. Interview with a member of the French data privacy authority, CNIL, Paris 2003.

83. Interview with Louis Joinet, Paris 2003. When asked if data privacy should cover both the public and private sectors, Joinet responded at the time, "How in the long run can there be two sets of rules? It is obvious that fundamental rules must be identical." Quoted in *Transnational Data Report,* "Louis Joinet: France's Astute Legal Expert and Diplomat," March 1978, 2.

84. Interview with French data privacy expert for the banking sector. Paris 2003.

85. See John Zysman, *Political Strategies for Industrial Order* (Berkeley: University of California Press, 1977).

86. See Moran, "State and the Financial Services Revolution."

87. The credit-reporting system in France is explained by members of the CNIL in Emile Passemard and Clarisse Girot, "Presentation of the FICP: The French Negative File on Credit Repayment Incidents," Warsaw, March 10, 2002.

88. Interviews with a member of the CNIL and Louis Joinet. Paris 2003.

89. Interview with a member of the CNIL. Paris 2003.

90. See *Le Monde,* "L'informatique et les libertés a l'Assemblée Nationale," October 6, 1977, 8.

91. See Spiros Simitis, *Kommentar zum Bundesdatenschutzgesetz* (Baden-Baden: Nomos, 2003).

92. The government and the legal community envisioned a commissioner enforcement system. Modeled on the data protection commissioner in Hesse, which Simitis helped devise, the legal experts hoped to create an advisory post that would act both as an ombudsman for disputes and a resource for new legislation. In the private sector, the legislation proposed the creation of internal data protection officers (IDPOs) who were charged with implementing the adoption of data protection rules within industry. These private-sector employees, however, were monitored by Länder regulators, who acted as a public-sector backstop to quasi-voluntary self-regulation. The expert community agreed that a registration system such as that proposed in France and the United Kingdom was too restrictive and preferred a model that would work with the federal governmental structure. This is explained by Herbert Auernhammer: "Therefore we have held extensive conversations with the Länder. We were instructed that it would be unconstitutional to contradict the federal principle by constructing federal regulations that interfered with the organizational integrity of the Länder." As far as Länder agencies carrying out Länder law, they did not fall under the Federal Data Protection Act. The federal government did not have jurisdiction here and therefore must rely on the existing or still-to-be constructed Länder Data Protection Acts. Bundesministerium des Innern, *Einer Anhörung zum Referententwurf eines Bundes-Datenschutzgesetzes,* Bonn, 1972, 6.

93. FDP politicians recognized the synergies between the themes of the Freiburg Theses and data protection. Limits on governmental and private-sector use of personal information represented a cornerstone in the promotion of societal democratization. As Scheidermann, FDP parliamentarian, argued at the 1972 public hearing on data protection:

> The draft is an excellent example of forward looking legislation even if there are naturally pieces to be discussed. Already there are countless personal data saved on computers. The real threat to the private sphere of individual citizens emerges when this information is networked to create comprehensive personal profiles. The protection of an untouchable area of individual liberty is a prerequisite for the maintenance of our liberal rule of law. Citizens must not be allowed to become the defenseless objects of information technology and data processing by public and private sector institutions. Additionally, the boundaries between industry and government were blurred by the numerous public/private partnerships inherent in the German political economy. Therefore it did not make any sense to exempt the private sector from strict regulations.

Ibid., 69.

94. See Herbert Auernhammer, "Überlegungen zu einem Bundesgesetz über Datenschutz," *Bulletin* 87 (1971): 923–26.

95. Bundesministerium des Innern, *Einer Anhörung,* 1.

96. Spiros Simitis, professor of law at the University of Frankfurt, began a dialogue in the late 1960s with his dissertation about the implications of computerization for the legal profession. See Spiros Simitis, *Informationskrise des Rechts und Datenverarbeitung* (Karlsruhe: CF Mueller, 1970). Simitis then became the second data protection

commissioner for Hesse in 1975 and created a program in data protection law at the university, training many future data protection experts in the country. During the debates over the legislation, Simitis was one of the key academic figures pushing for restrictive legislation.

Simultaneously, Professor Wilhelm Steinmüller at the law school in Regensburg organized a set of working groups that looked at the interaction between new technology and society. These groups examined how technology could be harnessed by the legal community and the challenges technology posed for law, regulation, and society. In addition to producing numerous data protection experts, Steinmüller's group was instrumental in setting the terms of the original legislative debate over the legislation through their *Recommendation on Data Protection*. See Wilhelm Steinmüller, *Stellungnahme zum Entwurf des Bundesdatenschutzgesetzes* (Regensburg: University of Regensburg, 1973). Steinmüller acted as a vital resource for many parliamentarians and advised them as they navigated the treacherous political debate.

The importance of the expert community for the legislative process was noted in multiple interviews. Hirsch labeled the interaction a learning process between the academic and the legislatures. Haenschke argued that he should consult with Steinmüller throughout the legislative effort. The following comments from a representative of the banking sector demonstrate the perceived influence of the academic community:

> The draft whose rules can only be sketched here were presented in 1972. Passages are heavily influenced by academic advisors who the ministry appointed to work on the legislation. They rely heavily on theoretical arguments although the draft could have reached out to experts from industry with more practical knowledge. Instead it relies on heavily laden theoretical ideas made by ideological sociologists, lawyers, and documentation scholars.

Klaus Flachmann, "Kreditwirtschaft und Datenschutz," *Zeitschrift für das Gesamte Kreditwesen* 2 (1973): 56.

97. For a synopsis of the results of the hearing, see *Die Welt*, "Benutzung von Datenbanken," 7.

98. Although I am treating industry together, a few sectors did not share the central industry position. The most vocal of these was the doctors' association, which wanted strict data privacy rules that would limit the oversight powers of insurance providers.

99. See Bundesministerium des Innern, *Einer Anhörung*, 35.

100. Trade associations from a broad spectrum of the economy argued to limit regulation to the public sector. See the remarks of the Bundesverband der Deutschen Industrie, Zentralverband der Elektrotechnischen Industrie, Deutscher Industrie und Handelstag, Vertein Deutscher Maschinenbau-Anstalten, Verband der Handelsauskunfteien, Rat des deutschen Handels, Gesamtverband der Versicherungswirtschaft, Zentralverband des Deutschen Handwerks, and Freier Ausschuss der Deutschen Genossenschaftsverbaende, in ibid. Hirsch argued more bluntly in an interview with the author that industry wanted to kill the legislation. Düsseldorf, 2003.

101. See the comments of the Freier Ausschuss der Deutschen Genossenschaftsverbände and the Gesamtverband der Versicherungswirtschaft, in Bundesministerium des Innern, *Einer Anhörung*. In addition, ten out of ten associations that responded to a question at the hearing concerning affiliate rules called for their elimination in the 1976 hearing on data privacy. See Deutscher Bundestag, *Öffentliche Anhörung zu Fragen*

der Datenschutzgesetzgebung, Protokoll der 104, Sitzung des Innenausschusses und der 83, Sitzung des Ausschusses fuer Wirtschaft, Bonn, 1976.

102. See the comments of the Bundesverband der Deutschen Industrie, Zentraler kreditausschuss, and Zentralverband der Elekrotechnischen Industrie, in Bundesministerium des Innern, *Einer Anhörung.*

103. Germany has one of the most fragmented banking sectors in the world, with the largest five banks holding only 20 percent of market assets (compare this with the Swedish market, in which the largest five banks hold 80 percent of the market assets). In addition, the three-tiered structure promotes aggressive decentralization of bank autonomy and the extensive use of affiliates and branching. This has led Richard Deeg to characterize the German banking system as federalist. Richard Deeg, *Financial Capitalism Unveiled: Banks and the German Political Economy* (Ann Arbor: University of Michigan Press, 1999), 45.

104. For a description of the *Regionalprinzip,* see William Coleman, *Financial Services, Globalization, and Domestic Policy Change* (New York: St. Martin's Press, 1996).

105. The Schutzgemeinschaft für Absatzfinanzierung und Kreditsicherung (SCHUFA), which was established in 1927, acts as a credit clearinghouse for German banks. The need for the SCHUFA demonstrates the inability of the banks to independently cover their information needs. For a description of the organization and its function within the financial services sector, see Schutzgemeinschaft für Absatzfinanzierung und Kreditsicherung, *Geschaeftsbericht 2001* (Wiesbaden: SCHUFA Holding AG, 2002).

106. See Bundesministerium des Innern, *Einer Anhörung,* 78.

107. An article published shortly after the hearing in the banking sector industry magazine summarizes industry position on the external control of private-sector operations: "The increasing tendency of the state to control personal freedom is not acceptable just because it claims to protect that freedom." Flachmann, "Kreditwirtschaft und Datenschutz," 56. At a 1976 hearing, eleven of twelve industry associations rejected the external control of private-sector activity.

108. Owing to the bicameral nature of the German federal legislature, data protection required approval from both houses to become law. In contrast to the U.S. Senate, in which members are directly elected, the German Bundesrat is composed of representatives from the Länder governments. Because FDP ministers sat in Länder coalition governments with both the CDU and the SPD, they were able to leverage Länder politics to achieve results at the federal level.

109. See *Die Welt,* "Datenschutz-Gesetz droht zu scheitern," April 21, 1975, 1.

110. See *Computerwoche,* "Datenschutzgesetz: Novellierung Eingeplant," October 17, 1975 [online].

111. The direct marketing industry claimed that the legislation would cost 20 billion marks and that the banks would take the brunt of the regulation. Credit agencies foresaw one-time costs of 32 million marks plus annual recurring costs of four and one-half million. See *Capital,* "Datenschutz scheitert an den Kosten," 1 (1976), 61–63. Of the thirteen associations present at the hearing, all rejected the inclusion of internal data, ten rejected the treatment of affiliates as third parties, and eleven rejected external governmental control of private-sector activity. See Deutscher Bundestag, *Öffentliche Anhörung zu Fragen der Datenschutzgesetzgebung.*

112. For an explanation of the work of the compromise committee, see Burkhard Hirsch, "Datenschutz im Computer-Zeitalter—eine internationale Herausforderung," in *Datenschutz,* ed. Friedrich Naumann Stiftung, 19–24 (Bonn: Friedrich Naumann Stiftung, 1980).

113. See *Computerwoche*, "Datenschutz ein 'Buendel von Interessenkonflikten'," April 4, 1976 [online]; *Computerwoche*, "Zehn CDU/CSU Änderungen via Bundesrat," May 28, 1976 [online].

114. For the FDP rejection of weakening private-sector regulations see *Fdk Tagesdienst*, "Wir sind für die Fortentwicklung des Datenschutzrechts offen," June 10, 1976, 1–2. The uncertain future of the bill at the close of the parliamentary session is reported in *Computerwoche*, "Im November letzte Chance für das BDSG," August 6, 1976 [online].

115. For the final CDU position in the Bundestag, see the comments of CDU Representative Johannes Gerster, "The appointment of data protection officials...for the public and private sectors will create more than a thousand additional government positions in the federal and state administrations which means more bureaucracy, creating more government but hardly better data protection." Similarly, the CSU state secretary of Bayern, who led the opposition in the Bundesrat, warned, "the government enforcement of private sector regulation must not create a large bureaucracy." Both quoted in *Das Parlament*, "Schutz des Bürgers vor dem Computer," November 27, 1976, 1.

116. For the tension of the last minutes before passage, see *Computerwoche*, "Bundes-Datenschutzgesetz verabschiedet," November 19, 1976 [online].

117. See ibid.; *Das Parlament*, "Schutz des Bürgers vor dem Computer."

118. Similarly, several years after the adoption of the initial legislation, the issue of data privacy was brought before the German Constitutional Court. In response to a census that asked several intimate questions, a citizens' movement formed to reduce government data monitoring. Far from striking down the legislation, the court found that there existed a fundamental right that guaranteed individuals control over their personal information (*informationelle Selbstbestimmung*). Judicial review, then, enhanced the standing of data privacy law in German politics, especially in the public sector. See Simitis, "Die informationelle Selbstbestimmung."

119. On a range of issues, including the right to die, the drug war, corporate governance, privacy, civil unions, and stem cell research, coalitional possibilities extend across traditional left-right boundaries.

120. For the original appeal of privacy to the social libertarian agenda, see Thomas Ronan, "Certain Legislation Gets Backers Left and Right," *New York Times*, May 17, 1975, 12. For the resurgence of the coalition in the new security environment, see, for example, Michael Tomasky, "Strange Bedfellows," *American Prospect*, September 2003 [online].

121. The standard focus on left-right dynamics is evident in recent efforts to map political party preferences and voter ideology across advanced industrial democracies. See Mathew Gabel and John Huber, "Putting Parties in Their Place: Inferring Party Left-Right Ideological Positions from Party Manifestos Data," *American Journal of Political Science* 44 (2000): 94–103; Ian Budge and Hans-Dieter Klinemann, *Mapping Policy Preferences: Estimates for Parties, Electors, and Governments 1945–1998* (Oxford: Oxford University Press, 2001).

122. See Herbert Kitschelt, "Left-Libertarian Parties: Exploring Innovation in Competitive Party Systems," *World Politics* 40 (1988): 194–234.

123. See Ronald Inglehart and Christian Welzel, *Modernization, Cultural Change and Democracy* (Cambridge, UK: Cambridge University Press, 2005).

124. See Richard Clarke, "Collusion and the Incentives for Information Sharing," *Bell Journal of Economics* 14 (1983): 383–94; Tullio Jappelli and Marco Pagano, "Information Sharing in Credit Markets," *Journal of Finance* 48 (1993): 1693–1718.

125. This informs and bridges the debate between theorists who argue for the importance of veto points and those who focus on veto players. On the former, see Immergut, "Rules of the Game"; on the latter, see George Tsebelis, *Veto Players: How Political Institutions Work* (Princeton: Princeton University Press, 2002).

126. Kagan, *Adversarial Legalism.*

127. See Mathew McCubbins and Thomas Schwartz, "Congressional Oversight: Police Patrols versus Fire Alarms," *American Journal of Political Science* 28 (1984): 165–79; Barry Weingast, "The Congressional-Bureaucratic System: A Principal-Agent Perspective," *Public Choice* 44 (1984): 147–91.

128. See Howell and Lewis, "Agencies by Presidential Design."

129. See Gilardi, "Institutional Foundations of Regulatory Capitalism."

Chapter 4. The EU Data Privacy Directive

This chapter expands on an article-length version of the argument presented in Abraham Newman, "Building Transnational Civil Liberties: Transgovernmental Entrepreneurs and the European Data Privacy Directive," *International Organization* 62 (2008): 103–30.

1. During the debate over the directive, the political entity known as the European Community changed its name to the European Union. I have paralleled this change in the empirical narrative. I apologize for any confusion.

2. In contradiction to harmonization arguments that isolate the role of supranational institutions or industry in raising regulatory standards, the European Commission and international businesses often argued that the first goal should be prioritized, whereas national data protection officials stressed the second goal. See European Parliament and the Council of the European Union, Directive 95/46/EC, Recital 8 and 9.

3. See Andrew Moravcsik, *The Choice for Europe: Social Purpose and State Power from Messina to Maastricht* (Ithaca: Cornell University Press, 1998).

4. This follows the logic of the trading-up argument found in Vogel, *Trading Up.*

5. See Peter Evans, *Embedded Autonomy: States and Industrial Transformation* (Princeton: Princeton University Press, 1994).

6. See Graham Pearce and Nicholas Platten, "Achieving Personal Data Protection in the European Union," *Journal of Common Market Studies* 36 (1998): 529–47.

7. See Wayne Sandholtz and John Zysman, "1992: Recasting the European Bargain," *World Politics* 42 (1989): 95–128; Nicolas Jabko, *Playing the Market: A Political Strategy for Uniting Europe* (Ithaca: Cornell University Press, 2006).

8. See Elliot Posner, "Sources of Institutional Change: The Supranational Origins of Europe's New Stock Markets," *World Politics* 58 (2005): 1–40; Elliot Posner, The Origins of Europe's New Stock Markets (Cambridge, Mass.: Harvard University Press, 2008).

9. See Heisenberg, *Negotiating Privacy.*

10. See Kal Raustiala, "The Architecture of International Cooperation," Virginia Journal of International Law 43 (2002): 1–92; Slaughter, *New World Order.* For an earlier effort see Raymond Hopkins, "The International Role of 'Domestic' Bureaucracy," *International Organization* 30 (1976): 405–432.

11. Keohane and Nye define transgovernmental relations as the "set of direct interactions among sub-units of different governments that are not controlled or closely guided by the policies of the cabinets or chief executives of those governments." Keohane and Nye, "Transgovernmental Relations and International Organizations," 43.

Slaughter 2004 argues that "the most highly developed and innovative transgovernmental system is the European Union" (50).

12. See generally Raustiala, "The Architecture of International Cooperation"; and Slaughter, *New World Order.* In Europe, see specifically Renaud Dehousse, "Regulation by Networks in the European Community," *Journal of European Public Policy* 4 (1997): 246–61; Burkard Eberlein and Abraham Newman, "Escaping the International Governance Dilemma? Incorporated Transgovernmental Networks in the European Union," *Governance* 21 (2008): 25–52; and the work of Coen and Thatcher as part of the new governance project, available at: http://www.eu-newgov.org.

13. In their original article, Keohane and Nye 1974 distinguished between transgovernmental policy coordination and transgovernmental coalition builders. While much recent research has focused on the former, this article builds on the latter.

14. See Andrew Moravcsik, "A New Statecraft? Supranational Entrepreneurs and International Cooperation," *International Organization* 53 (1999): 267–306; quotation from 271.

15. See Barnett and Finnemore, *Rules for the World;* Carpenter, *Bureaucratic Autonomy.*

16. See Haas, "Introduction"; Nicholas Ziegler, "Institutions, Elites, and Technological Change in France and Germany," *World Politics* 47 (1995): 341–72.

17. See Robert Keohane, *After Hegemony* (Princeton: Princeton University Press, 1984); Moravcsik, "A New Statecraft?"

18. See Kathleen McNamara, "Consensus and Constraint: Ideas and Capital Mobility in European Monetary Integration," *Journal of Common Market Studies* 37 (1999): 455–76.

19. Hooghe and Marks, *Multi-Level Governance and European Integration.*

20. For a detailed discussion of policy networks in general, see Tanja Börzel, "Organizing Babylon: On Different Conceptions of Policy Networks," *Public Administration* 76 (1998): 253–73.

21. See Keohane and Nye, "Transgovernmental Relations and International Organizations"; Thomas Risse-Kappen, *Bringing Transnational Relations Back In: Non-state Actors, Domestic Structures and International Institutions* (Cambridge, UK: Cambridge University Press, 1995).

22. See Slaughter, *New World Order.*

23. See John Padgett and Chris Ansell, "Robust Action and the Rise of the Medici," *American Journal of Sociology* 98 (1993): 1259–319; Chris Ansell, "The Networked Polity: Regional Development in Western Europe," Governance 13 (2000): 303–33.

24. See *Transnational Data Report,* "The Battle Over Data Processing and Freedom," March 1, 1978, 1–8.

25. The European Parliament passed a series of resolutions calling for supranational action, including those of May 3, 1976, O.J. (C 100) 27; May 8, 1979, O.J. (C 140) 147; and March 9, 1982, O.J. (C 87) 39.

26. The countries that ratified the convention prior to the presentation of the draft of the European privacy directive in 1990 were Austria, Denmark, France, Germany, Luxembourg, Norway, Spain, Sweden, and the United Kingdom.

27. See Commission Recommendation 1981 O.J. (L246) 31.

28. The Commission position is described by a Commission official in George Papapavlou, "Latest Developments Concerning the EC Draft Data Protection Directives," in *Recent Developments in Data Privacy Law,* edited by Jan Dumortier (Leuven: Leuven University Press, 1992); Spiros Simitis, "Data Protection in the European Union—the Quest for Common Rules," *Courses of the Academy of European Law* 8 (1997): 95–142.

29. See *European Report,* "UNICE Calls for Changes in Proposal on Personal Data," 1651, 1991, 3.

30. See *Marketing,* "EC Scheme for Data Protection Stuns UK," July 12, 1990, 3; *Transnational Data and Communications Report,* November–December 1992, 43–45. Interestingly, it was not until after the passage of the directive that U.S. firms took an active interest in the European privacy debate.

31. As reported to the author in interviews with data privacy experts in Germany and France. Frankfurt and Paris, 2003.

32. For the comments of Wolfgang Schäuble, then interior minister, see "Datenschützer warnt vor 'Freihafen' der Informationsweitergabe," *Frankfurter Rundshau,* August 8, 1989, 1.

33. The results of a one-tailed two-sample t test confirm that the mean public opinion for national action was significantly greater in countries with legislation than in countries without regulation ($t = -2.52$, $p > 0.02$).

34. See *Marketing,* "EC Scheme"; *Computerwoche,* "Wirtschaft fürchtet Nachteile durch verschärften Datenschutz," December 21, 1990 [online].

35. See Friedrich Kretschmer, "Europäische Datenschutznormen aus sicht der deutschen Industrie" (paper presented at DAFTA, Königswinter, Germany, November 16, 1989). Translation by the author.

36. See Gesellschaft für Datenschutz und Datensicherung, *Erhebung über die möglichen Auswirkungen der geplanten EG-Datenschutzrichtlinie auf die Wirtschaft* (Königswinter: GDD, 1992).

37. *Transnational Data Report,* "European Data Protection Chiefs to Meet in Bonn," March 1, 1979, 1.

38. See Jacques Fauvet, "Privacy in the New Europe," *Transnational Data and Communications Report* (November 1989): 17–18; Spiros Simitis, "Data Protection: Transcending the National Approach," *Transnational Data and Communications Report* (November 1989): 23–28.

39. See the comments of the president of the CNIL in Fauvet, "Privacy in the New Europe."

40. According to a senior official at the German federal data privacy agency.

41. See *Transnational Data and Communications Report,* "Simitis Reports Data Protection Chaos" (June–July 1990): 26.

42. For a discussion of reversion points, see John Richards, "Toward a Positive Theory of International Institutions: Regulating International Aviation Markets," *International Organization* 53 (1999): 1–37.

43. *Journal Officiel de la République Française* 1978, Loi no. 78-17 du 6 janvier 1978 relative à l'informatique, aux fichiers et aux libertés.

44. See *Transnational Data and Communications Report,* "No Fiat for Fiat" (November 1989): 10; *Business Week,* "Privacy vs. Marketing: Europe Draws the Line," June 3, 1990, 124.

45. See Fauvet, "Privacy in the New Europe."

46. See *Transnational Data and Communications Report,* "CNIL Urges Belgian Data Law" (February 1990): 24.

47. The president of the CNIL made this argument at the Eleventh International Data Commissioners Conference; see Fauvet, "Privacy in the New Europe."

48. Simitis, the leading German data privacy expert, argued, "These provisions were introduced on the demand of the data protection authorities of the Member States." In *Transnational Data and Communications Report,* "Simitis Reports Data Protection Chaos." This was confirmed by senior officials at the German federal data privacy agency in Bonn 2003 and the French CNIL in Paris 2003.

49. As explained by a Commission official in the Internal Market Directorate responsible for data privacy.

50. See *RAPID,* "Modification of the Commission's Proposal on Data Protection," October 23, 1992, 59.

51. Interview with the author. Brussels, 2003.

52. Internal Market Commissioner Mogg emphasizes the expert role of data privacy authorities, "For the Commission, the question is now where do we go from here? The Commission is in a learning process, ready to hear from those who have the experience, and first of all the Data Protection Commissioners." John Mogg, "Initiatives Taken by the European Communities in the Field of Data Protection: New Developments" (remarks presented at the 13th Conference of the Data Protection Commissioners, Strasbourg, October 2–4, 1991).

53. For example, the European Chamber of Commerce called on the European Community to recognize national peculiarities in data protection and promote subsidiarity in the draft, see *European Report,* "Chambers of Commerce Demand Review of Data Protection Proposal," April 8, 1993, 1850. In an interview with the author, an official from a European trade association argued that business supported subsidiarity because it feared the costs of regulatory change. Brussels, 2003.

54. For the German government position, see *Transnational Data and Communications Report,* "Government's Position on the EC Data Protection Directive" (May–June 1991): 41.

55. The analysis presented here focuses on rules governing private-sector use of data. Member-state governments also actively lobbied to integrate subsidiarity rights for security and police issues. For a comprehensive discussion of the political wrangling among the member states in the Council of the European Community, see Spiros Simitis, "From the Market to the Polis: The EU Directive on the Protection of Personal Data," *Iowa Law Review* 80 (1995): 445–69.

56. See *VDI Nachrichten,* "Europäischer Datenschutz liegt weiter auf Eis," January 7, 1994, 4. For a comprehensive discussion of political fights among the member states in the Council of the European Community, see Simitis, "From the Market to the Polis."

57. See John Mogg, "Privacy Protection in the Information Society," *Transnational Data and Communications Report* 29 (November–December 1994): 29–32.

58. See Platten, "Background to and History of the Directive."

59. The implementation of the directive was quite controversial in a number of member states. The German reform took seven years and produced an intense debate over the future of data protection in the country. Member states that previously had had no regulations were the quickest to adopt rules and often took a strict interpretation in their application. Representatives of both the Internal Market Directorate and European Business lobbies confirmed this position.

60. The term *adequacy* was controversial in the development of the directive. Initially, the term *equivalent* was used, but this was seen as placing too high a barrier for other countries.

61. The creation of this article was highly contested by business interests, which feared that the group would obtain quasi-regulatory powers and wished to have industry representation on the committee. Industry lost both pursuits.

62. Article 28 specifies that data privacy authorities must be independent and enjoy the power to investigate and enforce national laws.

63. See Union of Industrial and Employers' Confederations of Europe, *Implementation of Directive 95/46/EC on the Protection of Individuals with Regard to the Processing of*

Personal Data and on the Free Movement of Such Data of 24 October 1995, Brussels, UNICE, 2002, 1–10.

64. The power of the Working Party to affect business behavior was echoed in numerous interviews with European trade associations.

65. The Article 29 Working Party has produced over one hundred opinions, recommendations, and working documents since 1997. They are available at: http://europa.eu.int/comm/internal_market/en/dataprot/wpdocs/index.htm. Its continued influence with the Commission was confirmed by a representative from the Information Society directorate, who explained, "They [the Article 29 Working Party] are influential because they know much better than we do how national rules function." Brussels, 2003. This was echoed by both German and British civil servants serving in their interior ministries. Berlin and London 2003.

66. For example, a recent article in the *International Herald Tribune* discussing an Article 29 Working Party investigation was titled, "EU Panel to Question US Spying on Banks," September 26, 2006, 4. Similarly, an article in the *Washington Post* discussing a recent opinion of the Working Party reads, "IP Addresses are Personal Data, EU Regulator Says," January 22, 2008, D1.

67. The need for a European data protection supervisor was first mentioned in the Amsterdam Treaty and then created in subsequent implementation legislation. See European Parliament and the Council of the European Union, *The Regulation 2001/45/EC on the Protection of Individuals with Regard to the Processing of Personal Data by the Community Institutions and Bodies and on the Free Movement of Such Data, Official Journal of the European Communities* L1. Brussels, 2001.

68. See Vogel, *Trading Up.*

69. This resonates with recent work on regulator preferences in international cooperation. See David Andrew Singer, *Regulating Capital: Setting Standards for the International Financial System* (Ithaca: Cornell University Press, 2007).

Chapter 5. The Spread of Comprehensive Rules

1. See Richards, "Toward a Positive Theory"; Dan Drezner, "Globalization and Policy Convergence," *International Studies Review* 3 (2001): 53–78; Dan Drezner, *All Politics Is Global: Explaining International Regulatory Regimes* (Princeton: Princeton University Press, 2007).

2. See Roy Ginsberg, "Conceptualizing the European Union as an International Actor: Narrowing the Theoretical Capability-Expectations Gap," *Journal of Common Market Studies* 73 (1999): 429–54.

3. See Shaffer, "Globalization and Social Protection."

4. Industry research conducted by Forrester Research Group estimates that global electronic commerce grew to $12 trillion by 2004. Of this, the U.S. market was $7 trillion, compared to $3 trillion in Europe. The data are available from the author.

5. Israel was the only non–western European nation to adopt comprehensive privacy rules prior to the adoption of the EU privacy directive.

6. I employ here active vocabulary to describe regulatory adjustments, but I recognize that extraterritorial effects are often unintentional. Regulators may actively promote their rules internationally or national rules may spill over, forcing other countries to adjust. In future work, I intend to problematize the issue of intentionality to determine its effect on international market governance.

7. For a review of the various mechanisms employed in diffusion processes, see Elkins and Simmons, "On Waves, Clusters, and Diffusion."

8. See Thelen and Steinmo, "Historical Institutionalism in Comparative Politics."

9. See Kathleen Thelen, "How Institutions Evolve: Insights from Comparative Historical Analysis," in *Comparative Historical Analysis in the Social Sciences,* edited by James Mahoney and Dietrich Rueschemeyer, 208–40 (Cambridge, UK: Cambridge University Press, 2003).

10. See Pierson, "When Effect Becomes Cause."

11. See Majone, *Regulating Europe.*

12. This argument was inspired by many conversations with David Bach and Elliot Posner. See Bach and Newman, "The European Regulatory State." For an analogous argument in the U.S. context, see Ann-Marie Burley, "Regulating the World: Multilateralism, International Law, and the Projection of the New Deal Regulatory State," in *Multilateralism Matters,* edited by John Ruggie, 125–56 (New York: Columbia University Press, 2003).

13. See Jabko, *Playing the Market.*

14. See Suzanne Berger and Ronald Dore, eds., *National Diversity and Global Capitalism* (Ithaca: Cornell University Press, 1996).

15. The data privacy case contradicts the accepted wisdom in international relations research that process standards do not produce regulatory convergence at a high level of protection. By linking process regulations to market access, the European Union rules enjoy extraterritorial effects, something observable in an increasing number of sectors.

16. Information on the cross-national adoption of data privacy legislation can be found in Council of Europe, *National Laws,* 2006, available at: http://www.coe.int/t/e/legal_affairs/legal_co%2Doperation/data_protection/documents/national_laws/NATIONAlLAWS_en.asp#TopOfPage.

17. Making regulatory reform a condition of EU enlargement played a large role in this adjustment in the central European nations. It is important to note, however, that Slovakia and Lithuania shifted systems prior to opening formal enlargement negotiations.

18. See Asia-Pacific Economic Cooperation, *APEC Privacy Framework.*

19. The different preferences of domestic and multinational firms concerning the Safe Harbor Agreement (the solution to this threat) are examined in Heisenberg, *Negotiating Privacy.*

20. See William Clinton, *Framework for Global Electronic Commerce* (Washington, D.C.: Federal Government, 1997).

21. See Swire and Litan, *None of Your Business.*

22. Michael Barnett and Martha Finnemore, *Rules for the World: International Organizations in Global Politics* (Ithaca: Cornell University Press, 2004) focus on expertise, delegation, and values as the three roots of authority. Carpenter, *Forging of Bueacratic Autonomy,* by contrast, identifies the legitimacy provided by networks. For a detailed analysis of forms of power, see Michael Barnett and Raymond Duvall, *Power in Global Governance* (Cambridge, UK: Cambridge University Press, 2005).

23. For the adequacy decision, see the Article 29 opinions, available at: http://europa.eu.int/comm/internal_market/en/dataprot/wpdocs/index.htm.

24. For the historical details surrounding the 1988 Privacy Act in Australia, see Margaret Jackson, "Data Protection Regulation in Australia after 1988," *International Journal of Law and Information Technology* 5 (1997): 158–91; Roger Clarke, "A History of Privacy in Australia," 2002, available at: http://www.anu.edu.au/people/Roger.Clarke/DV/OzHistory.htm.

25. For the role of the EU directive in shifting the Australian position, see Philippa Yelland, "EU Laws May Prompt Data Exchange Reform," *The Australian,* June 11, 1996 [online].

26. See Attorney General Department, *Discussion Paper: Privacy Protection in the Private Sector* (Canberra, Australia: Commonwealth Government, 1996); Janet Fife-Yeomans, "Sweeping Changes for Laws on Privacy," *The Australian,* September 13, 1996, 3.

27. See Office of the Prime Minister, *Privacy Legislation* (Camberra, Australia: Commonwealth Government, 1997).

28. The chief executive of the Australian Chamber of Commerce and Industry warned, "The Government ought to move with extreme caution to ensure that they do not overreact and therefore take information that is commercially critical out of the hands of the business community." Quoted in Christopher Dore, "Privacy Laws Will Extend to Private Sector," *The Australian,* December 11, 1995 [online].

29. See John Hilvert, "EU 'White List' to Test Our Data Security," *The Australian,* August 19, 1997, 36.

30. The Australian Computer Society argued,

> While some of the ideas of privacy may seem esoteric, the current impetus for action in Australia is a real, commercial one. Western countries, particularly in Europe, have adopted privacy laws. Those laws not only govern internal handling of personal information in the country, but export of information. The European Union Data Protection Directive comes into force 24 October 1998. Some sectors of Australian industry could be severely disadvantaged by the lack of complementary legislation.

Position on Privacy, June 24, 1998; on file with the author.

31. See John Hilvert, "Report Urges Action on Electronic Privacy," *The Australian,* December 16 1997, 31.

32. See AAP Newsfeed, "New Voluntary Laws Criticised," February 20, 1998 [online].

33. Attorney General Daryl Williams argued during the legislative debate,

> The Bill is intended to facilitate trade in information between Australia and foreign countries. Without such legislative measures, this trade may be adversely affected. The 1995 European Union directive on the protection of individuals with regard to the processing of personal data and on the free movement of such data restricts the transfer of personal information from member countries to other countries unless adequate privacy safeguards are in place.

Official Hansard, April 12, 2000, 15749. The legal affairs spokesman for the opposition Labor party underlined the importance of EU pressure: "Regrettably the government has been dragged kicking and screaming into making the decision.... The government's attempt to portray the decision as a natural extension of its proposals for self-regulation is dishonest." Quoted in Fiona Hamilton, "Government Introduces Privacy Scheme to Cover Private Sector," AAP Newsfeed, December 16, 1998 [online].

34. See House of Representatives, *Privacy Amendment (Private Sector) Bill 2000: Explanatory Memorandum,* Camberra, Australia, 2000, 11–12.

35. See ibid., 32.

36. For a summary of the Australian system, see the remarks of Australian Privacy Commissioner Karen Curtis, "The Importance of Self-Regulation in the Implementation of Data Protection Principles: The Australian Private Sector Experience" (address to the 27th International Conference of Data Protection and Privacy Commissioners, Montreux, Switzerland, September 15, 2005).

37. See Office of the Privacy Commissioner, *Getting in on the Act: The Review of the Private Sector Provisions of the Privacy Act 1988*, Sydney, March 2005.

38. For the industry position, see Mark Paterson, *Australian Chamber of Commerce and Industry Statement on Privacy Legislation*, Camberra, Australia, 2000. For a critique of the legislation, see Roger Clarke, "Privacy Bill Needs Much More Work," *The Australian*, February 15, 2000, 4. The small-business exemption applies to firms with revenue up to 3 million Australian dollars.

39. A spokesman for the European delegation argued, "We are trying to be constructive.... It's pointless for us to stay silent and then come in later and say the legislation doesn't meet our requirements." Quoted in Simon Hayes, "Privacy bill Not up to Standard," *The Australian*, June 27, 2000, 35.

40. See Article 29 Data Protection Working Party, *Opinion 3/2001 on the Level of Protection of the Australian Privacy Amendment Act 2000* (Brussels: European Community, 2001); Emma Macdonald, "Privacy Laws under Attack," *Canberra Times*, March 27, 2001, 5.

41. See Karen Dearne, "Privacy Cop on Warpath," *The Australian*, January 28, 2003, 19.

42. The Commission will rely on this expert study to make a final adequacy ruling. The importance of the Working Party in this process was explained to the author in an interview with a Commission official. Brussels 2005.

43. In a 2005 Senate inquiry into the privacy laws, a privacy advocate from the Law Institute of Victoria argued:

> In terms of business, our submission deals with the need for Australia to have a privacy system that complies with the EU directive. It is particularly important for Australian businesses that are collecting information and want to deal transnationally. If we do not comply with the EU directive, Australian businesses are going to be impacted in terms of the extent to which they can work offshore and deal with other jurisdictions.

Bill O'Shea in Senate Legal and Constitutional References Committee, *The Real Big Brother: Inquiry into the Privacy Act 1988*, Canbbera, June 2005, 88.

44. A 2005 Senate review of Australian privacy laws concluded:

> Further, the committee considers that protecting the privacy of personal information also makes good commercial sense for all businesses, large and small. The committee notes that the privacy regimes of other jurisdictions, such as New Zealand, operate effectively without any small business exemption. Finally, the committee received evidence that the small business exemption is one of the key outstanding issues in negotiations with the European Union for recognition of Australia's privacy laws under the EU Data Protection Directive. Therefore, notwithstanding the proposed ALRC review, the committee recommends that the small business exemption be removed altogether from the Privacy Act.

Ibid., 157.

45. See Australian Law Reform Commission, "Review of Australian Privacy Law an Overview," Discussion Paper no. 72, Sydney, Australian Law Reform Commission, 2007.

46. See Christopher Kuner and Aaron Simpson, "Managing Privacy Enforcement Risks in Europe," *Risk Management* (February 2005): 42–44.

47. For a list of enforcement examples, see Article 29 Data Protection Working Party, *Recent Examples of Enforcement Actions Carried out by Data Protection Authorities* (Brussels: European Commission, January 2005).

48. The general director of the European direct marketing association argued, "If Microsoft was processing its Spanish data in the US, then it is probably doing it in other countries as well. Signing up for the Safe Harbor is a logical step, because it seems the Data Protection Commissioners have abandoned their unofficial moratorium on the agreement and may well start prosecuting those who contravene it, especially big companies." Quoted in *Precision Marketing*, "Microsoft Signs Safe Harbour Following Fine," May 18, 2001, 1.

49. Heisenberg, *Negotiating Privacy,* presents a cautious interpretation of European influence on domestic U.S. regulatory change.

50. See Anna Diamantopoulou, "The European Social Model and Enlargement" (paper presented at the Seminar on the Harmonisation of Turkey's Social Policy and Legislation with EU Standards, Istanbul, 2000).

51. See Frank Schimmelfennig and Ulrich Sedelmeier, *The Europeanization of Central and Eastern Europe* (Ithaca: Cornell University Press, 2005).

52. See Heather Grabbe, "How Does Europeanization Affect CEE Governance? Conditionality, Diffusion, and Diversity," *Journal of European Public Policy* 8 (2001): 1013–31.

53. Aside from Hungary, which has an extensive data protection tradition, EU accession seems to be driving the adoption of comprehensive legislation in new member countries. See Nick Platten, "Poland Legislates on Data Protection to Pace Its Way for EU Membership," *Privacy Law and Business International Newsletter* 44, July (1998), [online]; Laszlo Majtenyi, "Ensuring Data Protection in East-Central Europe," in *Privacy in Post-Communist Europe* (Social Research Conference Series), edited by Arien Mack, *Social Research* 69 (spring 2002): 151–78.

54. See, for example, *CTK News Agency,* "European Parliament Urges Czechs to Act in Keeping with European Standards," April 19, 1999 [online]; *European Report,* "Riga Claims to Have Met All Requirements for Closer EU Ties," February 24, 1999 [online].

55. The industry lack of interest is expressed in Stephen Mihailovich, "New Privacy Bill Could Hurt Direct Marketing," *Budapest Business Journal* 27, 1997 [online].

56. This was confirmed in an interview with a civil servant from the EU Reform Ministry in Albania. The civil servant argued that firms were not yet at a stage at which data processing figured into their business and therefore were not critically involved in the legislative process.

57. Article 70 of the Stabilization and Association Agreement between the European Union and Albania, for example, requires Albania to adjust its data privacy laws.

58. Between 1998 and 2000, the European Union conducted over three hundred formal twinning programs. For a description of twinning programs, see Commission of the European Communities, *Twinning in Action* (Brussels: European Commission, 2001).

59. See *CTK News Agency,* "European Experts Monitor Protection of Personal Information," June 21, 2002 [online].

60. See Delegation of the European Commission to the Czech Republic, "European Union Helps the Czech Republic to Strengthen Regulation and to Enforce Personal Data Protection" (press release, September 23, 2004).

61. For a detailed description of the projects carried out in the Czech Republic, Latvia, and Lithuania, see the PHARE Standard Summary Project fiches CZ2000/IB/OT/03, LI 2002/000.601.03.02, and LV2002/IB/OT-01.

62. The study is available at: http://www.privacyinternational.org/article.shtml?cmd [347]=x-347-559597.

63. For a nuanced discussion of EU authority in the trade setting, see Meunier and Nicolaidis, "Who Speaks for Europe?"; Meunier, *Trading Voices*.

64. See Bretherton and Vogler, *European Union as a Global Actor;* Smith, *Europe's Foreign and Security Policy.*

65. The close ties between competition regulators are described by Devuyst, "Transatlantic Competition Relations"; more generally, see Slaughter, *New World Order.*

66. See Commission of the European Communities, "European Commission Requests Denunciation of Open Sky Agreement" (press release, November 20, 2002); Paul Meller, "Europeans Propose to End 'Open Skies' Deals," *New York Times,* February 27, 2002, 1.

67. See Bernard Hoekman, "Assessing the General Agreement Trade in Services," in *The Uruguay Round and the Developing Economies,* edited by Will Martin and L. Alan Winters, 125–55 (Washington, D.C.: World Bank, 1995).

68. See William Drake and Kalypso Nicolaidis, "Ideas, Interests, and Instituionalization: 'Trade in Services' and the Uruguay Round," *International Organization* 46 (1992): 37–100.

69. The senior EU negotiator for the Internal Market argued that the European Union went to GATS negotiations with the goal of exempting privacy rules. The United States, not understanding the implications, raised no argument. Interview with Commission official responsible for the directive, Brussels 2003.

70. The United States initially viewed European privacy efforts as an intra-European trade issue. It was only as the European Union moved to implement the directive in 1998 that the United States understood the extraterritorial trade implications. See Solveig Singleton, *Privacy as a Trade Issue.*

71. See Swire and Litan, *None of Your Business.*

72. During 1998, the U.S. government repeatedly threatened to go to the WTO to resolve privacy disputes. See Guy de Jonquières, "Bid to Avert Threat of 'Cyber Trade War'," *Financial Times,* September 10, 1998, 6.

73. Frits Bolkestein, the head of the Internal Market Directorate, argued quite forcefully that the privacy directive is in full compliance with European GATS commitments. Frits Bolkestein, "Is Europe Ready for the New Economy?" (speech, Nijenrode, Breukelen, March 27, 2000).

74. The deliberations that produced the Safe Harbor Agreement were possible only because Europe had closed the window on multilateral strategies; Farrell, "Constructing the International Foundations of E-Commerce."

75. See Burkard Eberlein and Abraham Newman, "Escaping the International Governance Dilemma?"

76. For the importance of soft law in international governance, see Kenneth Abbott and Duncan Snidal, "Hard and Soft Law in International Governance," *International Organization* 54 (2000): 421–56; in the context of the European Union, see Gerda Falkner, Oliver Treib, Miriam Hartlapp, and Simone Leiber, *Complying with Europe: EU Harmonization and Soft Law in the Member States* (Cambridge, UK: Cambridge University Press, 2005).

77. For the opinions of the Article 29 Group, see http:/europa.eu.int/comm/internal_market/en/dataprot/wpdocs/index.htm.

78. See Article 29 Working Party, *Report 1/2007 on the First Joint Enforcement Action: Evaluation and Future Steps* (Brussels, 2007).

79. See *New York Times*, "Microsoft Faces European Commission Inquiry on Privacy Concerns," May 28, 2002 [online].

80. See Article 29 Data Protection Working Party, *Working Document on On-line Authentication Services* (Brussels: European Union, 2003).

81. See Matt Loney, "Microsoft Passport Compromise after EU Scrutiny with Global Consequences," *Silicon.com,* January 31, 2003 [online].

82. See Peter Schaar, "Letter to Peter Fleischer," Brussels, May 16 2007.

83. See Union of Industrial and Employers' Confederations of Europe, *Implementation of Directive 95/46/EC,* 1–10.

84. The power of the opinions of the Working Party on business behavior was echoed by representatives of numerous European trade associations representing the telecommunications, banking, and direct marketing industries. Interviews, Brussels 2003.

85. For a general discussion see Mitchener, "Increasingly, Rules of Global Economy"; Parker and Buck, "Washington Bridles at EU's Urge"; Bach and Newman, "European Regulatory State."

86. See Shefter, "Party and Patronage."

87. See, for example, Katzenstein, "International Relations and Domestic Structures."

88. This is a response to a theoretical gap clearly identified by Milner: "Following studies of domestic politics, IR [international relations] might move toward more comparative institutional analysis at both the domestic and international levels. Scholars might explore the effects that different political institutions have on policy choices and how these policies are implemented." "Rationalizing Politics," 786.

89. This idea is explored in greater detail in Abraham Newman and Elliot Posner, "Rethinking Market Power: Authority, Territoriality, and the International Economy" (paper presented at the 101st Annual American Political Science Association Conference, Washington, D.C., September 1, 2005).

Chapter 6. The Struggle over Transnational Civil Liberties

1. See Stephen Kobrin, "Territoriality and the Governance of Cyberspace," *Journal of International Business Studies* 32 (2001): 687–704.

2. Policymaking within the European Union is organized around three pillars: the European Communities, the Common Foreign and Security Policy, and police and judicial cooperation. The legislative process differs within each pillar. The third pillar, concerned with internal security, was first created in 1993 with the signing of the Maastricht treaty. For a detailed discussion of EU competencies in different issue areas, see Simon Hix, *The Political System of the European Union* (New York: Palgrave, 2005); Helen Wallace, William Wallace, and Mark A. Pollack, eds., *Policy-Making in the European Union* (Oxford: Oxford University Press, 2005).

3. A cynical reading might suggest that privacy regimes legitimize government surveillance. I believe, by contrast, that these regulations create a system to balance the interests of organizations and individuals. Comprehensive privacy regimes create a framework for responsible data collection, providing a benchmark from which to protest abusive behavior.

4. The transgovernmental network of data privacy authorities founded the International Working Group on Data Protection in Telecommunications as part of the International Conference of Data Protection Commissioners in 1983. In 1989, at the Eleventh International Conference of Data Protection Commissioners, the working group passed a resolution that called on the European Union to pass specific data privacy legislation for the telecommunications sector. The resolution called for stringent regulations that forced the erasure of customer data after billing had been completed and strong opt-in rules for marketing purposes. The resolution is available on the Data Protection Commission of Berlin website (www.datenschutz-berlin.de). At the same time, data privacy authorities lobbied at the national level to integrate restrictive sectoral provisions into national telecommunications deregulation. In Germany, for example, data privacy officials successfully integrated detailed rules on the retention and erasure of personal information into the 1996 reform of the telecommunications sector. The text of the Telecommunications Carrier Data Protection Ordinance (*Telekommunikationsdienstunternehmen—Datenschutzverordnung*, TDSV), which was passed in 1996, is available at: http://www.online-recht.de/vorges.html?TDSV.

5. This sentiment was most clearly expressed in the Lisbon agenda formulated in March 2000, which attempted to craft a strategy for expanding competitiveness in the European Union over the following decade. A recent evaluation of the agenda reaffirmed the commitment of the Commission to privacy protection and its effect on trust: "The use of the Internet is beginning to penetrate the daily life of citizens. A precondition for it to become more widespread is that it proves worthy of our trust. Security, privacy protection, property protection and general governance of the sector are indispensable for building citizens' confidence in the Information Society." Commission of the European Communities, *Challenges for the European Information Society beyond 2005*, Brussels, 2004, section 4.7: [online].

6. See European Parliament and the Council of the European Union, *Directive 97/66/EC Concerning the Processing of Personal Data and the Protection of Privacy in the Telecommunications Sector, Official Journal of the European Communities L24/1*, Brussels, January 30, 1997.

7. See European Parliament and the Council of the European Union, *Directive 2002/58/EC on Privacy and Electronic Communications. Official Journal of the European Communities L201*, Brussels, July 31, 2002 [hereafter: Directive 2002/58/EC].

8. For the distinction between *data retention* and *data preservation*, see John Schwartz, "German and U.S. Telecommunications Privacy Law: Legal Regulation of Domestic Law Enforcement Surveillance," *Hastings Law Journal* 54 (2003): 751; Abu Bakar Munir and Siti Hajar Yasin, "Retention of Communications Data: A Bumpy Road Ahead," *John Marshall Journal of Computer and Information Law* 22 (summer 2004): 731. Recent revelations in the United States, however, demonstrate that the government may have secretly imposed a retention system after September 11, 2001. See Leslie Cauley, "NSA Has Massive Database."

9. The resistance by the civil rights community is chronicled at: www.state watch.org.

10. The commissioners released a statement at the International Conference of Data Protection Commissioners that concluded,

Where traffic data are to be retained in specific cases, there must therefore be a demonstrable need, the period of retention must be as short as possible and the practice must be clearly regulated by law, in a way that provides sufficient safeguards against unlawful access and any other abuse. Systematic retention of all kinds of traffic data for a period of one year of more would be clearly disproportionate and therefore unacceptable in any case.

Article 29 Data Protection Working Party, *Opinion 5/2002 on the Statement of the European Data Protection Commissioners at the International Conference in Cardiff on Mandatory Systematic Retention of Telecommunications Traffic Data* (Brussels: European Union, 2002), 3.

11. Directive 2002/58/EC.

12. See International Chamber of Commerce, *Common Industry Statement on Storage of traffic Data for Law Enforcement Purposes*, Brussels, 2003.

13. See Council of the European Union, *Draft Framework Decision on the Retention of Data Processed and Stored in Connection with the Provision of Public Communications Networks for the Purpose of Prevention, Investigation, Detection and Prosecution of Crime and Criminal Offences Including Terrorism*, 8958/04, Brussels, April 28, 2004.

14. The German Telecommunications Association (BITKOM) conducted a study that forecast the cost of retention to be in the hundreds of millions of marks. See *Frankfurter Allgemeine Zeitung*, "Telekom-Branche gegen Datensammler," September 23, 2004, 13.

15. See Article 29 Data Protection Working Party, *Opinion 9/2004 on a Draft Framework Decision on the Storage of Data Processed and Retained for the Purpose of Providing Electronic Public Communications Networks with a View to the Prevention, Investigation, Detection, and Prosecution of Criminal Acts, Including Terrorism* (Brussels: European Commission, 2004).

16. In June, the data protection commissioners of Germany called on the federal government to reject the EU data retention proposal; see Datenschutzbeauftragte Deutschlands, "Presseinformation," Bonn, June 25, 2004. The federal data protection commissioner's warning to Minister Schily was reported in *Die Stern*, "Schily weist Datenschuetzer-Kritik zurueck," April 20, 2005 [online].

17. The German parliament passed a resolution rejecting EU data retention plans; see *Heise Online*, "Bundestag will Datenschutzreform anmahnen," December 1, 2004 [online].

18. The parliamentarian responsible for the issue emphasized in an interview with the author the importance of the positions of the Article 29 Working Party as a critical source of information and argumentation, Brussels, 2005.

19. The position paper of Alexander Alvaro, MdEP, is available at: http://www.edri.org/issues/dataretention/alvaropaper.

20. See Tatum Anderson, "Major European Institutions Divided on Data Retention," *Telecom Markets*, February 22, 2005 [online].

21. See Council of the European Union, *The European Union Counter-Terrorism Strategy*, Brussels, December 1, 2005.

22. The 2006 proposal was a far cry from the initial four-year retention period in the framework proposal.

23. See European Data Protection Supervisor, *Opinion of the European Data Protection Supervisor on the Proposal for a Directive of the European Parliament and of the Council on the Retention of Data Processed in Connection with the Provision of Public Electronic Communication Services and Amending Directive 2002/58/EC*, Brussels, 2005.

24. See Article 29 Data Protection Working Party, *Opinion 4/2005 on the Proposal for a Directive of the European Parliament and of the Council on the Retention of Data Processed in Connection with the Provision of Public Electronic Communication Services and Amending Directive 2002/58/EC* (Brussels: European Commission, 2005).

25. In contrast to the earlier vote, the new German parliament supported Schäuble's position on retention.

26. See European Parliament and the Council of the European Union, *Directive 2006/24/EC on the Retention of Data Generated or Processed in Connection with the Provision of Publicly Available Electronic Communications Services or of Public Communications Networks and Amending Directive 2002/58/EC, Official Journal of the European Communities* L105(54), Brussels, March 15, 2006.

27. See Article 29 Data Protection Working Party, *Opinion 3/2006 on the Directive 2006/24/EC of the European Parliament and of the Council on the Retention of Data Generated or Processed in Connection with the Provision of Publicly Available Electronic Communications Services or of Public Communications Networks and Amending Directive 2002/58/EC* (Brussels: European Commission, 2006).

28. For the importance of environmental uncertainty for political entrepreneurship see Neil Fligstein, "Markets as Politics: A Political-Cultural Approach to Market Institutions," *American Sociological Review* 61 (1996): 656–73.

29. See Kathleen McNamara, "Rational Fictions: Central Bank Independence and the Social Logic of Delegation," *West European Politics* 25, no. 1 (2002): 47–76.

30. Peter Hustinx, the EDPS, summed up the opinion of the data privacy authorities, arguing that the passage of the retention directive was, "a sad moment for the EU. . . . the safeguards are weak and member states have too much flexibility." Quoted in *European Report* "EU Supervisor Lambasts Data Retention Directive," April 20, 2006 [online].

31. In 2006, for example, the Department of Justice proposed the creation of a retention regime in the United States.

32. See Commission of the European Communities, *Joint Statement*, Brussels, 2003.

33. See Article 29 Data Protection Working Party, *Opinion 6/2002 on Transmission of Passenger Manifest Information and Other Data from Airlines to the United States* (Brussels: European Commission, 2002).

34. See Stefano Rodota, "Letter to European Parliament Committee on Citizens' Freedom and Rights," Brussels, March 3, 2003.

35. See Sarah Ludford, *Debate on the Resolution concerning PNR*, Plenary Session of the European Parliament, Brussels, March 12, 2003.

36. The Working Party detailed its concerns in June 2003. It focused on the pull system, which allowed direct U.S. access to European databases; the lack of an enforcement or audit system; the possibility that data would be shared with other agencies; the collection of sensitive data; the retention period; and the lack of correction rights for passengers. Article 29 Data Protection Working Party, Opinion 4/2003 on the Level of Protection ensured in the US for the Transfer of Passengers' Data, Brussels, 2003.

37. See Frits Bolkestein, Letter to Tom Ridge, June 12, 2003, available at: http://www.statewatch.com.

38. See Bruno Waterfield, "MEPs Defy Air Passenger Data Deal." *Eupolitix,* March 13, 2004, 13.

39. See Rodota, "Letter to European Parliament Committee."

40. See Frits Bolkestein, *EU/US Talks on Transfers of Airline Passengers' Personal Data,* testimony before the Committee on Citizens' Freedoms and Rights, European Parliament, Brussels, September 9, 2003.

41. Bolkestein argued, "But the US leadership were finally persuaded of the need for flexibility. I might say here that Parliament's strong pressure has played a very important role." Ibid., [online].

42. See Article 29 Data Protection Working Party, *Opinion 3/2004 on the Level of Protection Ensured in Canada for the Transmission of Passenger Name Records and Advanced Passenger Information from Airlines* (Brussels: European Commission, February 11, 2004); Article 29 Data Protection Working Party, *Opinion 1/2004 on the Level of Protection Ensured in Australia for the Transmission of Passenger Name Records from Airlines* (Brussels: European Commission, 2004).

43. See Council of the European Union, *Case before the Court of Justice—Case C-317/04*, 11876/04, Brussels, August 6, 2004.

44. The European Court of Justice, in the 2003 Lindqvist case, ruled that the European Convention on Human Rights protects individual privacy within Europe. See *Lindqvist*, case C-101/01, November 6, 2003.

45. As a formal supranational body, the EDPS has the authority to enter arguments to the Court in cases that directly fall under its jurisdiction. The case of PNR, which does not deal with the processing of personal information by EU institutions, does not fall under a strict reading of the EDPS mandate. The EDPS, however, has argued since its inception that it has the right to advise the bodies of the European Union on topics relevant to the development of data privacy regulation more broadly. And the EDPS has actively developed an agenda for the protection of personal information in the third pillar (concerned with home and justice affairs). For the EDPS effort to define a broad mission within Europe, see European Data Protection Supervisor, *The EDPS as an Advisor to the Community Institutions on Proposals for Legislation and Related Documents*, Brussels, March 18, 2005.

46. As explained by the EDPS to the author in an interview. Brussels, 2005.

47. See European Court of Justice, cases C-317/04 and C-318/04, May 30 2006. See also Nicola Clark, "EU Court Bars Giving Passenger Data to US," *International Herald Tribune*, May 31, 2006, 1 and 8.

48. The EU-15 countries are Austria, Belgium, Denmark, Finland, France, Germany, Greece, Republic of Ireland, Italy, Luxembourg, the Netherlands, Portugal, Spain, Sweden, and the United Kingdom.

49. See Department of Homeland Security, *Fact Sheet: Security Improvements to Visa Waiver Program*, Washington, D.C., November 30, 2006.

50. See Article 29 Data Protection Working Party, *Opinion 2/2007 on Information to Passengers about Transfer of PNR Data to US Authorities* (Brussels: European Commission, 2007).

51. See Peter Hustinx, "New PNR Agreement with the United States," letter to Wolfgang Schauble, Brussels, June 27, 2007.

52. See European Parliament, *Resolution of 12th July 2007 on the PNR agreement with the United States of America*, Brussels, July 12, 2007.

53. See Council of the European Union, *Agreement between the European Union and the United States of America on the Processing and transfer of Passenger Name Record (PNR) Data by Air Carriers to the United States Department of Homeland Security (DHS)*, 11595, Brussels, July 18, 2007.

54. The Privacy Act provision, however, is contained in an exchange of letters between the European Union and the United States and not in the agreement proper. As such, its standing under international law is unclear. Demonstrating this uncertainty, the Department of Homeland Security has already proposed an exemption to the Privacy Act for airline passenger data. See *Federal Register*, "Privacy Act: Implementation of Exemptions; Automated Targeting System," August 6, 2007, 43567–69.

55. See Parliament of the Czech Republic, *Declaration to the Agreement between the European Union and the United States of America on the Processing and Transfer of Passenger*

Name Record (PNR) Data by Air Carriers to the United States Department of Homeland Security (DHS), Brussels, July 19, 2007.

56. The Working Party has published an initial opinion in which it concludes that the new agreement provides fewer privacy protections than the earlier one, and it calls on the Commission to clarify many points of implementation. Article 29 Working Party, *Opinion 5/2007 on the Follow-Up Agreement between the European Union and the United States of America on the Processing and Transfer of Passenger Name Record (PNR) Data by Air Carriers to the United States Department of Homeland Security concluded in July 2007* (Brussels: European Commission, August 17, 2007).

57. See Article 29 Data Protection Working Party, *Press Release on the SWIFT Case Following the Adoption of the Article 29 Working Party Opinion on the Processing of Personal Data by the Society for Worldwide Interbank Financial Telecommunication (SWIFT)* (Brussels: European Commission, November 23, 2006).

Chapter 7. Regulatory Power in the Global Economy

1. See Majone, *Regulating Europe*.

2. For similar arguments that stress the importance of national and supranational European institutions for international affairs see Walter Mattli and Tim Büthe, "Setting International Standards: Technological Rationality or Primacy of Power," *World Politics* 56, no. 1 (2003): 1–42; Meunier, *Trading Voices;* Bach and Newman, "European Regulatory State."

3. The U.S. insider-trading case draws heavily from the empirical work in David Bach, "Varieties of Cooperation: Regulating Transnational Markets for Information Goods" (PhD diss., University of California, Berkeley, 2004). See also Laurence, "Spawning the SEC."

4. See Lotte Frach, "The Participation of Interest Groups in the Lamfalussy Process: A New Quality of Participatory Legitimacy," REGEM Analysis no. 13, University of Trier, February 2005.

5. The empirical examples of renewed European influence are inspired by and draw heavily from Elliot Posner, "Market Power without a Single Market: The New Transatlantic Relations in Financial Services" (paper presented at The New Transatlantic Agenda and the Future of Transatlantic Economic Governance workshop, Robert Schuman Center for Advanced Studies, Florence, Italy, June 18–19, 2004).

6. See, for example, *Economist*, "A Bit of Give and Take," October 17, 2002 [online].

7. See Floyd Norris, "US and European Securities Officials Vow Cooperation," *New York Times,* June 5, 2004, 3; Floyd Norris, "Europe Welcomes Accounting Plan," *New York Times,* April 23, 2005, B3.

8. See Robert Bruce, "The Road Map to Global Convergence with Backing from George Bush and the EU," *Financial Times,* July 7, 2005, 14.

9. See Bach and Newman, "European Regulatory State."

10. See Simon Evenett, Alexander Lehmann, and Benn Steil, *Antitrust Goes Global: What Future for Transatlantic Cooperation* (Washington, D.C.: Brookings Institution, 2000); *Tufts Center for the Study of Drug Development*, "European Approval of New Biotech Drugs Outpaces US Approval," 2 (2000): 1–3; Hendrik Glimstedt, "Competitive Dynamics of Technological Standardization: The Case of Third Generation Cellular Communications," *Industry and Innovation* 8, no. 1 (2001): 49–78; Mattli and Büthe, "Setting International Standards."

11. See Chris Ansell and David Vogel, *Why the Beef? The Contested Governance of European Food Safety* (Cambridge, Mass.: MIT Press, 2006).

12. See Mark Pollack and Gregory Shaffer, "The Challenge of Reconciling Regulatory Differences: Food Safety and GMOs in the Transaltantic Relationship," in *Transatlantic Governance in the Global Economy*, edited by Mark Pollack and Greg Shaffer, 153–78 (New York: Rowman and Littlefield, 2001).

13. Some authors contend that exactly this has happened with regulations concerning genetically modified food. See Yves Tiberghien, "The Battle for the Global Governance of Genetically Modified Organisms: The Roles of the European Union, Japan, Korea, and China in a Comparative Context," *Etudes du CERI*, no. 124 working paper (April 2006).

14. The history of the JAA is available at: http://www.jaa.nl.

15. See European Parliament and the Council of the European Union, *Regulation 1592/2002 on Common Rules in the Field of Civil Aviation and Establishing a European Aviation Safety Agency, Official Journal of the European Communities* L240 (1), July 15, 2002.

16. *European Report*, "Commission Updates Blacklist," June 21, 2006, 3109.

17. See Slaughter, "Agencies on the Loose?"; Slaughter, *New World Order*.

18. See Raustiala, "Architecture of International Cooperation."

19. See Carpenter, *Forging of Bureaucratic Autonomy*.

20. See Gilardi, "Institutional Foundations of Regulatory Capitalism."

21. See Renaud Dehousse, "Regulation by Networks in the European Community," *Journal of European Public Policy* 4, no. 2 (1997): 246–61; Slaughter, *New World Order*.

22. See Eberlein and Newman 2008, "Escaping the International Governance Dilemma?"

23. See McCubbins and Schwartz, "Congressional Oversight."

24. This argument is a logical international application and extension of an argument developed by Carpenter, *Forging of Bureaucratic Autonomy*, in the domestic context.

25. For a review of such monitoring mechanisms in the European context, see Mark Pollack, *The Engines of Integration? Delegation, Agency, and Agenda Setting in the European Union* (New York: Oxford University Press, 2003).

26. Although I focus my empirical analysis here on transgovernmental actors in European regional politics, the theoretical argument applies to other areas of the world. Collaboration among North American environmental agencies under the auspices of the North American Free Trade Agreement, for example, promises to contain similar patterns of political entrepreneurship.

27. See Haas, "Introduction: Epistemic Communities."

28. See Fligstein, "Markets as Politics"; Sandholtz and Zysman, "1992: Recasting the European Bargain."

29. See Slaughter, *New World Order*; Giandomenico Majone, "Two Logics of Delegation: Agency and Fiduciary Relations in EU Governance," *European Union Politics* 2 (2001): 103–21.

30. See Vogel, *Trading Up*; Tonnelson, *Race to the Bottom*.

31. See Berger and Dore, *National Diversity and Global Capitalism*; Geoffrey Garrett, "Global Markets and National Politics," *International Organization* 52, no. 4 (1998): 787–824.

32. See Stephen Krasner, *International Regimes* (Ithaca: Cornell University Press, 1983); James and Lake, "Second Face of Hegemony."

33. See Thelen and Steinmo, "Historical Institutionalism in Comparative Politics."

34. See Peter Evans, Dietrich Rueschemeyer, and Theda Skocpol, "On the Road to a More Adequate Understanding of the State," in *Bringing the State Back In*, edited by Peter Evans, Dietrich Rueschemeyer, and Theda Skocpol, 347–66. Cambridge, UK: University of Cambridge Press, 1985, quotation on 351.

35. See Lisa Martin and Beth Simmons, "Theories and Empirical Studies of International Institutions," *International Organization* 52, no. 4 (1998): 729–53.

36. For the debate on missing trade and border effects, see Daniel Trefler, "The Case of Missing Trade and Other Mysteries," *American Economic Review* 85 (1995): 1029–46.

37. See David Bach, Abraham Newman, and Steve Weber, "The International Implications of China's Fledgling Regulatory State: From Product to Rule Maker," *New Political Economy* 11 (2006): 499–518.

38. For the case of product standards, see Mattli and Büthe, "Setting International Standards." More generally, see *Economist,* "How the European Union Is Becoming the World's Chief Regulator," September 20, 2007 [online].

39. See Parker and Buck, "Washington Bridles at EU's Urge."

40. See Ian Mannners, "Normative Power Europe: A Contradiction in Terms?" *Journal of Common Market Studies* 40, no. 2 (2002): 235–58.

41. See Fritz Scharpf, "Community and Autonomy: Multilevel Policy Making in the European Union," *Journal of European Public Policy* 1 (1994): 219–42.

Bibliography

Abbott, Kenneth, and Duncan Snidal. "Hard and Soft Law in International Governance." *International Organization* 54, no. 3 (2000): 421–56.

Alter, Karen. "Who Are the 'Masters of the Treaty'? European Governments and the European Court of Justice." *International Organization* 52, no. 1 (1998): 121–47.

Ansell, Chris. "The Networked Polity: Regional Development in Western Europe." Governance 13, no. 3 (2000): 303–33.

Ansell, Chris, and David Vogel. *Why the Beef? The Contested Governance of European Food Safety.* Cambridge, Mass.: MIT Press, 2006.

Archick, Kristin. *US-EU Cooperation against Terrorism.* Washington, D.C.: Congressional Research Service, 2005.

Article 29 Data Protection Working Party. *Opinion 3/2001 on the Level of Protection of the Australian Privacy Amendment Act 2000.* Brussels: European Commission, 2001.

———. *Opinion 5/2002 on the Statement of the European Data Protection Commissioners at the International Conference in Cardiff on Mandatory Systematic Retention of Telecommunications Traffic Data.* Brussels: European Commission, 2002.

———. *Opinion 6/2002 on Transmission of Passenger Manifest Information and Other Data from Airlines to the United States.* Brussels: European Commission, 2002.

———. *Opinion 1/2003 on the Storage of Traffic Data for Billing Purposes.* Brussels: European Commission, 2003.

———. *Opinion 4/2003 on the Level of Protection Ensured in the US for the Transfer of Passengers' Data.* Brussels: European Commission, 2003.

Article 29 Data Protection Working Party. *Opinion 1/2004 on the Level of Protection Ensured in Australia for the Transmission of Passenger Name Records from Airlines.* Brussels: European Commission, 2004.

———. *Opinion 3/2004 on the Level of Protection Ensured in Canada for the Transmission of Passenger Name Records and Advanced Passenger Information from Airlines.* Brussels: European Commission, 2004.

———. *Opinion 9/2004 on a Draft Framework Decision on the Storage of Data Processed and Retained for the Purpose of Providing Electronic Public Communications Networks with a View to the Prevention, Investigation, Detection, and Prosecution of Criminal Acts, Including Terrorism.* Brussels: European Commission, 2004.

———. *Opinion 4/2005 on the Proposal for a Directive of the European Parliament and of the Council on the Retention of Data Processed in Connection with the Provision of Public Electronic Communication Services and Amending Directive 2002/58/EC.* Brussels: European Commission, 2005.

———. *Opinion 3/2006 on the Directive 2006/24/EC of the European Parliament and of the Council on the Retention of Data Generated or Processed in Connection with the Provision of Publicly Available Electronic Communications Services or of Public Communications Networks and Amending Directive 2002/58/EC.* Brussels: European Commission, 2006.

———. *Opinion 2/2007 on Information to Passengers about Transfer of PNR data to US Authorities.* Brussels: European Commission, 2007.

———. *Opinion 5/2007 on the Follow-Up Agreement between the European Union and the United States of America on the Processing and Transfer of Passenger Name Record (PNR) Data by Air Carriers to the United States Department of Homeland Security Concluded in July 2007.* Brussels: European Commission, 2007.

———. *Press Release on the SWIFT Case Following the Adoption of the Article 29 Working Party Opinion on the Processing of Personal Data by the Society for Worldwide Interbank Financial Telecommunication (SWIFT).* Brussels: European Commission, 2006.

———. *Recent Examples of Enforcement Actions Carried Out by Data Protection Authorities.* Brussels: European Commission, 2005.

———. *Working Document on On-line Authentication Services.* Brussels: European Commission, 2003.

Asia-Pacific Economic Cooperation. *APEC Privacy Framework.* Singapore: APEC Secretariat, 2005.

Attorney General Department. *Discussion Paper: Privacy Protection in the Private Sector.* Canberra, Australia: Commonwealth Government, 1996.

Auernhammer, Herbert. "Überlegungen zu einem Bundesgesetz über Datenschutz." *Bulletin* 87 (1971): 923–26.

Bach, David. "Varieties of Cooperation: Regulating Transnational Markets for Information Goods." PhD diss., University of California, Berkeley, 2004.

Bach, David, and Abraham Newman. "The European Regulatory State and Global Public Policy: Micro-Institutions, Macro-Influence." *Journal of European Public Policy* 14, no. 6 (2007): 827–46.

Bach, David, Abraham Newman, and Steve Weber. "The International Implications of China's Fledgling Regulatory State: From Product Maker to Rule Maker." *New Political Economy* 11, no. 4 (2006): 499–518.

Barnett, Michael, and Raymond Duvall. *Power in Global Governance.* Cambridge, UK: Cambridge University Press, 2005.

Barnett, Michael, and Martha Finnemore. *Rules for the World: International Organizations in Global Politics.* Ithaca: Cornell University Press, 2004.

Baum, Gerhart. "Auszug aus der Rede am 10.6.1976." In *Datenschutz,* ed. Friedrich Naumann Stiftung. Bonn: Friedrich Naumann Stiftung, 1980: 14.

Bellman, Steven, Eric J. Johnson, Stephen J. Kobrin, and Gerald L. Lohse. "International Differences in Information Privacy Concerns: A Global Survey of Consumers." *Information Society* 20 (2004): 313–24.

Bennett, Colin. *Regulating Privacy: Data Protection and Public Policy in Europe and the United States.* Ithaca: Cornell University Press, 1992.

———. "What Is Policy Convergence and What Causes It?" *British Journal of Political Science* 21, no. 2 (1991): 215–33.

Bennett, Colin, and Charles Raab. *The Governance of Privacy: Policy Instruments in Global Perspective.* Boston: MIT Press, 2006.

Berger, Suzanne, and Ronald Dore, eds. *National Diversity and Global Capitalism.* Ithaca: Cornell University Press, 1996.

Bergkamp, Lucas. "EU Data Protection Policy: The Privacy Fallacy." *Computer Law and Security Report* 18, no. 1 (2002): 31–47.

Bessette, Rändi, and Virginia Haufler. "Against All Odds: Why There is no International Information Regime." *International Studies Perspectives* 2 (2001): 69–92.

Bignami, Francesca. "Transgovernmental Networks vs. Democracy. The Case of the European Information Privacy Network." *Michigan Journal of International Law* 26 (2005): 806–68.

Bolkestein, Frits. *EU/US Talks on Transfers of Airline Passengers' Personal Data.* Testimony before the Committee on Citizens' Freedoms and Rights, European Parliament, Brussels, September 9, 2003.

———. "Is Europe Ready for the New Economy?" Speech, Nijenrode, Breukelen, March 27, 2000.

———. Letter to Tom Ridge, June 12, 2003. Available at: http://www.statewatch.com.

Börzel, Tanja. "Organizing Babylon: On Different Conceptions of Policy Networks." *Public Administration* 76 (1998): 253–73.

Börzel, Tanja, and Madeleine Hosli. "Brussels between Bern and Berlin: Comparative Federalism Meets the European Union." *Governance* 16, no. 2: 179–202.

Bracher, Karl, Wolfgang Jaeger, and Werner Link, eds. *Republik im Wandel 1969–1974.* Mannheim: Deutsche Verlags-Anstalt, 1986.

Bretherton, Charlotte, and John Vogler. *The European Union as a Global Actor.* London: Routledge, 1996.

Budge, Ian, and Hans-Dieter Klinemann. *Mapping Policy Preferences: Estimates for Parties, Electors, and Governments 1945–1998.* Edited by Andrea Volkens, Judith Bara, and Eric Tanenbaum. Oxford: Oxford University Press, 2001.

Bull, Hans Peter. *Datenschutz oder die Angst vor dem Computer.* Muenchen: Piper, 1984.

Bundesministerium des Innern. *Einer Anhörung zum Referententwurf eines Bundes-Datenschutzgesetzes.* Bonn, 1972.

Bundesverband der Deutschen Industrie. *Stellungnahme des EP-Rechtausschusses zur Datenschutz-Richtlinie.* Cologne, 1992.

Burkert, Herbert. "Privacy—Data Protection." In *Governance of Global Networks in the Light of Different Local Values,* edited by Christoph Engel and Kenneth H. Keller, 43–70. Baden-Baden: Nomos, 2000.

Burley, Ann-Marie. "Regulating the World: Multilateralism, International Law, and the Projection of the New Deal Regulatory State." In *Multilateralism Matters,* edited by John G. Ruggie, 125–56. New York: Columbia University Press, 1993.

Burley, Ann-Marie, and Walter Mattli. "Europe before the Court: A Political Theory of Legal Integration." *International Organization* 47 (winter 1993): 41–76.

Büthe, Tim. "Taking Temporality Seriously: Modeling History and the Use of Narratives as Evidence." *American Political Science Review* 96 (2002): 481–93.

Cameron, David. "The Dynamics of Presidential Coalition Formation in France." *Comparative Politics* 5 (1977): 253–79.

Carpenter, Daniel. *Forging of Bureaucratic Autonomy: Reputations, Networks, and Policy Innovation in Executive Agencies.* Princeton: Princeton University Press, 2001.

Cate, Fred. *Privacy in the Information Age.* Washington, D.C.: Brookings Institution, 1997.

Cauley, Leslie. "NSA Has Massive Database of Americans' Phone Calls." *USA Today,* May 11, 2006, 1.

Clark, William, Erick Duchesne, and Sophie Meunier. "Domestic and International Asymmetries in United States–European Union Trade Negotiations." *International Negotiations* 5 (2000): 69–95.

Clarke, Richard. "Collusion and the Incentives for Information Sharing." *Bell Journal of Economics* 14 (1983): 383–94.

Clarke, Roger. "A History of Privacy in Australia." 2002. Available at: http://www.anu.edu.au/people/Roger.Clarke/DV/OzHistory.htm.

Clinton, William. *Framework for Global Electronic Commerce.* Washington, D.C.: Federal Government, 1997.

Cohen, Richard. "Protection of Citizens' Privacy Becomes Major Federal Concern." *National Journal* 6 (1974): 1521–30.

Coleman, William. *Financial Services, Globalization, and Domestic Policy Change.* New York: St. Martin's Press, 1996.

Commission of the European Communities. *Challenges for the European Information Society beyond 2005.* COM(2004)757, Brussels, November 19, 2004.

——. "European Commission Requests Denunciation of Open Sky Agreement." Press release, Brussels, November 20, 2002.

——. *Final Report of the Committee of Wise Men on the Regulation of European Securities Markets.* Brussels, 2001.

——. *The Implementation of Commission Decision 520/2000/EC on the Adequate Protection of Personal Data Provided by the Safe Harbour Privacy Principles and Related Frequently Asked Questions Issued by the US Department of Commerce.* Brussels, October 20, 2004.

——. *Joint Statement.* Brussels, 2003.

——. "Modification of the Commission's Proposal on Data Protection." Press release, RAPID database, October 23, 1992.

——. *Twinning in Action*. Brussels, 2001.

Congressional Quarterly Almanac. "Senate Hearings on Invasion of Privacy." 27 (1971): 772–79.

——. "Privacy Act." 30 (1974): 292–94.

Council of Europe. *National Laws*. 2007. Available at: http://www.coe.int/t/e/legal_affairs/legal_co%2Doperation/data_protection/documents/national_laws/NATIONAlLAWS_en.asp#TopOfPage.

——. *Convention for the Protection of Individuals with Regard to Automatic Processing of Personal Data*. Strasbourg, 1981.

Council of the European Union. *Agreement between the European Union and the United States of America on the Processing and Transfer of Passenger Name Record (PNR) Data by Air Carriers to the United States Department of Homeland Security (DHS)*. 11595/07. Brussels, July 18, 2007.

——. *Case before the Court of Justice—Case C-317/04*. 11876/04. Brussels, August 6, 2004.

——. *Draft Framework Decision on the Retention of Data Processed and Stored in Connection with the Provision of Public Communications Networks for the Purpose of Prevention, Investigation, Detection and Prosecution of Crime and Criminal Offences Including Terrorism*. 8958/04. Brussels, April 28 2004.

——. *The European Union Counter-Terrorism Strategy*. Brussels, December 1, 2005.

Datenschutzbeauftragte. *Ersten Tätigkeitsbericht*. Wiesbaden: Hessischer Landtag, 1972.

Datenschutzbeauftragte Deutschlands. "Presseinformation." Bonn, June 25, 2004.

Davies, Simon, Gus Hosein, and Edgar Whitley. *The LSE Identity Project Report*. London: London School of Economics, 2005.

Deeg, Richard. *Financial Capitalism Unveiled: Banks and the German Political Economy*. Ann Arbor: University of Michigan Press, 1999.

Dehousse, Renaud. "Regulation by Networks in the European Community." *Journal of European Public Policy* 4, no. 2 (1997): 246–61.

Delegation of the European Commission to the Czech Republic. "European Union Helps the Czech Republic to Strengthen Regulation and to Enforce Personal Data Protection." Press release, September 23, 2004.

Department of Homeland Security. *Fact Sheet: Security Improvements to Visa Waiver Program*. Washington, D.C., November 30, 2006.

Deutscher Bundestag. *Öffentliche Anhörung zu Fragen der Datenschutzgesetzgebung. Protokoll der 104. Sitzung des Innenausschusses und der 83. Sitzung des Ausschusses fuer Wirtschaft*. Bonn, 1976.

Devuyst, Youri. "Transatlantic Competition Relations." In *Transatlantic Governance in the Global Economy*, edited by Mark A. Pollack and Gregory C. Shaffer, 127–52. Lanham: Rowman and Littlefield, 2001.

Diamantopoulou, Anna. "The European Social Model and Enlargement." Paper presented at the Seminar on the Harmonisation of Turkey's Social Policy and Legislation with EU Standards, Istanbul, 2000.

Drake, William, and Kalypso Nicolaidis. "Ideas, Interests, and Institutionalization: 'Trade in Services' and the Uruguay Round." *International Organization* 46, no. 1 (1992): 37–100.

Drezner, Dan. *All Politics Is Global: Explaining International Regulatory Regimes.* Princeton: Princeton University Press, 2007.

——. "Globalization and Policy Convergence." *International Studies Review* 3 (spring 2001): 53–78.

Dumortier, Jan. "The Protection of Personal Data in the Schengen Convention." *International Review of Law, Computers & Technology* 11 (1997): 93–106.

Eberlein, Burkard, and Abraham Newman. "Escaping the International Governance Dilemma? Incorporated Transgovernmental Networks in the European Union." *Governance* 21 (2008): 25–52.

Economides, Nicholas, R. Glenn Hubbard, and Darius Palia. "The Political Economy of Branching Restrictions and Deposit Insurance." *Journal of Law and Economics* 39 (October 1996): 667–704.

Electronic Privacy Information Center. *Privacy and Human Rights 2005.* Washington, D.C.: EPIC, 2006.

Elkins, Zachary, and Beth Simmons. "On Waves, Clusters, and Diffusion: A Conceptual Framework." *Annals of the American Academy of Political and Social Science* 598, no. 1 (2005): 33–51.

Ervin, Sam. "The First Amendment: A Living Thought in the Computer Age." *Columbia Human Rights Law Review* 4, no. 1 (1972): 13–47.

Esping-Andersen, Gosta. *The Three Worlds of Welfare Capitalism.* Princeton: Princeton University Press, 1990.

European Data Protection Supervisor. *The EDPS as an Advisor to the Community Institutions on Proposals for Legislation and Related Documents.* Brussels, March 18, 2005.

——. *Opinion of the European Data Protection Supervisor on the Proposal for a Directive of the European Parliament and of the Council on the Retention of Data Processed in Connection with the Provision of Public Electronic Communication Services and Amending Directive 2002/58/EC.* Brussels, 2005.

European Parliament. *Resolution of 12th July 2007 on the PNR Agreement with the United States of America.* Brussels, July 12, 2007.

European Parliament and the Council of the European Union. *Directive 95/46/EC on the Protection of Individuals with Regard to the Processing of Personal Data and on the Free Movement of Such Data. Official Journal of the European Communities* L281. Brussels, November 23, 1995.

——. *Directive 97/66/EC Concerning the Processing of Personal Data and the Protection of Privacy in the Telecommunications Sector. Official Journal of the European Communities* L24/1. Brussels, January 30, 1997.

——. *Directive 2002/58/EC on Privacy and Electronic Communications. Official Journal of the European Communities* L201. Brussels, July 31, 2002.

——. *Directive 2006/24/EC on the Retention of Data Generated or Processed in Connection with the Provision of Publicly Available Electronic Communications Services or of Public Communications Networks and Amending Directive 2002/58/EC. Official Journal of the European Communities* L105(54). Brussels, March 15, 2006.

——. *Directive on the Retention of Data Generated or Processed in Connection with the Provision of Publicly Available Electronic Communications Services or of Public Communications Networks and Amending Directive 2002/58/EC. Official Journal of the European Communities* L105. Brussels, 2002.

——. *Regulation 1592/2002 on Common Rules in the Field of Civil Aviation and Establishing a European Aviation Safety Agency. Official Journal of the European Communities* L240 (1). July 15, 2002.

——. *Regulation 2001/45/EC on the Protection of Individuals with Regard to the Processing of Personal Data by the Community Institutions and Bodies and on the Free Movement of Such Data. Official Journal of the European Communities* L1. Brussels, 2001.

Evans, Peter. *Embedded Autonomy: States and Industrial Transformation.* Princeton: Princeton University Press, 1994.

Evans, Peter, Dietrich Rueschemeyer, and Theda Skocpol. "On the Road to a More Adequate Understanding of the State." In *Bringing the State Back In,* edited by Peter Evans, Dietrich Rueschemeyer, and Theda Skocpol, 347–66. Cambridge, UK: University of Cambridge Press, 1985.

Evenett, Simon, Alexander Lehmann, and Benn Steil. *Antitrust Goes Global: What Future for Transatlantic Cooperation?* Washington, D.C.: Brookings Institution, 2000.

Experian. *Corporate Fact Sheet.* Costa Mesa, 2004.

Falkner, Gerda, Oliver Treib, Miriam Hartlapp, and Simone Leiber. *Complying with Europe: EU Harmonisation and Soft Law in the Member States.* Cambridge, UK: Cambridge University Press, 2005.

Farrell, Henry. "Constructing the International Foundations of E-Commerce: The EU-US Safe Harbor Arrangement." *International Organization* 2 (2003): 277–306.

——. "Governing Information Flows: States, Private Actors, and E-Commerce." *Annual Review of Political Science* 6 (2006): 353–74.

Farrell, Henry, and Abraham Newman. "Domestic Determinants of International Market Regulation." Paper presented at the 103rd American Political Science Association Conference, Chicago, September 2, 2007.

Fauvet, Jacques. "Privacy in the New Europe." *Transnational Data and Communications Report* (November 1989): 17–18.

Fdk Tagesdienst. "Wir Sind für die Fortentwicklung des Datenschutzrechts Offen," June 10, 1976, 1–2.

FDP Kreisverband Nuerberger Land. *25 Ordentlicher Landesparteitag.* Augsburg, 1975.

Federal Trade Commission. *The Information Marketplace: Merging and Exchanging Consumer Data.* Washington, D.C.: Government Printing Office, 2001.

Flachmann, Klaus. "Kreditwirtschaft und Datenschutz." *Zeitschrift für das Gesamte Kreditwesen* 2 (1973): 56–58.

Flaherty, David. *Protecting Privacy in Surveillance Societies.* Chapel Hill: University of North Carolina Press, 1989.

Fligstein, Neil. "Markets as Politics: A Political-Cultural Approach to Market Institutions." *American Sociological Review* 61: 656–73.

Fligstein, Neil, and Iona Mara Drita. "How to Make a Market: Reflections on the European Union's Single Market Program." *American Journal of Sociology* 102 (1996): 1–33.

Frach, Lotte. "The Participation of Interest Groups in the Lamfalussy Process: A New Quality of Participatory Legitimacy." REGEM Analysis no. 13. University of Trier, February 2005.

Frears, John. "Liberalism in France." In *Liberal Parties in Western Europe,* edited by Emil Kirchner, 124–50. Cambridge, UK: Cambridge University Press, 1988.

Gabel, Mathew, and John Huber. "Putting Parties in Their Place: Inferring Party Left-Right Ideological Positions from Party Manifestos Data." *American Journal of Political Science* 44, no. 1 (2000): 94–103.

Gandy, Oscar. *Panoptic Sort: A Political Economy of Personal Information.* Boulder: Westview Press, 1993.

Garrett, Geoffrey. "Global Markets and National Politics." *International Organization* 52, no. 4 (1998): 787–824.

Gerschenkron, Alexander. *Economic Backwardness in Historical Perspective.* Cambridge, Mass.: Belknap Press, 1962.

Gesellschaft für Datenschutz und Datensicherung. *Erhebung über die möglichen Auswirkungen der geplanten EG-Datenschutzrichtlinie auf die Wirtschaft.* Königswinter: GDD, 1992.

——. *Stellungnahmen der GDD um ersten Entwurf einer EG-Datenschutzrichtlinie.* Königswinter: GDD, 1992.

——. *Vorschlag für eine Richtlinie des Tates zum Schutz von Personen bei der Verarbeitung personenbezogener Daten.* Bonn: GDD, 1992.

Gilardi, Fabrizio. "The Institutional Foundations of Regulatory Capitalism: The Diffusion of Independent Regulatory Agencies in Western Europe." *Annals of the American Academy of Political and Social Science* 598 (2005): 84–101.

——. "Policy Credibility and Delegation to Independent Regulatory Agencies: A Comparative Empirical Analysis." *Journal of European Public Policy* 9 (2002): 873–93.

Ginsberg, Roy. "Conceptualizing the European Union as an International Actor: Narrowing the Theoretical Capability-Expectations Gap." *Journal of Common Market Studies* 73 (1999): 429–54.

Glassman, Cynthia. *Customer Benefits from Current Information Sharing by Financial Services Companies.* Financial Services Roundtable. New York: Ernst & Young, 2000.

Glimstedt, Hendrik. "Competitive Dynamics of Technological Standardization: The Case of Third Generation Cellular Communications." *Industry and Innovation* 8, no. 1 (2001): 49–78.

Global Business Dialogue. *Paris Recommendations 1999.* Paris: Global Business Dialogue, 1999.

Goodman, John. "The Politics of Central Bank Independence." *Comparative Politics* 23, no. 3 (1991): 329–49.

Grabbe, Heather. "How Does Europeanization Affect CEE Governance? Conditionality, Diffusion, and Diversity." *Journal of European Public Policy* 8, no. 6 (2001): 1013–31.

Grunberg, Gerard. "Liberal Parties in Europe: The Case of France." In *Liberalism and Liberal Parties in the European Union,* edited by Lieven De Winter, 201–17. Barcelona: Institut de Ciències Polítiques i Socials, 2000.

Haas, Peter. "Introduction: Epistemic Communities and International Policy Coordination." *International Organization* 46, no. 1 (1992): 1–35.

Hall, Peter, and David Soskice. *Varieties of Capitalism*. Oxford: Oxford University Press, 2001.

Haufler, Virginia. *A Public Role for the Private Sector: Industry Self-Regulation in a Global Economy*. Washington, D.C.: Carnegie Endowment for International Peace, 2001.

Heisenberg, Dorothee. *Negotiating Privacy: The European Union, the United States, and Personal Data Protection*. Boulder: Lynne Rienner, 2005.

Heritier, Adrienne. "Public Interest Services Revisited." *Journal of European Public Policy* 9, no. 6 (2002): 995–1019.

Hessischer Ministerpraesident. *Der Grosse Hessenplan*. Wiesbaden, 1968.

Hirsch, Burkhard. "Datenschutz im Computer-Zeitalter—eine internationale Herausforderung." In *Datenschutz*, ed. Friedrich Naumann Stiftung, 19–24. Bonn: Friedrich Naumann Stiftung, 1980.

Hix, Simon. *The Political System of the European Union*. New York: Palgrave, 2005.

Hoekman, Bernard. "Assessing the General Agreement on Services." In *The Uruguay Round and the Developing Economies*, edited by Will Martin and L. Alan Winters. Washington, D.C.: World Bank, 1995.

Hoelder, Egon. *Bericht der interministeriellen Arbeitsgruppe Datenbanksystem*. Bonn: M. Rottmann, 1971.

Hondius, Fritz. *Emerging Data Protection in Europe*. New York: Elsevier, 1975.

Hooghe, Liesbet, and Gary Marks. *Multi-Level Governance and European Integration*. Lanham: Rowan & Littlefield, 2000.

Hopkins, Raymond. "The International Role of 'Domestic' Bureaucracy." *International Organization* 30, no. 3 (1976): 405–32.

Howell, William, and David Lewis. "Agencies by Presidential Design." *Journal of Politics* 64, no. 4 (2002): 1095–114.

Huber, Evelyne, Charles Ragin, and John Stephens. *Comparative Welfare States Data Set*. Chicago: Northwestern University and University of North Carolina, 1997.

——. "Social Democracy, Christian Democracy, Constitutional Structure, and the Welfare State." *American Journal of Sociology* 99, no. 3 (1993): 711–49.

Hustinx, Peter. "New PNR Agreement with the United States." Letter to Wolfgang Schauble, Brussels, June 27, 2007.

Ikenberry, G. John. *Reasons of State: Oil Politics and the Capacities of American Government*. Ithaca: Cornell University Press, 1988.

Immergut, Ellen. "The Rules of the Game: The Logic of Health Policy-Making in France, Switzerland, and Sweden." In *Structuring Politics*, edited by Kathleen Thelen, Sven Steinmo, and Frank Longstreth, 57–89. Cambridge, UK: Cambridge University Press, 1992.

Inglehart, Ronald, and Christian Welzel. *Modernization, Cultural Change and Democracy*. Cambridge, UK: Cambridge University Press, 2005.

International Chamber of Commerce. *Common Industry Statement on Storage of Traffic Data for Law Enforcement Purposes*. Brussels, 2003.

Jabko, Nicolas. *Playing the Market: A Political Strategy for Uniting Europe*. Ithaca: Cornell University Press, 2006.

——. "The Political Foundations of the Regulatory State." In *The Politics of Regulation: Examining Regulatory Institutions and Instruments in the Age of Governance*, edited by Jacint Jordana and David Levi-Faur, 200–217. Northampton, UK: Edward Elgar, 2003.

Jackson, Margaret. "Data Protection Regulation in Australia after 1988." *International Journal of Law and Information Technology* 5, no. 2 (1997): 158–91.

Jacoby, Wade. *The Enlargement of the EU and NATO: Ordering from the Menu in Central Europe.* New York: Cambridge University Press, 2006.

James, Scott, and David Lake. "The Second Face of Hegemony: Britain's Repeal of the Corn Laws and the American Walker Tariff of 1846." *International Organization* 43, no. 1 (1989): 1–29.

Jappelli, Tullio, and Marco Pagano. "Information Sharing in Credit Markets." *Journal of Finance* 48 (1993): 1693–718.

Johannes, Rubina. *Identity Fraud Survey Report.* Javelin Strategy Group, 2006.

Journal Officiel de la Republique Francaise. "Loi No. 78–17 du 6 janvier 1978 relative a l'informatique, aux fichiers et aux libertes." Paris, 1978.

Juliussen, Egil, and Karen Petska-Juliussen. *The 8th Annual Computer Industry Almanac.* Incline Village, Nev.: Computer Industry Almanac, 1996.

Jupille, Joseph. "The European Union and International Outcomes." *International Organization* 53, no. 2 (1999): 409–21.

Kagan, Robert. *Adversarial Legalism: the American Way of Law.* Cambridge, Mass.: Harvard University Press, 2001.

Katzenstein, Peter. "International Relations and Domestic Structures: Foreign Economic Policies of Advanced Industrial States." *International Organization* 30 (winter 1976): 1–45.

Keleman, Daniel. "The Politics of Eurocracy: Building a New European State?" In *State of the European Union, Vol. 7: With US or against US: European Trends in American Perspective,* edited by Nicolas Jabko and Craig Parsons, 173–89. Oxford: Oxford University Press, 2005.

Keohane, Robert. *After Hegemony.* Princeton: Princeton University Press, 1984.

Keohane, Robert, and Joseph Nye. "Transgovernmental Relations and International Organizations." *World Politics* 27 (1974): 39–62.

Kirchner, Emil, and David Broughton. "The FDP in the Federal Republic of Germany: The Requirements of Survival and Success." In *Liberal Parties in Western Europe,* edited by Emil Kirchner, 62–92. Cambridge, UK: Cambridge University Press, 1988.

Kitschelt, Herbert. "Left-Libertarian Parties: Exploring Innovation in Competitive Party Systems." *World Politics* 40, no. 2 (1988): 194–234.

Kobrin, Stephen. "Territoriality and the Governance of Cyberspace." *Journal of International Business Studies* 32, no. 4 (2001): 687–704.

——. "Safe Harbours are Hard to Find: The Trans-Atlantic Data Privacy Dispute, Territorial Jurisdiction and Global Governance." *Review of International Studies* 30 (2004): 111–31.

Koontz, Linda. *Personal Information: Agencies and Resellers Vary in Providing Privacy Protections.* Washington, D.C.: Government Accounting Office, 2006.

Kovacs, Janos. "Approaching the EU and Reaching the US? Rival Narratives on Transforming Welfare Regimes in East-Central Europe." *West European Politics* 25, no. 2 (2002): 175–208.

Krasner, Stephen. *International Regimes*. Ithaca: Cornell University Press, 1983.

Kretschmer, Friedrich. "Europäische Datenschutznormen aus sicht der deutschen Industrie." Paper presented at DAFTA, Königswinter, Germany, November 16, 1989.

Kuner, Christopher, and Aaron Simpson. "Managing Privacy Enforcement Risks in Europe." *Risk Management* (February 2005): 42–44.

Laurence, Henry. "Spawning the SEC." *Indiana Journal of Global Legal Studies* 6, no. 2 (1999): 647–83.

Levy, Jonah, Robert Kagan, and John Zysman. "The Twin Restorations: The Political Economy of the Reagan and Thatcher 'Revolutions'." In *Ten Paradigms of Market Economies*, edited by Lee-Jay Cho and Yoon Hyung Kim, 3–58. Seoul: Korea Research Institute for Human Settlements, 1997.

Libin, Nancy, and Jim Dempsey. *Mandatory Data Retention—Invasive, Risky, Unnecessary, and Ineffective*. Washington, D.C.: Center for Democracy and Technology, 2006.

Liedtke, Werner. *Das Bundesdatenschutzgesetz: Fallsudie zum Gesetzgebungsprozess*. Düsseldorf: Mannhold, 1980.

Loesche, Peter, and Franz Walter. *Die FDP: Richtungsstreit und Zukunftszweifel*. Darmstadt: Wissenschaftliche Buchgesellschaft, 1996.

Long, J. Scott. *Regression Models for Categorical Dependent Variables Using STATA*. College Station, Tex.: STATA Press, 2003.

Long, William and Marc Pang Quek. "Personal Data Privacy Protection in an Age of Globalization." *Journal of European Public Policy* 9 (2002): 325–44.

Ludford. Sarah. *Debate on the Resolution Concerning PNR*. Plenary Session of the European Parliament, Brussels, March 12, 2003.

Lyon, David. *The Electronic Eye: The Rise of Surveillance Society*. Minneapolis: University of Minnesota Press, 1994.

Mahoney, James. "Strategies of Causal Assessment in Comparative Historical Analysis." In *Comparative Historical Analysis in the Social Sciences*, edited by James Mahoney and Dietrich Rueschemeyer, 337–72. Cambridge, UK: Cambridge University Press, 2003.

Majone, Giandomenico. *Regulating Europe*. New York: Routledge, 1996.

——. "Two Logics of Delegation: Agency and Fiduciary Relations in EU Governance." *European Union Politics* 2 (2001): 103–21.

Majtenyi, Laszlo. "Ensuring Data Protection in East-Central Europe." In *Privacy in Post-Communist Europe* (Social Research Conference Series), edited by Arien Mack. *Social Research* 69 (spring 2002): 151–78.

Makinson, Larry. *Open Secrets: The Encyclopedia of Congressional Money and Politics*. Washington, D.C.: Congressional Quarterly, 1992.

Manners, Ian. "Normative Power Europe: A Contradiction in Terms?" *Journal of Common Market Studies* 40, no. 2 (2002): 235–58.

Martin, Lisa, and Beth Simmons. "Theories and Empirical Studies of International Institutions." *International Organization* 52, no. 4 (1998): 729–53.

Mattli, Walter, and Tim Büthe. "Setting International Standards: Technological Rationality or Primacy of Power." *World Politics* 56, no. 1 (2003): 1–42.

McCubbins, Mathew, and Thomas Schwartz. "Congressional Oversight: Police Patrols versus Fire Alarms." *American Journal of Political Science* 28, no. 1 (1984): 165–79.

McGinness, John. *What's Up in the Asia Pacific? APEC Privacy Initiatives.* Wellington, New Zealand: Privacy Issues Forum, 2003.

McNamara, Kathleen. "Consensus and Constraint: Ideas and Capital Mobility in European Monetary Integration." *Journal of Common Market Studies* 37 (1999): 455–76.

——. "Rational Fictions: Central Bank Independence and the Social Logic of Delegation." *West European Politics* 25, no. 1 (2002): 47–76.

Meunier, Sophie. *Trading Voices: The European Union in International Commercial Negotiations.* Princeton: Princeton University Press, 2005.

Meunier, Sophie, and Kalypso Nicolaidis. "Who Speaks for Europe? The Delegation of Trade Authority in the EU." *Journal of Common Market Studies* 37, no. 3 (1999): 477–501.

Mihailovich, Stephen. "New Privacy Bill Could Hurt Direct Marketing." *Budapest Business Journal* 27, 1997 [online]. http://www.bbj.hu/.

Milberg, Sandra, H. Jeff Smith, and Sandra Burke. "Information Privacy: Corporate Management and National Regulation." *Organization Science* 11, no. 1 (2000): 35–57.

Miller, Arthur. *The Assault on Privacy: Computers, Data Banks, and Dossiers.* Ann Arbor: University of Michigan Press, 1971.

Milner, Helen. "Rationalizing Politics: The Emerging Synthesis of International, American, and Comparative Politics." *International Organization* 52, no. 4 (1998): 759–86.

Mitchener, Brandon. "Increasingly, Rules of Global Economy Are Set in Brussels." *Wall Street Journal,* April 23, 2002 [online].

Mogg, John. "Privacy Protection in the Information Society." *Transnational Data and Communications Report* 29 (November–December 1994): 29–32.

Moran, Michael. "The State and the Financial Services Revolution: A Comparative Analysis." *European Politics* 17, no. 3 (1994): 158–77.

Moravcsik, Andrew. *The Choice for Europe: Social Purpose and State Power from Messina to Maastricht.* Ithaca: Cornell University Press, 1998.

——. "A New Statecraft? Supranational Entrepreneurs and International Cooperation." *International Organization* 53, no. 2 (1999): 267–306.

Mueller-Rommel, Ferdinand. "The FDP: Small but Beautiful." In *Liberalism and Liberal Parties in the European Union,* edited by Lieven De Winter, 85–118. Barcelona: Institut de Ciencies Politiques i Socials, 2000.

Munir, Abu Bakar, and Siti Hajar Yasin. "Retention of Communications Data: A Bumpy Road Ahead." *John Marshall Journal of Computer and Information Law* 22 (summer 2004): 731.

Müthlein, Thomas. "Für die Wirtschaft nicht praktikabel," *WIK* (January, no. 1 1993): 12–15.

Newman, Abraham. "Building Transnational Civil Liberties: Transgovernmental Entrepreneurs and the European Data Privacy Directive." *International Organization* 62, no. 1 (2008): 103–30.

——. "Protecting Privacy in Europe: Administrative Feedbacks and Regional Politics." In *Making History: European Integration and Institutional Change at Fifty,* edited by Sophie Meunier and Kathleen McNamara, 123–39. New York: Oxford University Press, 2007.

Newman, Abraham, and David Bach. "Self-Regulatory Trajectories in the Shadow of Public Power: Resolving Digital Dilemmas in Europe and the United States." *Governance* 17 (2004): 387–414.

Newman, Abraham, and Elliot Posner. "Rethinking Market Power: Authority, Territoriality, and the International Economy." Paper presented at the 101st American Political Science Association Conference, Washington, D.C., September 1, 2005.

Newman, Abraham, and John Zysman. "Transforming Politics in the Digital Era." In *How Revolutionary Was the Digital Revolution? National Responses, Market Transitions, and Global Technology*, edited by John Zysman and Abraham Newman, 391–411. Palo Alto: Stanford University Press, 2006.

Nora, Simon, and Alain Minc. *L'Informatisation de la Societe*. Paris: La Documentation Francaise, 1978.

Oberthuer, Sebastian. "The EU as an International Actor: The Protection of the Ozone Layer." *Journal of Common Market Studies* 37, no. 4 (1999): 641–59.

Office of Management and Budget. *Historical Tables*. Washington, D.C.: U.S. Government Printing Office, 2004.

Office of the Prime Minister. *Privacy Legislation*. Camberra, Australia: Commonwealth Government, 1997.

Office of the Privacy Commissioner. *Getting in on the Act: The Review of the Private Sector Provisions of the Privacy Act 1988*. Sydney, March 2005.

O'Harrow, Robert. *No Place to Hide*. New York: Free Press, 2005.

Organisation for Economic Cooperation and Development. *Guidelines on the Protection of Privacy and Transborder Flows of Personal Data*. Paris: OECD, 1980.

——. *Inventory of Data Banks in the Public Sector*. Paris: OECD, 1971.

——. *The Usage of International Data Networks in Europe*. Paris: OECD, 1979.

Padgett, John, and Chris Ansell. "Robust Action and the Rise of the Medici." *American Journal of Sociology* 98, no. 6 (1993): 1259–319.

Papapavlou, George. "Latest Developments Concerning the EC Draft Data Protection Directives." In *Recent Developments in Data Privacy Law*, edited by Jan Dumortier, 29–57. Leuven: Leuven University Press, 1992.

Parker, George, and Tobias Buck. "Washington Bridles at EU's Urge to Regulate." *Financial Times*, May 12, 2006 [online].

Parliament of the Czech Republic. *Declaration to the Agreement between the European Union and the United States of America on the Processing and Transfer of Passenger Name Record (PNR) Data by Air Carriers to the United States Department of Homeland Security (DHS)*. Brussels, July 19, 2007.

Passemard, Emile, and Clarisse Girot. "Presentation of the FICP: The French Negative File on Credit Repayment Incidents." Warsaw, March 10, 2002.

Paterson, Mark. *Australian Chamber of Commerce and Industry Statement on Privacy Legislation*. Camberra, Australia, 2000.

Pearce, Graham, and Nicholas Platten. "Achieving Personal Data Protection in the European Union." *Journal of Common Market Studies* 36, no. 4 (1998): 529–47.

Pierson, Paul. *Politics in Time: History, Institutions, and Social Analysis*. Princeton: Princeton University Press, 2004.

——. "When Effect Becomes Cause: Policy Feedback and Political Change." *World Politics* 45 (1993): 595–628.

Platten, Nick. "Background to and History of the Directive." In *The EC Data Protection Directive*, edited by David Bainbridge, 13–32. London: Butterworths, 1996.

———. "Poland Legislates on Data Protection to Pace Its Way for EU Membership." *Privacy Laws and Business International Newsletter* 44, 1998.

Pollack, Mark. *The Engines of Integration? Delegation, Agency, and Agenda Setting in the European Union*. New York: Oxford University Press, 2003.

Pollack, Mark, and Gregory Shaffer. "The Challenge of Reconciling Regulatory Differences: Food Safety and GMOs in the Transatlantic Relationship." In *Transatlantic Governance in the Global Economy*, edited by Mark Pollack and Gregory Shaffer, 153–78. New York: Rowman and Littlefield, 2001.

Posner, Elliot. "Market Power without a Single Market: The New Transatlantic Relations in Financial Services." Paper presented at The New Transatlantic Agenda and the Future of Transatlantic Economic Governance workshop, Robert Schuman Center for Advanced Studies, Florence, Italy, June 18–19, 2004.

———. *The Origins of Europe's New Stock Markets*. Cambridge, Mass.: Harvard University Press, 2008.

———. "Sources of Institutional Change: The Supranational Origins of Europe's New Stock Markets." *World Politics* 58 (October 2005): 1–40.

Privacy Protection Study Commission, *Personal Privacy in an Information Society*, Washington, D.C., 1977.

Prosser, William. "Privacy." *California Law Review* 48, no. 3 (1960): 383–423.

Raustiala, Kal. "The Architecture of International Cooperation: Transgovernmental Networks and the Future of International Law." *Virginia Journal of International Law* 43 (2002): 1–92.

———. "Domestic Institutions and International Regulatory Cooperation: Comparative Responses to the Convention on Biological Diversity." *World Politics* 49, no. 4 (1997): 482–509.

Regan, Priscilla. *Legislating Privacy: Technology, Social Values, and Public Policy*. Raleigh: University of North Carolina Press, 1995.

———. "Safe Harbors or Free Frontiers? Privacy and Transborder Data Flows." *Journal of Social Issues* 59 (2003): 263–82.

Reidenberg, Joel. "Resolving Conflicting International Data Privacy Rules in Cyberspace." *Stanford Law Review* 52 (2000): 1315–371.

Richards, John. "Toward a Positive Theory of International Institutions: Regulating International Aviation Markets." *International Organization* 53, no. 1 (1999): 1–37.

Risse-Kappen, Thomas. *Bringing Transnational Relations Back In: Non-State Actors, Domestic Structures and International Institutions*. Cambridge, UK: Cambridge University Press, 1995.

Rodota, Stefano. "Letter to European Parliament Committee on Citizens' Freedom and Rights." Brussels, March 3, 2003.

———. *Testimony to the Committee on Citizens' Freedom and Rights*. Brussels, November 25, 2003.

Sabel, Charles, and Jonathan Zeitlin. "Learning from Difference: The New Architecture of Experimentalist Governance in the European Union." La Follette School Working Paper No. 2007-20.

Sandholtz, Wayne, and John Zysman. "1992: Recasting the European Bargain." *World Politics* 42, no. 1 (1989): 95–128.

Scharpf, Fritz. "Community and Autonomy: Multilevel Policy Making in the European Union." *Journal of European Public Policy* 1 (1994): 219–42.

———. *Governing in Europe: Effective and Democratic?* Oxford: Oxford University Press, 1999.

Schimmelfennig, Frank, and Ulrich Sedelmeier. *The Europeanization of Central and Eastern Europe.* Ithaca: Cornell University Press, 2005.

Schutzgemeinschaft für Absatzfinanzierung und Kreditsicherung. *Geschaeftsbericht 2001.* Wiesbaden: SCHUFA Holding AG, 2002.

Schwartz, John. "German and U.S. Telecommunications Privacy Law: Legal Regulation of Domestic Law Enforcement Surveillance." *Hastings Law Journal* 54 (April 2003): 751.

Schwartz, Paul, and Joel Reidenberg. *Data Privacy Law: A Study of United States Data Protection.* Charlottesville, Va.: Michie, 1996.

Sell, Susan. *Private Power, Public Law: The Globalization of Intellectual Property Rights.* Cambridge: Cambridge University Press, 2003.

Shaffer, Gregory. "Globalization and Social Protection: The Impact of EU and International Rules in the Ratcheting Up of US Privacy Standards." *Yale Journal of International Law* 25 (winter 2000): 1–88.

Shefter, Martin. "Party and Patronage: Germany, England, and Italy." *Politics and Society* 7 (1977): 403–51.

Shonfield, Andrew. *Modern Capitalism.* London: Oxford University Press, 1965.

Simitis, Spiros. "Data Protection: Transcending the National Approach." *Transnational Data and Communications Report* (November 1989): 23–28.

———. "Data Protection in the European Union—the Quest for Common Rules." *Courses of the Academy of European Law* 8, no. 1 (1997): 95–142.

———. "From the Market to the Polis: The EU Directive on the Protection of Personal Data." *Iowa Law Review* 80 (1995): 445.

———. "Die informationelle Selbstbestimmung—Grundbedingung einer verfassungskonformen Informationsordnung." *Neue Juristische Wochenschrift* 37 (1984): 398–405.

———. *Informationskrise des Rechts und Datenverarbeitung.* Karlsruhe: CF Mueller, 1970.

———, ed. *Kommentar zum Bundesdatenschutzgesetz.* Baden-Baden: Nomos, 2003.

Simmons, Beth. "The International Politics of Harmonization: The Case of Capital Market Regulation." *International Organization* 55 (2001): 589–620.

Singer, David Andrew. *Regulating Capital: Setting Standards for the International Financial System.* Ithaca: Cornell University Press, 2007.

Singleton, Solveig. "Privacy and Human Rights: Comparing the United States to Europe." In *The Future of Financial Privacy,* edited by Competitive Enterprise Institute. Washington, D.C.: Competitive Enterprise Institute, 2000: 186–203.

———. *Privacy as a Trade Issue: Guidelines for US Trade Negotiators.* Washington, D.C.: Heritage Foundation, 2002.

Skowronek, Stephen. *Building a New American State: The Expansion of National Administrative Capacities, 1877–1920.* Cambridge, UK: Cambridge University Press, 1982.

Slaughter, Ann-Marie. "Agencies on the Loose? Holding Government Networks Accountable." In *Transatlantic Regulatory Cooperation*, edited by George A. Bermann, Matthias Herdegen, and Peter L. Lindseth, 521–46. Oxford: Oxford University Press, 2001.

——. *A New World Order*. Princeton: Princeton University Press, 2004.

Smith, Michael E. *Europe's Foreign and Security Policy*. Cambridge, UK: Cambridge University Press, 2003.

Staten, Michael, and Fred Cate. *The Adverse Impact of Opt-In Privacy Rules on Consumers: A Case Study of Retail Credit*. New York: Privacy Leadership Initiative, 2002.

Steinmueller, Wilhelm. *Stellungnahme zum Entwurf des Bundesdatenschutzgesetzes*. Regensburg: University of Regensburg, 1973.

Stich, Otto. *Botschaft zum Bundesgesetz über den Datenschutz*. Bern, Swiss Bundesrat, 1988.

Sweet, Alec Stone, Wayne Sandholtz, and Neil Fligstein. *The Institutionalization of Europe*. Oxford: Oxford University Press, 2001.

Swire, Peter, and Robert Litan. *None of Your Business: World Data Flows, Electronic Communication, and the European Privacy Directive*. Washington, D.C.: Brookings Institution, 1998.

Swire, Peter, and Lauren Steinfeld. "Security and Privacy after September 11: The Health Care Example." *Minnesota Law Review* 86 (2002): 1515.

Thelen, Kathleen. "How Institutions Evolve: Insights from Comparative Historical Analysis." In *Comparative Historical Analysis in the Social Sciences*, edited by James Mahoney and Dietrich Rueschemeyer, 208–40. Cambridge, UK: Cambridge University Press, 2003.

Thelen, Kathleen, and Sven Steinmo. "Historical Institutionalism in Comparative Politics." In *Structuring Politics: Historical Institutionalism in Comparative Analysis*, edited by Kathleen Thelen, Sven Steinmo, and Frank Longstreth, 1–32. Cambridge, UK: Cambridge University Press, 2002.

Tiberghien, Yves. "The Battle for the Global Governance of Genetically Modified Organisms: The Roles of the European Union, Japan, Korea, and China in a Comparative Context." *Etudes du CERI* no. 124 working paper (April 2006).

Tonnelson, Alan. *The Race to the Bottom*. Boulder: Westview Press, 2000.

Trefler, Daniel. "The Case of Missing Trade and Other Mysteries," *American Economic Review*, 85 (1995): 1029–46.

Tricot, Bernard. *Rapport de la Commission Informatique et Libertes*. Paris: La Documentation Francaise, 1975.

Tsebelis, George. *Veto Players: How Political Institutions Work*. Princeton: Princeton University Press, 2002.

Tufts Center for the Study of Drug Development. "European Approval of New Biotech Drugs Outpaces US Approval." 2 (March 2000): 1–3.

Turner, Michael. *The Impact of Data Restrictions on Consumer Distance Shopping*. New York: Privacy Leadership Initiative, 2001.

Turner, Michael, and Lawrence Buc. *The Impact of Data Restrictions on Fundraising for Charitable and Nonprofit Institutions*. New York: Privacy Leadership Initiative, 2002.

Uncapher, Mark. *Global E-Data: Continental Divide—Will Europe Lag behind the US.* Arlington: ITAA, 2000.

Union of Industrial and Employers' Confederations of Europe. *Implementation of Directive 95/46/EC on the Protection of Individuals with Regard to the Processing of Personal Data and on the Free Movement of Such Data of 24 October 1995.* Brussels: UNICE, 2002.

U.S. Department of Health, Education, and the Welfare Secretary's Advisory Committee on Automated Personal Data Systems. *Records, Computers, and the Rights of Citizens.* Washington, D.C.: Government Printing Office, 1973.

U.S. Privacy Protection Study Commission. *Personal Privacy in an Information Society.* Washington, D.C., 1977.

U.S. Senate. *Federal Data Banks, Computers, and the Bill of Rights.* Committee on the Judiciary, Subcommittee on Constitutional Rights. Washington, D.C.: Government Printing Office, 1971.

———. *Privacy: The Collection, Use, and Computerization of Personal Data. Joint Hearings before the Ad Hoc Subcommittee on Privacy of the Committee on Government Operations and Information Systems and Subcommittee on Constitutional Rights of the Committee on the Judiciary.* Washington, D.C.: Government Printing Office, 1974.

Vogel, David. "The Power of Business in America: A Re-appraisal." *British Journal of Political Science* 13 (1983): 19–43.

———. "The Public-Interest Movement and the American Reform Tradition." *Political Science Quarterly* 95, no. 4 (1981): 607–27.

———. *Trading Up: Consumer and Environmental Regulation in a Global Economy.* Cambridge, Mass.: Harvard University Press, 1995.

———. "Trading Up and Governing Across: Transnational Governance and Environmental Protection." *Journal of European Public Policy* 4 (1997): 556–71.

Vogel, Steve. *Freer Markets, More Rules: Regulatory Reform in Advanced Industrial Countries.* Ithaca: Cornell University Press, 1996.

Wallace, Helen, William Wallace, and Mark A. Pollack, eds. *Policy-Making in the European Union.* Oxford: Oxford University Press, 2005.

Wallace, Helen, and Alasdair Young. *Regulatory Politics in the Enlarged European Union.* Manchester: Manchester University Press, 2001.

Warren, Samuel, and Louis Brandeis. "The Right to Privacy." *Harvard Law Review* 4 (1890): 193–220.

Weber, Steve, and Elliot Posner. "Creating a Pan-European Equity Market: The Origins of the EASDAQ." *Review of the International Political Economy* 7, no. 4 (2000): 529–73.

Weiler, Joseph. "The Transformation of Europe." *Yale Law Journal* 100 (1991): 2403–83.

Weingast, Barry. "The Congressional-Bureaucratic System: A Principal-Agent Perspective." *Public Choice* 44 (1984): 147–91.

Weir, Margaret, and Theda Skocpol. "State Structures and the Possibilities for 'Keynesian' Responses to the Great Depression in Sweden, Britain and the United States." In *Bringing the State Back In,* edited by Peter Evans, Dietrich Rueschemeyer, and Theda Skocpol, 107–63. Cambridge, UK: Cambridge University Press, 1985.

Westin, Alan. *Privacy and Freedom.* New York: Atheneum, 1967.

Whitaker, Reg. *The End of Privacy.* New York: New Press, 2000.

Wuermeling, Ulrich. "Betriebliche Datenschützer fürchten um ihre Existenz," *Handelsblatt,* October 28, 1993, 6.

Young, Alasdair. "Political Transfer and 'Trading Up'? Transatlantic Trade in Genetically Modified Food and US Politics." *World Politics* 55 (July 2003): 457–84.

Ziegler, Nicholas. "Institutions, Elites, and Technological Change in France and Germany." *World Politics* 47 (1995): 341–72.

Zysman, John. *Governments, Markets, and Growth.* Ithaca: Cornell University Press, 1983.

——. "How Institutions Create Historically Rooted Trajectories of Growth." *Industrial and Corporate Change* 3 (1994): 243–83.

——. *Political Strategies for Industrial Order.* Berkeley: University of California Press, 1977.

Index

Note: Page numbers with an *f* indicate figures; those with a *t* indicate tables.